Jiggle

Jiggle

(Re)Shaping American Women

Wendy Burns-Ardolino

LEXINGTON BOOKS

A division of
ROWMAN & LITTLEFIELD PUBLISHERS, INC.
Lanham • Boulder • New York • Toronto • Plymouth, UK

LEXINGTON BOOKS

A division of Rowman & Littlefield Publishers, Inc.
A wholly owned subsidiary of The Rowman & Littlefield Publishing Group, Inc.
4501 Forbes Boulevard, Suite 200
Lanham, MD 20706

Estover Road
Plymouth PL6 7PY
United Kingdom

British Library Cataloguing in Publication Information Available

Library of Congress Cataloging-in-Publication Data

Burns-Ardolino, Wendy A.
  Jiggle : (re)shaping American women / Wendy Burns-Ardolino.
     p. cm.
  Includes bibliographical references and index.
  ISBN-13: 978-0-7391-1298-4 (cloth : alk. paper)
  ISBN-10: 0-7391-1298-8 (cloth : alk. paper)
  ISBN-13: 978-0-7391-1299-1 (pbk. : alk. paper)
  ISBN-10: 0-7391-1299-6 (pbk. : alk. paper)
  1. Foundation garments—History. 2. Foundation garments—Social aspects. 3.
Women's clothing—Psychological aspects. 4. Body image in women. I. Title.
  TT677.B87 2007
  687.082—dc22
                                                        2007033191

Printed in the United States of America

∞™ The paper used in this publication meets the minimum requirements of American
National Standard for Information Sciences—Permanence of Paper for Printed Library
Materials, ANSI/NISO Z39.48–1992.

May 7, 2012

For John

To Milt:
Who will teach me to better
understand myself and
others.

[signature]

Contents

Figures

Tables

Acknowledgments

This project is the culmination of so many hours of reading, researching and writing; however, it is also the result of living and learning within academic and personal communities that have fostered the growth and development of this project and its writer. Certainly, I could never have undertaken this work without much personal and professional support. It is to these many people that I offer my sincere thanks and gratitude.

A number of people in the George Mason Cultural Studies Doctoral Program have given to me the gifts of time, energy, and commentary. In particular, members of my writing group, Cynthia Patterson and Chris Sutch, the Feminist Cultural Studies Group and the Cultural Studies Student Organizing Committee have provided me with peers/colleagues who have tirelessly served as sounding boards, comrades, critics, and staunch supporters. In every way, their commitment to community has benefited us all.

The diverse faculty base in the Cultural Studies Doctoral Program at George Mason also provided me with a breadth of interdisciplinary experience. Few programs allow for the kind of interaction among the disciplines. I know that I am more than fortunate to have engaged in conversations with experts in the fields of sociology, philosophy, anthropology, history, English, and women's studies. This truly interdisciplinary community has permeated both my research and teaching goals, and I am deeply indebted to all who refused to allow me to see the world through only one disciplinary lens.

I would like to thank my mentors, Roger Lancaster, Debra Bergoffen, Larry Levine, and Greg Guagnano for their support and dedication to this project. Each of them provided me with a higher respect for their individual disciplinary craft, and perhaps most importantly they have been wonderful teachers. I am ultimately indebted to them because they did not attempt to have me reproduce their own knowledges, but rather they encouraged me to produce my own.

Additionally, I am grateful to my Department Head, Tom Barnett, and colleagues in the Department of Communicative Arts and Integrative Studies at Clayton State University in Georgia for giving me much needed time in the summers to see this project through to publication.

While this work is certainly the result of purposeful professional academic collaboration, factors of kismet including chance meetings and stumbling upon new sources (frequently described as the mystified element of research) have facilitated its development at every turn. My discovery of the Maidenform Collection at the Smithsonian may indeed be the greatest case in point. Hence, I offer special thanks to Professor John Cheng (History GMU) who suggested I consult the American History Archives at the Smithsonian, Charlie McGovern (Smithsonian Archivist now Professor of History at William and Mary) who took time to read my research proposal and sign on as my advisor, and Claudia Kidwell (Fashion Historian and Smithsonian Archivist), who took time to discuss my larger project and who encouraged me to work with both human subjects and archival resources rather than dissuading me from this formidable task. The Maidenform Collection at the Smithsonian provided a rich text to read the history of the foundation garment industry as well as a potential source for future research and writing.

To the women who so graciously participated in my survey and interview research, this project would be incomplete and fragmented without you. Thank you for time, effort and your vivid accounts of feminine embodied experience.

To the Virginian, thanks for your ideas about girdling and the advertisements and scanning, and to Chris, James, and Alisa at CSU in the Center for Instructional Development, thank you for your technological support without which advertisements would not appear in this book.

I would also like to thank my friends and family for their longstanding support throughout the research and writing of this project. I offer sincere thanks to the following: to Todd and Sara, who are my best critics and only a phone call away; to Joy, my mother and my first mentor; to Jim, my brother and intellectual sparring partner; to Art, who trusted me; to Fred and Annabel, my grandparents, who always thought I could; to Dad who taught me to do my best; to John, my partner who loved me through all the blood, sweat, and tears; and to my sons, Adrian and Adam, who daily rebuke the mind/body split between academia and mothering by demanding a smartly embodied motherlove.

Introduction

> Although young women today enjoy greater freedom and more options than their counterparts of a century ago, they are also under more pressure, and at greater risk, because of a unique combination of biological and cultural forces that have made the adolescent female body into a template for much of the social change of the twentieth century.
>
> Joan Jacobs Brumberg, *The Body Project*

Social, historical, and cultural critiques of fashion and beauty cultures have sought to address women's participation in the practices, consumption and (re)production of these cultures in terms of consent, resistance and agency.[1] While each of these critiques uses different disciplinary lenses, relies on distinctive primary sources and focuses on separate elements of women's fashion and beauty cultures, together they underscore the long struggle of women to construct feminine identities through fashion and beauty practices and products. Situating women in a dialectical relationship with fashion and beauty cultures primarily mediated by the conventions of the dominant culture, fashion historians, sociologists and cultural theorists continue to identify the consumptive and performative practices of women's fashion and beauty cultures as offering both a site for social change and a means of constraining women's social agency.[2]

This element of contested agency stemming from various disciplinary studies of fashion and beauty cultures forms the foundation of this study which focuses on the relationship between American women and their bodies as mediated by shaping garments. As a post-corsetry study this project begins in the 1930s and continues into the twenty-first century taking up the study of shapewear: bras, girdles, panty girdles, all-in-ones and more contemporary versions of these foundations: slimmers, shaper-panties, power-slips and push-up bras (as opposed to underwear or intimate apparel) because these garments work to shape female bodies into ideal bodies. Focusing on the corporate, cultural and individual practices and meanings of women's experiences with shaping garments, and exploring how the contested terrains of fashion and beauty cultures reflect larger cultural power struggles, this study seeks to understand how women's consumption of shaping garments relates to cultural values, meanings and stigmas of the ideal female body, femininity itself, and the social construction of female subjectivity. Through this analysis I argue that the notions of the ideal female body and idealized femininity are most certainly culturally produced and that women participate in the continued consumption and (re)production of these ideals through vast networks of power including: popular media (particularly women's magazines and advertising), fashion and beauty cultures, and social institutions (family, church and school); however, I also maintain that women should *not* be complicit in alienating themselves from the physical capacities, strengths, beauties and transformative powers of their bodies.

In keeping with my training in cultural studies, I have approached this project using interdisciplinary research methods including: archival research in the Maidenform Collection at Archive Center in the Smithsonian American History Museum, survey research—267 telephone interviews with women from a national sample,[3] in-depth interviews with 40 women of varying ages, races, classes, and geographic locations, and semiotic and discourse analysis of historical and contemporary trade journals, popular women's magazine articles and foundationwear advertisements. Employing these methodologies, I work dialectically with empirical evidence and the theories of Butler, Bartky, Beauvoir, Young, Bordo, Foucault, and Bourdieu and others to organize evidence and test these theories. I examine the histories and meanings of shaping garments within the changing social context of the lives of American women while asking how these garments work *for* and/or *against* women as mechanisms of rebellion, protection, and subordination.

In asking this question, I first begin in chapter 1 "Not Your Grandma's Girdles!" with an examination of the practices of girdling. I discuss how the girdle, a more liberating form of corsetry, comes into being and explain cultural rationales for its decline in popularity some forty years later. While the significance of the girdle in the history of foundationwear of the twentieth century cannot be denied, the extent to which the girdle influences contemporary shapewear becomes the focus of the latter part of this chapter. Relying on interview data and the discourse of popular and trade magazines, I compare the current boom in contemporary shapewear to the ritualized practices of girdling.

Picking up the threads of the discussion in chapter 1 concerning girdling practices, chapter 2 "Dress Codes: Foundationwear Required" explores the issues linking definitions of acceptable femininity and social dress codes to formal occasions. Drawing on survey data and in-depth interviews, I allow women's embodied accounts of wearing foundation garments to explore and explain the relationship between women and the cultural requirements of feminine dress while treading lightly into the minefield of the discourse of sexual desire and objectification.

While chapters 1 and 2 examine the practices and rituals of wearing foundation garments in conjunction with acceptable codes of feminine dress, chapter 3 "Boomers and X-ers: Mothers and Daughters" defines and details the *ideal body* for both generation x-ers and baby boomers. Continuing to discuss the notion of a historical girdle resurgence arriving in the form of contemporary shapewear, I describe how the fetishization of the *ideal slender female body* is commodified in order to sell shaping garments that *solve the problem bodies* of both baby boomers and generation x-ers, who are at least potentially mothers and daughters.

Following the notion that there is an ideal feminine form for each historical moment and that the material conditions of culture produce this ideal body image, chapter 4 "The Myths of Control and Freedom: Constructing the Ideal Feminine Form in Foundationwear Advertising" provides a careful reading of foundationwear advertising from the late 1930s to today.[4] Representations of women's bodies clad in foundation garments demonstrate the elusiveness of the transient feminine form in fashion and convey the message that these garments can be used by women to transform their real bodies into ideal ones by controlling and/or shaping them. Additionally, I take up the issues of freedom and control as they are specifically proffered in these advertisements to an audience of women through their appearance in popular women's magazines, store catalogs, trade journals and newspapers.

Recognizing fashion's changing and elusive feminine body ideal, chapter 5 "Under Cover Agency?" focuses on the issue of women's capacity for agency from within historical structures of corporate, social and cultural power. The contested terrains of both the symbolic and social practices of wearing foundation garments point toward an understanding that these garments may function simultaneously as structures of domination and spaces of resistance. Findings from survey data and in-depth interviews demonstrate the conflicted agency experienced by women across the United States, by both those who wear foundations and those who do not.

Chapter 6 "Minding Our Bodies: Displacing the Foundations of Femininity" confronts the normative modes of feminine bodily comportment that women encounter as they control and shape their bodies with foundation garments. Examining accounts of feminine embodied experience and using them as lenses through which to look closely at women's bodily comportment in foundation garments and the language in fashion magazines which describes what foundation garments do to women's bodies, I explore ways in which women can subvert habituated practices and performances of normative femininity.

My conclusions and afterthoughts are the culmination of many hours of recounting the embodied experiences of women purchasing, wearing, and talking about foundation garments and the ways in which these garments shaped their bodies and their lives. Listening to women in in-depth interviews, conducting telephone survey interviews and performing archival research, I immersed myself in the lived personal accounts of female embodied experience with shaping garments. It is my hope to convey the collective experience of this research to a general audience of women, perhaps most especially young women, in order to provide an understanding of how women in the United States encounter, engage, and resist what may be considered the most intimate structures of femininity—foundation garments.

Survey Research

In order to test my test my critical analyses, I designed a survey instrument and conducted telephone interviews with a national sample of 267 women concerning their practices and habits past and present with foundation garments. The survey was voluntary and included standard demographic items such as race, class, age and geographic data for each respondent. I conducted the survey over a two-week period in July of 2000 in The Northern Virginia Survey Lab. Undergraduate students and some graduate students from George Mason University were trained to perform interviews for the study. I oversaw all two weeks of interviewing which were conducted nightly from 9:00 p.m. until midnight across U.S. time zones. A copy of the survey questionnaire is attached.

While feminists have used survey research to amass statistical data on the status of women,[5] to date only informal surveys have been conducted concerning the experience of women with their foundation garments. In their recent book, *Uplift: The Bra in America*, Jane Farrell-Beck and Colleen Gau perform such a survey regarding women's experiences with their bras by placing an informal questionnaire in retirement homes and handing them out to individual women in Rochester, Minnesota (2001, xiv). They assert that in their survey, "Respondents gave several reasons for wearing their first brassiere, including the desire to achieve a fashionable look, submission to peer or maternal pressure, or the need for support. Only a small number of women mentioned comfort as an inducement to start wearing a brassiere (2001, 71). Hence, the need for this study comes in response to Farrell-Beck and Gau's articulation of what has been done to solicit women's experiences and what still needs to be done.

Limitations

While this survey of American women's experiences with their foundation garments is much more formalized in its design and implementation than that of Farrell-Beck and Gau, it is by no means comprehensive or definitive. My aim in undertaking this research was to broaden the scope of my study since I could not possibly interview 267 women personally across the nation. When I began this study, it was my hope to conduct survey interviews with as many as 600 women. Ultimately, we interviewed less than half that number. Additionally, we found after the first couple nights of interviewing that we should not divulge the intention of our study to male members of the household who answered the phone. We changed our introduction to state that we were calling from George Mason University with a women's survey and asked to speak a female household member. In this way, we ended up completing many more successful interviews. Although women seemed to want to talk about their bodies and the garments that shape them, the men in many households were uncomfortable with women speaking about this subject.

However, I am less concerned about the size of this sample since it represents in many ways a breaking of new ground in experiential women's research. I am very pleased that we were able to talk to so many women. This certainly provided a much broader perspective on the issues and practices of wearing foundation garments, and made me more intent on finding new ways to elicit women's experiences. In the future, I would like to work collaboratively with feminist survey researchers to possibly gain a grant which would facilitate a larger sample size for further exploration into women's embodied experience.

Interviewing/Embodied Accounts

To add depth to the survey responses I performed 40 open-ended interviews over a 4-year period beginning in the fall of 1999 with women regarding their experiences with their bodies, foundation garments and clothing. The interviews were voluntary. Most interviewees were solicited from women's social groups and academic communities: e.g. church groups, garden clubs, and student organizations. In my analysis of the in-depth interviews, I paid particular attention to points where the private discourse of the interviewees intersected, reinforced or opposed the public discourse of popular culture in women's magazines and newspapers and the discourse of corporations in trade journals, sales and marketing information and ads. I also examined survey data against interview material looking for patterns. Using survey data and in-depth interviewing proved to be a most productive method of recording and examining experiential evidence. As I recorded lived accounts of female embodied experience with foundation garments, I appealed to theories of embodiment that carefully examine the cultural practices of femininity. In this way I was able to integrate methods of survey research and in-depth interviewing and work dialectically with theory to produce more specific knowledge about women's embodied experience with shaping garments.

Limitations

The open-ended, in-depth interviews typically lasting an hour, provided richer and more detailed accounts of individual women's experiences; however, they did not allow for a consistent line of questioning. My skills as an interviewer developed as I went along, so several of the first interviews seemed more like question and answer sessions. Later interviews, which yielded lengthy anecdotes seemed less structured, but by their nature were difficult to fit into the patterned research. In the end, I asked interviewees to tell me about memorable experiences up front and later followed up with questions regarding purchasing habits, my first bra stories, and information about current wearing habits. In the end, this material could be integrated with survey data to give greater weight to my claims, but it seemed rather incomplete and inconsistent standing on its own.

Considering the limitations of both survey and in-depth interviewing methods, race and class data, which were of great concern to my research agenda, became slippery entities which called for the use of larger samples and more detailed studies of this kind.

Race and Class in Survey and Interview Data

Race and class were self-reported variables in the telephone survey. Race statistics were reported as follows: 2 percent Native American, 5 percent African American, 2 percent Asian, 3 percent Hispanic, and 85 percent Caucasian. Class statistics were also self-reported in this form: -$20,000 = 12 percent; $20,000-40,000 = 18 percent; $40,000-60,000 =14 percent; $60,000-80,000 = 12 percent, +$100,000 = 5 percent. In terms of self-reported class: lower 1 percent, working 24 percent, middle 67 percent, and upper 6 percent.

In my in-depth interviews, I did not ask income, class or race questions; however, my observations are as follows: For race—72 percent Caucasian, 15 percent African American, 8 percent Hispanic, 5 percent Asian. In terms of class, the majority of women I interviewed (36 out of 40) could be considered middle to upper class. I only interviewed 4 women who could be considered working class and none who could be considered lower class. The reporting of class was definitely a vague and in many ways indeterminable factor in both the in-depth interviews and survey work. Even the self-reporting of class in the survey seems to be conflicted since 20 people who claimed to be middle class reported a household income of under $20,000 while 8 people who reported household income of over $100,000 claimed to be middle class.

However, my survey work and interviews do share common results for race and class in terms of fashion ideals and agendas. In all classes, over 75 percent of women strongly agreed with the statement that "The fashion industry places unrealistic demands on women's bodies."[6] With regard to race, 83 percent of Native American, 99 percent of African American, 40 percent of Asian American, 55 percent of Hispanic and 92 percent of Caucasian respondents agreed with the same statement. Hence, attitudes concerning the fashion industry and its control over women seem more varied in terms of race than in terms of class. Similarly, responses in terms of class correlate in answer to the statement "women wear shaping garments to mask figure flaws."[7] Eighty-eight percent of upper class, 84 percent of middle class, 82 percent of working class, and 100 percent of lower class respondents indicated that they agreed with the above statement while 83 percent of Native American, 83 percent of African American, 40 percent of Asian, 89 percent of Hispanic, and 85 percent of Caucasian respondents agreed with the above statement. Again the most variance is reflected by Asian women.[8] Although this data does not provide any conclusive evidence for this variance, perhaps Asian women feel less pressured to adhere to the demands of fashion, or perhaps they do not find it difficult to meet the demands of fashion. It is also possible that Asian women, who are statistically thinner and less voluptuous, may not feel the *need* to wear shaping garments as frequently as Hispanic, Caucasian, Native American, and African American women. Hence, class and to a lesser extent race do not indicate a substantial difference in terms of women's responses to the agenda of the fashion industry nor women's rationales for wearing shaping garments. This suggests that women's relationships to their shaping garments may be more likely to be a greater concern of gender than that of race or class. This may in fact be a function of codes of dress for women in U.S. society since a majority of women, 60 percent of respondents, agreed that shaping garments are yet another fashion requirement.[9]

In-depth Interview Questions

For the purposes of this interview, the term *shaping garments* refers to corsets, corselettes, all-in-ones, girdles, panty girdles, bras, long-line bras, push-up bras, control-top panty hose, shapewear, shapers, slimmers, smoothers, shaping panties, power slips and any other undergarment which shapes the body.

1. How did you first experience shaping garments? Brands? Colors? Styles?
2. How did these garments make you feel? When did you wear them?
3. What shaping garments have you worn/do you wear at present? When do you wear them? How do they make you feel?
4. Is there a difference in the way you experience your body with these garments and without them? What are the differences/similarities?
5. What do you look for in a shaping garment?
6. What brands are you most likely to purchase? Why?
7. Where do you shop for shaping garments? Why?
8. What do you think about shaping garments now—in the past?
9. How has wearing these garments changed from the past to present?
10. To what do you attribute this change/ lack of change?
11. What have you worn shaping garments in the past? Why do you wear them now?
12. What is your most memorable experience with shaping garments?

Telephone Survey Questions:

For the purposes of this survey, the term *shaping garments* refers to corsets, corselettes, all-in-ones, girdles, panty girdles, bras, long-line bras, push-up bras, control-top panty hose, shapewear, shapers, slimmers, smoothers, shaping panties, power slips and any other undergarment which shapes the body.

1. How many years of formal education have you had? _____
2. What is your occupation? _____
3. What year were you born? _____
4. Which best describes you?
   a) Native American, Indian
   b) African-American, Black
   c) Asian
   d) Hispanic
   e) Caucasian
   f) Mixed Race
   g) Other
5. What's your marital status?
   a) Married
   b) Divorced

   c) Separated
   d) Widowed
   e) Other

6. If you were asked to use one of four names for your social class, which would you say you belong in?
   a) the lower class
   b) the working class
   c) the middle class
   d) the upper class

7. At what age did you wear your first shaping garment? _____

8. Who helped you pick it out?
   a) Mother
   b) Father
   c) Sister
   d) Girl friend
   e) Other

9. What kinds of shaping garments do you wear now?
   a) Panty girdles
   b) Open-bottom girdles
   c) Control-top panty hose
   d) Shapers
   e) Slimmers
   f) Smoothers
   g) Push-up bras
   h) Non-underwire bras
   i) Control/Power slips
   j) Other

10. Was there a period before now when you wore different shaping garments? If no skip to question 12. If yes,

11. What kind of garments did you wear?
   a) Corsets
   b) Corselettes
   c) All-in-ones
   d) Long-line bras
   e) Girdles
   f) Open-bottom girdles
   g) Panty girdles
   h) Other

12. How often do you wear shaping garments?
   a) daily
   b) weekly

    c) monthly
    d) on special occasions
    e) never

Now I am going to read a list of statements. Tell me if you strongly agree, agree, disagree or strongly disagree with each statement.

13. Wearing shaping garments makes me feel feminine. SA   A   D   SD
14. Without these garments I feel exposed. SA   A   D   SD
15. I enjoy wearing shaping garments. SA   A   D   SD
16. When I wear shaping garments, I feel sexy. SA   A   D   SD
17. My clothes look better when I wear shaping garments. SA   A   D   SD
18. Women who don't wear shaping garments jiggle. SA   A   D   SD
19. People find me more attractive when I wear shaping garments.
    SA   A   D   SD
20. I am comfortable in my chosen shaping garments. SA   A   D   SD
21. I can move freely in my shaping garments. SA   A   D   SD
22. Most women wear some kind of shaping garments. SA   A   D   SD
23. Most women should wear shaping garments. SA   A   D   SD
24. All women look better when they wear shaping garments.
    SA   A   D   SD
25. Present day shaping garments shape women's bodies without limiting their range of movement. SA   A   D   SD
26. All women need to wear some kind of shaping garment. SA   A   D   SD
27. Women who wear shaping garments give up free range of motion in favor of a better-looking body. SA   A   D   SD
28. Women wear shaping garments to mask figure flaws. SA   A   D   SD
29. Shaping garments make women sexier. SA   A   D   SD
30. Shaping garments protect women's bodies. SA   A   D   SD
31. Shaping garments are yet another fashion requirement. SA   A   D   SD
32. Shaping garments enable women to achieve the body that nature did not give them. SA   A   D   SD
33. The fashion industry places unrealistic demands on women's bodies.
    SA   A   D   SD
34. Shaping garments help women keep up with the demands of fashion.
    SA   A   D   SD

NOTES

1. Banner 1983, Kidwell & Steele 1989, Brumberg 1997, Peiss 1998, Presley 1998, Steele 1997, 2001, Ko 2001, Farrell-Beck & Gau 2001, Fields 1997, Gimlin 2001, Crane 2000

2. See McRobbie 1991, 1993, 1999, Enstad 1998, Entwistle 1997, 2000, and Entwistle and Wilson 2001 for a full discussion of relationship between the consumption of fashion and beauty culture and construction of female subjectivity.

3. See Appendix A, Telephone Survey Data for more information regarding variables and frequencies.

4. See Heywood and Dworkin *Built to Win* 2003 and Bordo *Unbearable Weight* 1993 for examples of careful readings of advertisements in terms of ideal bodies.

5. Roberta Spalter-Roth 1997 has conducted similar survey work concerning women and work.

6. See Appendix A, Telephone Survey Data variable v42.

7. See Appendix A, variable v36.

8. Only 6 Asian women were surveyed comprising only 2 percent of the total 267 respondents.

9. Again the majority seemed to answer on the basis that a bra is a required element of feminine dress.

Chapter One

Not Your Grandma's Girdles!

Innovations in dress which supported women's desires for comfort would
continue because industrialists sought not to end women's desires for fashion change, but to contain them.

Jill Fields, *An Intimate Affair*

The significance of girdles in American fashion culture cannot be denied, as
they emerged from a history of traditional corsetry, which constrained and
contained the female body primarily with a focus on the waist. The girdle,
long considered a cousin of the corset, is described as an elasticized or rub-
berized light-weight corset extending from waist to upper thigh. Certainly, it
is not coincidence that the girdle arrived along with an increase in women's
physical activity. In their pictorial history of lingerie, Karen Bressler, Karoline Newman, and Gillian Proctor note, "As sports gained in popularity, many
of the women playing tennis, cycling, riding, and skiing wore specialist underwear such as the 'sport corset' of 1934. This shorter corset controlled the
hips and was cut higher on the thigh" (1997, 17).

While this history seems to suggest the freeing proposition of girdles—at
least freeing in the sense that more movement was made possible by girdles
than by that of traditional corsets—the history of girdles has been somewhat
tempestuous. Girdles were simultaneously embraced and required in the
1940s and 1950s because they controlled jiggling and bulging while keeping
stockings up. Fabrics such as Lastex, Nylon and then Lycra increased the
comfort, construction and design of girdles during this time. Such new technologies spurred on by the progress of post-war industrialization (World
War II) showed up in an array of styles to fit the varying sizes of waists,
thighs and bottoms of all women. Hence, girdles became a necessity for

1

women of all ages and marked a rite of passage from girlhood to womanhood. When wearing girdles, girls felt like women and women felt like ladies. Historian Ellen Melinkoff explores this rite of passage in her social history, *What We Wore*. Melinkoff explains:

> For years girdle manufacturers had touted them [girdles] as necessary for every woman from sixteen to the grave. If we bought that line, then we had to wear girdles to hang laundry on the line and go bowling, for hiking, gardening, as well as for work. The ads showed smiling, spirited twenty-year-olds wearing girdles for all these activities. There was official acknowledgment that women were enduring a ridiculous amount of discomfort. (1984, 124)

Women and girls understood that they participated in a practice that was to be borne in the name of femininity and propriety. Indeed, women and girls wore the girdle as a badge of femininity. What Melinkoff suggests is the brewing of a controversy during the early 1960s concerning the practice of girdling. Women who had been previously taught that girdling was the only option began to question this practice on the grounds of comfort and practicality, particularly in light of the invention of pantyhose. Rosemary Hawthorne's popular history of stockings and suspenders confirms this as she examines DuPont's question in the mid-1970s: "What has happened to the girdle?"(1993, 112).

> It was important, as the manufacturers of Lycra, to know the answer [to this question]. The evidence they [DuPont] brought back showed that "rejection" was the keyword—in all age groups, but particularly between 15 and 35 years. These women said, quite rightly, that pantie-hose [sic] eliminated the girdle because you didn't have to hold up your stockings any more. What was more, they claimed that women didn't like girdles and never had, and only wore them because there had been nothing else available. Wearing a girdle had been "almost a legal requirement"—you had to, everyone did. . . But now, oh wonderful, there was choice. (1993, 113)

Hence, as Hawthorne points out, women chose pantyhose. The end of the 1960s and early 1970s meant a decline in girdles, and a virtual end to their prescribed rituals and practices. Although this garment underwent many changes—from open-bottom, to boy-leg, to panty-girdle; from rubber, to Lastex, to Lycra; from paneled to single-seamed to seamless—it continued to hold-up stockings, flatten tummies, and provide light, but firm control for the waists, hips, and buttocks of American women for almost three decades (Brumberg 1997, 114). In this way, the girdle marks a history of feminine bodily control and constraint which is as indicative of its power as it is of cultural attitudes toward girdling itself.

These cultural attitudes are perhaps most clearly reflected in popular women's magazines. The mystifying practices of girdling and the visual representations of the apparatuses that held women in and kept their bodies under control fill the pages of popular women's magazines. In order to analyze these representations and the public discourse of girdling, I have reviewed popular women's magazines dating from 1935 to the present.[1] I have also interviewed women about their own experiences with girdles,[2] and I have been surprised by the reasons that women have worn girdles, including issues of health, hygiene, posture, deportment, and aesthetics. An example of the health discourse of girdling comes from an article entitled "Corset Comfort" from a 1935 issue of *The Parents' Magazine*. In this article, journalist Jeanette Eaton suggests, "Girdles are recommended for even young girls since a properly designed support corrects bad posture . . . and all the vital organs are actually pulled out of place by continued bad posture"(1935, 74). In this way, Eaton speaks to the parents of young girls and underscores the relationship between wearing a girdle and good health. Eaton advises parents that learning to wear foundations correctly is a critical part of becoming a woman.

Eaton's advisor-like tone is typical of the prescriptive language that pervades popular women's magazines and is a key element of constructing the popular discourse of girdling. Exploring and demystifying the practices of girdling in terms of enculturation, socialization, and as a rite of passage, stand at the center of this chapter. What follows is a critical interrogation of girdling as a public and private phenomenon. Using popular magazines, trade journals and newspapers from 1935 to the present, I (re)construct the public discourse of girdling. In addition, I juxtapose this public discourse with the personal narratives of women who recall the heydays of girdling. I compare the public and private discourses of girdling and locate them along the historical trajectory of girdling including an in-depth analysis of the contemporary phenomenon of girdle resurgence in U.S fashion culture.

Trade journalists Susan Chandler and Ann Therese Palmer articulate the trend toward girdle resurgence in a 1995 issue of *Business Week*. They note, "Girdles, now spun out of new lightweight, colorful materials such as stretch satin laced with superstrong Lycra, have morphed into the 90s" (1995, 37). When considering the act of girdling, it is common to assume it as a past phenomenon that involved constraining and controlling women's bodies for reasons of health, etiquette, and appearance. However, this past phenomenon becomes even more complex when viewed in light of the present phenomenon of girdle resurgence. Chandler and Palmer's article from *Business Week* announces, "Girdles and corsets—once hated for their flesh-constricting features—are turning from avant-garde fashion into mainstream pieces" (1995, 37). This resurgence of girdles, which comes to the market under the guise of "shapers," "slimmers," "briefers" and "smoothies," marks not only a second wave in the history of girdles but complicates the study of the practices and rationales for purchasing and wearing contemporary versions of the girdle.

In spite of the contemporary conception that girdles are inventions of days gone by, the practical significance of the work performed by girdles, to hold up stockings is worth noting. As an English professor in her late forties stated, "I never wore a girdle while I was a teenager living in Florida because I never wore stockings. It was too hot. It wasn't until I went away to college in Chicago in 1964 that I bought my first girdles from Sear's and Penney's. I had to. I had to have something to attach to my stockings or even to my over-the-knee socks" (personal interview). While this story might be common in terms of experience, it is a detail, which is both essential to an understanding of girdle history and the history of the practice of girdling. It is significant precisely because it explains the practical necessity of girdles at a time when there were few choices available, other than garter belts, to hold up women's stockings. Fashion writer Hyman Goldberg emphasizes this point in a 1954 article entitled "The Big Squeeze" from *Cosmopolitan*. Goldberg exclaims "In the 1890s, some genius attached garters to the bottoms of corsets to serve two purposes—to keep stockings up and corsets down" (1954, 24). This little fact kept most women and their daughters and their daughter's daughters in girdles until the advent of pantyhose and tights.[3] All-in-one hosiery gained popularity in the late 1960s and early 1970s. As the younger generation rejected traditional corsetry, they became increasingly body, diet, exercise, and health conscious and chose to don dancewear, leotards and tights (Bressler 1997, 137). This idea that the generation of the 1960s just let it all hang out seems a bit contrived and false, since younger women did wear pantyhose, tights and even control-top pantyhose. However, the fact that these inventions brought other options to women in the late 1960s and 1970s does not change the fact that women of the 1930s, 1940s, 1950s and even into the 1960s wore girdles religiously for many reasons besides holding up their stockings.

Many of the reasons can be directly linked to social and cultural practices that eliminated the option of alternate choices. In fact, many of the women I interviewed articulated this lack of choice in the face of social conventions. They commented, "The practice was just assumed. It was the right thing to do. No questions were asked" (personal interviews). The practice of girdling in both the public and private spheres operates within the parameters of social control. There are rationales given and accepted from authorities ranging from societal norms voiced by parents, aunts and grandmothers, to medical and scientific discourses, all of which advocate girdling as a regulated practice. In his seminal text, *Outline of a Theory of Practice*, sociologist Pierre

Bourdieu details the significance of repeated and habitual practices in day-to-day life noting, "The homogeneity of habitus is what within the limits of the group of agents possessing the schemes (of production and interpretation) implied in their production—causes practices and works to be immediately intelligible and foreseeable, and hence taken for granted" (1977, 80). Working from Bourdieu's framework of the habitus, I argue that as the practice of girdling becomes one that is assumed or taken for granted it becomes part of a feminine habitus for women during the 1930s, 1940s, and 1950s, and even into the sixties. Women are complicit in the practice of girdling because it is a social convention advocated by public medical, scientific, health, fashion and beauty discourses and reinforced by the private discourses of femininity and women's culture.

The medical and scientific discourses which finds their way into popular women's magazines are designed to persuade women to wear girdles for their health. Journalist Carrie McMichael described such a rationale in a 1941 issue of *The Journal of Home Economics* where she argued for the need for wearing proper corsetry. She explained, "Corsets must safely enclose the vital organs, giving pressure where it is needed and avoiding pressure where it will do harm . . . The important abdominal organs must never be pressed downward. They are safest when pressed upward" (1941, 29–30). The concept was that women's organs were not safe where they existed naturally. This was but one example of medical and scientific rationales that was used as reinforcement for the practice of girdling. In a 1942 issue of *Hygeia* columnist Jane Dixon expounded upon the weakness of the female frame based on an evolutionary argument. She declared:

> The human body is not designed to stand and walk upright. The vital organs, it is true, are sheathed with muscular straps which in youth are firm and strong and, if the general posture is erect, hold the abdomen in a flat line. As the years go by, these muscles generally become more or less flaccid, letting the abdomen protrude gradually. Men grow 'corporations.' Women develop 'middle-aged spread.' The spine grows tired of supporting in an erect position the body that was intended to go on all fours. Unless something is done about it, the spine gradually sways forward at the small of the back where the strain of supporting the abdomen gives the backbone its most severe work, and as the incurved lordosis backline appears the abdomen protrudes in a compensating curve. Neither exercise nor any other known remedy can restore the again muscles . . . The only other solution to the problem is externally supplied support. (1942, 621–622)

Even women who were post-partum could not escape the practice of girdling. As journalist Helene Obolensky pointed out in a 1964 issue of *Redbook*, "It is advocated that after pregnancy women wear girdles with heavier control than the usual pre-pregnancy styles, for faster recovery of pre-pregnancy contours. Your doctor probably will advise you on the best type of maternity garments" (1964, 88). Prescribing a girdle to women post-pregnancy was a commonplace practice. One of my interviewees, a woman from the midwest in her early fifties, recalled her doctor telling her to get a girdle after pregnancy. She explained, "In 1981 I had a stillborn, and I had to go back to work, the doctors told me to get a good long-line girdle to get my figure back and to support my body until I could get my figure back. I wore it once, maybe twice and I knew it wasn't for me. I knew I couldn't spend my life inside one of those things." Similarly, in a 1954 edition of *Cosmopolitan*, fashion writer Hyman Goldberg made allusion to the medical rationale behind girdling as he stated, "Nowadays women wear foundation garments as much for health as for style. Doctors say they lessen fatigue, hold abdominal organs in place and protect delicate tissues. Women are happy that doctors say this, because these same garments make them smaller in some places and larger in others, as the women desire" (1954, 24). While it seems important to note that the woman in 1981 ultimately went against the medical discourse and chose not to wear the long-line girdle (though she did buy one), it is also significant that the public discourse from *Cosmopolitan* in 1954 and the medical discourse from 1981 resembled one another. However, what is even more significant is that these medical/scientific discourses are privileged even in popular women's magazines not just in health journals, and that these health/medical/scientific discourses are propagated by non-medical personnel including journalists and fashion writers.

But wearing a girdle was not just prescribed by these discourses in women's magazines, some employers also required women to wear girdles to work. Two of the forty women I interviewed noted that girdles were required as part of their uniform at work. A fifty-one year-old woman from New Jersey stated, "At Howard Johnson's they required us [waitresses] to wear girdles. There was talk they didn't want any jiggling. I was too skinny to be checked, but the word was if you were jiggling too much they would take you aside and tell you to wear the proper undergarments—which meant girdles" (personal interview). Another woman in her late fifties remembered a similar requirement when she worked in a women's shoe department in Pittsburgh in 1960. She explained, "I had to wear a girdle under my skirt or dress to work at Kaufmann's because they [the management] said we shouldn't be bending over without some kind of support. I think it was even printed in our work packets—girdles were required" (personal interview). Another comment on this issue is posted on the *Zona: The Girdle Zone* website.[4] Lillian writes, "Late in my sophomore year I started working at the branch of the public library and came under the influence of the head librarian, Miss Petersen . . .

Real girdles, not panty girdles were de rigueur. Miss Petersen's pages were to be young ladies and she saw that they acted as such" (Lillian). These experiences of enforced dress codes right down to the underclothing perform what Bourdieu describes as a process of deculturation and reculturation which set store on the seemingly most insignificant details of *dress, bearing,* physical and verbal manners (1977, 94). Bourdieu explains how these kinds of rules governing social dress, gestures, and deportment that have the greatest effect on people in society. Hence, in this case requiring young women to don undergarments suitable for their positions as pages and waitresses and store clerks, and perhaps more importantly young ladies, employers participated in what Bourdieu articulates as, "an implicit pedagogy, capable of instilling a whole cosmology, an ethic, a metaphysic, a political philosophy" (1977, 94). In this case an implicit pedagogy of girdling, capable of instilling a whole cosmology, an ethic, a metaphysic, a political philosophy of girdling might be claimed. I argue that the practice of girdling may be seen as a part in a process of deculturation, wherein girls become women by discarding the underwear of their youth, and reculturation, whereby women take up the foundation garments of womanhood—girdles and bras.

However, women did not only wear girdles in order to fulfill the prescriptives of the institutions of health and work, women also wore girdles in order to follow the demands of fashion and etiquette. As a fifty year-old woman from South Georgia recalled, "Girdles were what we wore. Anything less—for instance garter belts—would have made us jezebels. We were supposed to be young ladies, proper girls. Those were the rules. That was what we knew" (personal interview). In Ellen Melinkoff's Social History, *What We Wore*, several women described similar experiences. Rose Mary Kimble commented, "We had to wear girdles because God forbid someone should see something move" (Melinkoff 1984, 152). Tristine Berry supported such a supposition as she noted, "I remember panty girdles in the ninth grade, in 1962. We wore straight skirts and without a girdle your fanny would move. Considered very crude. In the late seventies we all wore straight skirts with our suits—and never considered a panty girdle. Interesting" (Melinkoff 1984, 152). These personal accounts suggest the absolute necessity for wearing a girdle at least until the late 1960s because nice girls did not wear garter belts, and they did not jiggle.

Similarly the popular literature reinforced this notion as a 1954 issue of *Good Housekeeping* maintained, "There isn't a woman who can possibly look or feel her best without the aid of a foundation garment. No matter how slim you are, no matter how perfect your figure, these scientifically designed garments are absolutely vital to a trim appearance and to an attractive carriage" ("It's a perfect fit" 1954, 79). A woman would not have wanted to be caught jiggling around and thus deemed not to have had an "attractive carriage." An article entitled "Build Your Own Best Silhouette" from a 1956 issue of *Woman's Home Companion* likewise declared, "When you buy a dress, fit it over the right foundation, wear it that way for your best silhouette" (1956, 92). This article was concerned with the appearance with fashion and fashion's mandates. This kind of reference to appearance, fashion and women's figures pervaded the public discourse. As fashion writer Ruth Hogeland noted in a 1954 issue of *Country Gentleman*, "To look lovely in today's fashions, you must try to achieve a natural silhouette—a high bust; a controlled, not pinched waistline; and slightly rounded hips. The secret lies in choosing the right foundation garment for your figure" (1954, 99). The language here seems contradictory as the notion of a "natural silhouette" was described as something women must achieve—not something they came by naturally. This example illustrates precisely what Bourdieu describes as being "the whole trick of pedagogic reason" (1977, 95). He notes that this trick "Lies precisely in the way it extorts the essential while seeming to demand the insignificant" (1977, 95). While women wearing girdles may seem to be an insignificant detail of social life, this practice of girdling indicates an element of social control, a demand, which although placed on the physical body, is constrained by social conventions that do not leave free the social or political body either.

Societal demands surfaced in popular media that laid out the protocols and etiquette of girdling for women. Women's journals and magazines operated as reinforcements for the already prescribed practice of girdling, indeed the feminine habitus. These media served as Bourdieu suggests, "Through the habitus, the structure which has produced it governs practice not by the processes of a mechanical determinism, but through the mediation of the orientations and limits it assigns to the habitus's operations of invention" (1977, 95). Hence, the role of women's journals during the 1930s, 1940s, 1950s and into the 1960s was to mediate the orientations and limits assigned by society. These limits—appearing as prescriptives, protocols, and etiquettes—clearly presented themselves in articles that were concerned specifically with the practice of girdling. An article entitled "How to Fit a Foundation" from a 1948 issue of *Woman's Home Companion* illustrated this point as it warned, "A good well-fitting girdle or all-in-one makes any woman's figure look trimmer and smarter than it really is—unless of course, she's an Olympic diver. But one that's badly fitted can produce more bumps and bulges than you'd believe" (1948, 164). This article sets the limits of fit, and this was only one of many articles which set the limits for purchasing and wearing girdles.

These limits were expounded upon by fashion writer Edna Sommerfeld in an article entitled "Buying and Wearing a Foundation Garment" in a 1941 issue of *Consumer's Digest* where criteria for purchasing and wearing a girdle were presented in the form of a checklist. Number ten on the purchasing checklist reminded women, "No figure is perfect and, therefore, seldom will a garment be found that fits perfectly. Minor adjustments are usually necessary for any type of figure" (1941, 26). This reminder signified a social impetus behind girdling—a desire to mask figure flaws, indeed to solve problem body. One response to this conditioning was articulated by Audrey on *The Girdle Zone* website where she stated, "Like other girls I thought it was my fault that a girdle was uncomfortable—I was the wrong shape, and the girdle was the right shape. This shows something of the mindsets we had" (Audrey).[5] These mind-sets were not some kind of natural insecurity. They were those mind-sets which were prescribed into existence.

An unsigned article entitled "Is Your Figure a Problem to Fit?" from a 1954 issue of *Woman's Home Companion* exemplified this point as it suggested, "Maybe you're higher-waisted than the average, longer waisted, or have a definite figure fault, a foundation fitted especially to you is the way to bring your figure in line with spring fashion" (1954, 88). *Woman's Home Companion* suggested that whatever the figure flaw, choosing the right foundation could correct what was wrong with a woman's figure. Two years later, the same message was sent by the same magazine. In a 1956 issue of *Woman's Home Companion* fashion writer Joan Baum's "How to Choose the Right Foundation For You," explained that the garments of 1956 were designed ". . . with built-in corrective features. They take account of high waists, low waists, wide hips and narrow, bust sizes from AA to D. It's all done to make sure that you can find the garments that are exactly right for your figure" (1956, 94). Baum noted that there had been a change, a shift in sizing to accommodate a wider variety of figures—all of course flawed in some way, but what Baum described as being most significant was that the "built-in correctives" could actually provide a solution to every woman's figure flaw. Audrey's personal account was reinforced by the public prescriptives. Women were admonished that their figures were inherently imperfect, and these imperfections became one reason for purchasing girdles.

But, purchasing also meant trying on, and there existed an entire list of protocols for this practice as well. In 1968 an unsigned article from *Good Housekeeping* entitled "Right Girdle and Bra" emphasized the point of trying on girdles before buying. The article declared, "Unless you are buying a style you have worn before, always try on a garment to check its fit and feel. Move around in it—sit, bend, walk. Don't expect to 'break it in' with wear. It should flatter your figure and fit comfortably when you first try it on" (1968, 174). This prescriptive suggested that by trying it on a woman would know what she was getting and what she was in for; however, as a forty-two-year-old woman from Florida pointed out, "It's a far different thing when you have the

thing on for five or ten minutes in a dressing room than when you have to
wear it all day. I remember dying to get out of my girdle, and I know that they
say that if it's uncomfortable, it doesn't fit. Mine fit fine, but after about an
hour of sitting, I always got the feeling that I couldn't breathe (personal interview)." Similarly, fashion writer Janet Livingston's "How to Tell Whether
You're Wearing the Wrong Girdle and Bra" from a 1958 issue of *Good
Housekeeping* commanded, "Never buy a girdle or bra without trying it on.
Absolutely never. In a girdle, make sure that the waistline fit is snug both
when you sit and when you stand, and that the boning follows the contours of
your body, and that the garment is long enough to stay down" (1958, 70). Finally, fashion writer Jack Fenstermacher's "The "Do's, Don'ts and Dressing
Room Decorum of Buying Bras and Girdles" from a 1964 issue of *Seventeen*
warned young women to "Make doubly sure that girdles and panty girdles fit
well; they're rarely returnable. And please take your shoes off before you try
them on. Use the paper panties most stores supply. If none are available, leave
your own on" (1964, 67). This set up etiquette for trying on before the purchase. The language used by Baum, Livingston, Fenstermacher, Sommerfeld
and other authors in popular women's magazines was more than suggestive,
it was actively prescriptive in its use of the second person command "you."

The prescriptive language used to teach women how to choose foundation
garments and how to try on foundation garments was a critical part of the discourse of girdling. The next step in the practice of girdling was the actual
wearing of girdles. Fashion writer Edna Sommerfeld prescribed how a
woman should put on a girdle: "The individual should get the body in the correct posture before putting on the garment . . . if the individual is large busted,
she should step into the garment to prevent unnecessary strain. If she is small
busted, she should slip the garment on over her head" (1941, 27). The minut-
est detail was not left unmentioned; the method of putting on a girdle was one
of the most frequently talked about events in the public girdling discourse.
This event was replayed as one woman wrote in to an advice section entitled
"The Fitting Room" from a 1953 issue of *Mademoiselle*, and she asked,
"What's the best way to put on a girdle? I'm forever puncturing them" (1953,
26). Advice columnist Miriam Howard responded admonishingly, "Fold the
girdle in half, turning the top toward the bottom. Step in and pull the bottom
up to the right place on your hips. Then unroll the top carefully, and use your
finger tips, *not* your nails" (1953, 26). The *not* emphasized here in the original text, illustrates the prescriptive nature, the language of limits, protocols,
and habitus. The negative was also used by fashion writer Helene Obolensky
as she described the way a woman should put on a girdle. She declared,
"*Never* use your nails to pull it on; be careful to use only the balls of your fin-
gers and your palms. Do *not* clutch the top or yank down the bottom" (1964,

88). The warnings concerning what one should *not* do suggested the serious-
ness of this art of practice, of putting on a girdle. The sense was that purchasing, putting on, and wearing a girdle were all important parts of the cultural experience of being woman, which must be entertained as seriously as
any other.

The negative form in the prescriptive, this sense of prescribing, of detailing
exactly what to do, how to do it and perhaps most provocatively what *not* to
do, emerges as a common thread in the popular discourse of girdling. Women
are warned of the consequences of engaging in girdling in the wrong way. I include here a depiction (see Figure 1.1) of such negative prescriptives from a
1938 *Ladies' Home Journal* article entitled "Are You a Corset Contortionist?"
which ascribed names to the women according to their girdling problems—the
yanker, the bulger, the roller, the gouger, and the groper (*LHJ* 1938, 68). So it
would seem that the *don'ts* far outweigh the *dos*. Such negative reinforcement
solidified the limits, the options, and operated as an authority in the public discourse of girdling. In this way, women who did these things—construed as
don't actions—were marked by society. The marks were named—the yanker,
the bulger, the roller, the gouger, and the groper—by the magazines, so the
limits of the feminine habitus through the practice of girdling would be publicly spoken through the social practice of name calling.

A girdle was prescribed, sought out, tried on, purchased, worn, and finally
cared for. The prescriptives for girdle care surfaced in a 1952 issue of
Woman's Home Companion entitled "Stretch the life of Your Girdle Three
Ways." Here the protocols for keeping girdles clean and elastic were outlined
in three parts.

> 1) Bathe your girdle frequently. Soil and perspiration left in a girdle for any
> length of time soon cut the life of it. For a good wash job use warm water,
> detergent and a small brush for more soiled areas. 2) Rinse your girdle
> thoroughly—especially when using a synthetic detergent, or you may find that
> unsightly colored streaks appear in your girdle and it may lose some of its elas-
> ticity. 3) Always dry it away from heat. That means don't dry it in the sun, in a
> dryer or over a radiator. When you're in a hurry to dry the girdle, put a fan close
> by. It cuts drying time considerably. (1952, 98)

This description of the final action of cleaning involved in the cycle of girdle
purchasing and wearing signaled the repetition of the habituated act of
girdling. This cycle of seeking out the right style, trying on for a correct fit,
purchasing a well-made garment, and then wearing and cleaning and wearing
again was continued and perpetuated by the women who wore them and who
initiated their daughters and their daughter's daughters into the practice of
girdling.

Are You A CORSET CONTORTIONIST?

THE YANKER.

Offender No. 1—she's perpetually tugging at the lower edge of her girdle. We've all seen her, we all know her; too many of us are her. So let's do something about it. Let's, the next time we go corset shopping, pick a model that is long enough to fit well over the danger point. If it is the proper length, your anatomy will see to it that the girdle stays where it belongs.

THE BULGER. A distressing sight, that of the lady who, beneath sleek hips, suddenly bursts out with too, too thriving thighs. She has erred in choosing a corset that is too tight, forcing the unfortunate flesh to find an outlet below. To avoid that lowly bulging, be sure that your new girdle allows room for everything you have to stay in its proper place. **THE ROLLER.** This is another all-too-frequent casualty—the waistline excess commonly known as "spare tire." The remedy demands both length and width; either an all-in-one foundation garment or a girdle that rises well above the sit-down bend, one which will not compress and force your tummy upward. A couple of light bones in front may also help.

THE GOUGER. Here we have the lady who, every time she sits or stands, adjusts the top front of her corset with a most ungraceful gesture of thumbs-in-and-up. As in the case of the Roller, an all-in-one is the logical solution to her problem. If she wants a girdle, too, it should be high and flexible in front. Then she won't have to dig for it. **THE GROPER.** Last but not least, the shoulder-strap adjuster, always fishing around for an elusive bit of ribbon or elastic. Some people feel she should just be quietly put out of the way in the most merciful manner possible. We suggest that she get a well-fitted bra, so cut that it conforms to her rather than expecting her to conform to it. If she has sloping Venus de Milo shoulders that simply refuse to bear the slightest burden, then she must have little bands sewed inside every dress to snap around her shoulder straps. Indeed, it's a wise precaution for you all. ∎

Figure 1.1. Are You a Corset Contortionist?
Source: *LHJ* April 1938

Still, many young girls questioned the practice of girdling as they discovered their bodies and the practices, which were to be performed upon them. Simone de Beauvoir describes the process in which "One is not born, but rather becomes a woman" (1989, 267). This process, a kind of initiation, is the way in which girls become initiated into the practices of womanhood. Beauvoir explains how young girls are initiated into womanhood by their senior counterparts—mothers, aunts, grandmothers and female teachers (1989, 281). Beauvoir notes, "the treasures of feminine wisdom are poured into her ears, feminine virtues are urged upon her, she is taught cooking sewing, housekeeping, along with care of her person charm, and modesty; she is dressed in inconvenient and frilly clothes" (1989, 282). In this way Beauvoir explains how girls are brought into the world of women, how a girl receives her "vocation" (1989, 283).

This process of becoming woman was often encouraged by older women to be looked upon as a moment of passage, when many rituals of femininity and womanhood were passed on to young women. During interviews, many women commented that girdling existed for them in their girlhood as markers of womanhood, which wearing a first girdle was understood as a rite of passage. One thirty-five-year-old woman remembered, "When I tried on my mother's girdles as a child, I knew that one day I would wear one as a woman. It made me proud to think I would grow up and wear one of these white supports. As it turns out that never happened since by the time I was of age girdles were on the way out and pantyhose were on the scene" (personal interview). Suzanne's experience, which she articulated on *The Girdle Zone* website, similarly confirmed this moment of ritual as she noted, "The first girdle for me, and I suspect many other women, was a genuine entry into well, for lack of a better term, ladyhood. It immediately made me feel, walk, sit, and act like a grown woman, a lady (Suzanne)."[6]

While the practice of girdling from the 1930s through to the 1960s was the habitus of grown women, it was a practice into which young women were initiated. Joan Brumberg's seminal text, *The Body Project*, points out the extent to which the young girl's initiation into womanhood was certainly nudged if not pushed by the beauty and fashion industries that sought to hawk their wares including underwear to younger audiences (1997). This also meant that advertisements for specific products accompanied or followed etiquette articles for wearing girdles and bras.[7] Women's and young women's journals reinforced those teachings and trainings from home and prescribed specific protocols for teenagers' introduction into girdling. In *Good Housekeeping* from 1949 fashion editor Shirley Mapes discussed the appropriate age for teens to begin wearing foundations. "Under certain circumstances a doctor may advise that a young girl from 11 to 16 years of age be fitted for a foundation

garment. A light, free-action garment is recommended, if needed, for controlling the teen-age figure" (1949, 301-302). This suggestion of a potential possibility for a need for teenage foundations became a mandate just seven years
later in an unsigned article entitled "Bras and Girdles for Teen-Agers" appearing in *Good Housekeeping* November 1956 which stated, "It is just as important for a teenager as it is for her mother to try on a girdle or bra before
she buys it. A proper fitting is the only way to tell whether a particular garment will control as it should. Because her figure is changing rapidly, she
should be fitted often and she should not buy more than one or two garments
at a time" (1956, 289). In fact, the public discourse on girdling for teens
seemed to proliferate in the 1950s and even into the 1960s. Another unsigned
article entitled "Foundations for Figure Types" from a 1955 issue of *Practical Home Economics* described the needs of teens for foundations that offered
effective support. *Practical Home Economics* explained, "Teaching girls with
such variant figures about foundation garments is a large assignment. Teen-
agers need a great deal of advice on the undergarments which will smooth
their youthful curves, make their clothes fit more attractively, and help them
to attain proportioned bust, waist, and hips at maturity" (1955, 14). What
Practical Home Economics did not explain was that the teachers were to be
adult women already knowledgeable and practiced in girdling. These teens
with their varied figures were in these articles the objects to be trained, to be
brought into the practice of girdling, the limited space of womanhood.

Beauvoir articulates this space as "The sphere to which she [the young girl]
belongs . . . [a space that] is everywhere enclosed, limited and dominated, by
the male universe" (1989, 297). Beauvoir recognizes that the limits placed on
girls are trained, learned and initiated by women, but it is patriarchy which
she sees prescribing the limits for all of womanhood. Just as women must
bring their daughters into the limits of womanhood, so must the daughters accept this rite of passage, this training—they have no choice. This is corrobo-
rated both by the public discourse in women's and young women's magazines, but also by the lived experiences of most women I interviewed who
were aged fifty or older. A fifty-one-year-old from New York noted that her
girdling experience began "with my being a teenager and thinking that long
line girdles were appropriate wear . . . at 110 pounds. It was the right thing to
do, so we wore girdles (personal interview)." The whole of society signified
to them that this womanhood that they moved toward was inevitable, it was
their vocation. In this way the public discourse in women's and young
women's journals took up the burden of training teenagers.

As mentioned earlier the prescriptives for older women called for the
proper preparation and training of teens into the practice of girdling; however,
simultaneously teens were taught the practice of girdling in their own maga-

zines. Fashion writer Jack Fenstermacher in a 1964 issue of *Seventeen* maintains, "You're a growing girl, so always have your measurements taken. And let your sales lady show you foundations designed for your specific figure requirements as well as your specific fashion requirements" (1964, 67). Many of my interviews supported this suggestion that teens were appealed to both in their own social circles and in media to put on girdles as an initiating ritual for womanhood. Even athletic girls could not escape "the control" of girdling on some level. An article entitled "The Most Valuable Players in Your Sports Wardrobe Are Foundations that Make You Look Like a Winner" from another 1964 issue of *Seventeen* noted the importance of panty girdles for athletes.

> Panty girdles play the game too—and their importance is not to be underestimated. Under a one or two-piece swimsuit a sporting panty brief in a light elasticized or rubberized fabric gives a smooth look. A good choice is a seamless panty (above) or one with paneled support wherever you need it most. If your midriff needs a bit of control a high-rise panty girdle under a one-piece suit will taper your waistline. Light, brief, stretchy panty girdles move easily and feel comfortable under almost all your active sportswear. (1964, 206)

Teenage girls especially during the 1950s and 1960s were trained in the practice of girdling by older women in their lives and this training was reinforced by public media that addressed their own age group. Social historian Joan Brumberg notes, "by the early 1950s, a reenergized corset and brassiere industry was poised for extraordinary profits. If 'junior figure control' became the ideal among the nation's mothers and daughters, it would open up sales of bras and girdles to the largest generation of adolescents in American history, the so-called baby boomers" (1997, 113). Thus teens in the 1950s grew up knowing that girdling was a part of their passage to womanhood and that they would not be considered proper women if they did not learn to purchase and wear the correct foundations for their figures, fashions and activities. As Beauvoir notes, "The little girl . . . in order to change into a grownup person, must be confined within the limits imposed upon her by her femininity" (1989, 315). The practice of girdling powerfully mirrors Beauvoir's concept as girls become teens and are girdled [confined], so then they can become women.

However, the girdle began to come into question in the early 1960s once pantyhose became a viable option. Garter belts were typically not worn except under very full skirts, which were not in fashion. In the meantime, girdles became more modern and manufacturers attempted to make changes in design that made them more desirable. Social historian Ellen Melinkoff explains, "As girdle legs became longer (and finally finished off with a two-inch cuff of lacy elastic) garter tabs were put up inside the cuff rather than at the bottom. It was a major aesthetic breakthrough. The stocking top, the ugly brown part, went up inside the garter and made a smooth line. We were in girdle heaven. We couldn't ask for anything more (except not to wear a girdle) (1989, 124). But, even these changes could not keep women and especially young women in girdles. Pantyhose took control of women's bodies. Melinkoff maintains, "Pantyhose, once the shaping and sizing were gotten down pat were a miracle. They could cover, control, and look natural at the same time" (Melinkoff 1984, 124). The advent of pantyhose also facilitated the wearing of the 1960s hit "the mini-skirt." Fashion historian Elizabeth Ewing concurs with Melinkoff. She states, "The stocking, entrenched in centuries of unquestioned acceptance, at once necessary and ornamental, met its Waterloo in the mini-skirt" (1978, 182). In many ways, the mini-skirt was a 1960s fashion articulation of the feminist movement. The traditions of women tending to the domestic sphere in long-style 1950s skirts, was being overthrown by a generation of women who recognized that their sexuality and their femininity had been too long contained and restrained under waist-cinching belts, poodle skirts and girdles. The mini-skirt and pants meant sexual, social and political freedom. Women could demonstrate their political and social strength and power while exhibiting their sexual freedom. Girdles represented prudery and restraint. Pantyhose allowed women to show off their legs, knees and even their thighs. They no longer had to hide inside of garments that were constructed to keep them safe and chaste. The feminist movement facilitated change in codes of dress and fashion and made pantyhose a fashion necessity.

Since tights and pantyhose came on the scene, the gap between stocking and garter ceased to be an issue, and hemlines became shorter and shorter as evidenced by the micro-mini. Melinkoff explains, "Pantyhose made the miniskirt phenomenon possible (and vice versa). We could let men see our pantyhose—on and off our bodies. Some women, excessively concerned about jiggling flesh, wore panty girdles over the hose. Manufacturers didn't seem to catch on that women no longer needed garter tabs and didn't eliminate them from girdles until the late seventies" (1989, 124). By the 1970s the girdle had declined significantly in terms of sales and consumption. Melinkoff concludes, "But most women, having flirted with the possibilities of wearing no or almost no underwear have decided that bra-wearing is for them. The girdle, however is dead, except for the most tradition-bound women who still think that discomfort is an acceptable price to pay for thinking they look thinner" (1989, 176).

If girdling then has been understood as a practice of the past, one which women of the 1960s and early 1970s rejected once they had better options, why would the potential exist for a resurgence of such a garment? In order to answer such a question, an analysis of contemporary trends in foundations must be examined carefully first to evaluate if there has been a resurgence, and second to gain insight into the reasons for such a resurgence. While I contend that there has been without a doubt a kind of foundation resurgence in contemporary shapewear, I do not claim that this resurgence comes from the same place as the girdling of the 1930s, 1940s, 1950s and 1960s. I claim instead that these are very different phenomena; furthermore, I maintain that the current resurgence is at least potentially something even more dangerous to women than the trained and habituated practices of the older girdling phenomenon.

However, in order to explain these claims, I must first explain what is meant by girdle resurgence. I rely here largely on the contemporary popular women's magazines and trade magazines to analyze this trend. While these sources address very different audiences, both confirm a resurgence of girdles in terms of sales figures and in terms of fashion. A 1991 issue of *Newsweek* identified the trend and warned, "If you thought it was safe to assume that women would never allow themselves to be squashed into an ideal form again, you were wrong. Believe it or not, girdles are back" (Darnton 1991, 63). Rationales for this phenomenon vary, but it seems clear that this trend seems to be picking up momentum. Women's Undergarments (Table 1.1) from a Specialists in Business Information Report illustrates a decline of girdles and other foundations from 1967 to 1972, while figures dive slowly and then remain relatively stable until 1988. Since 1988 these figures have been generally climbing. The table reflects an increase of almost one hundred million dollars between 1993 and 1994. These totals are estimated and forecasted to continue to climb into the next century (1995, 9). Contemporary girdles and shapewear (without other foundations) have shown significant growth as the sales figures from *American Demographics* point out, "Sales of shapers increased for $338 million in 1992 to $350 million in 1993, according to Field of the Intimate Apparel Council" (Braus 1995, 55). And in fact these numbers are still growing according to an article entitled, "Remember When Bras Were for Burning?" from a 1995 issue of *Business Week* which notes, "Since 1991, U.S. Sales of shapewear alone have risen 12 percent, to $350 million" (Chandler 1995, 37). This trend still continues into the late 1990s where intimate apparel sales in general are definitely on the rise. From a November 1997 issue of *Women's Wear Daily,* an article entitled "Little Nothings Are Big Business" confirms that, "With $10.3 billion in retail sales in 1996, the U.S. market for intimate apparel represents 11.7 percent of the women's apparel market . . . The intimate apparel market increased an impressive 14 percent in the last two years—a 7 percent annual growth rate—outpacing women's apparel which was up 3 to 4 percent each year" (Monget 1997, 48).

WOMEN'S UNDERGARMENTS

TABLE 1.1. U.S. WOMEN'S UNDERGARMENT MARKET SALES BY MAJOR PRODUCT SECTOR, 1967–2005

(DOZEN IN THOUSANDS, VALUE IN MILLIONS)

	WOMEN'S & GIRLS' UNDERWEAR[1]		BRASSIERES[1]		GIRDLES & OTHER FOUNDATION GARMENTS[1]	
	DOZEN	VALUE	DOZEN	VALUE	DOZEN	VALUE
1967	58,392	$507.4	22,499	$356.8	8,283	$309.2
1972	59,385	494.9	22,201	460.9	5,469	242.2
1977	57,761	636.9	19,125	576.5	3,887	196.4
1978	57,070	690.8	22,935	599.5	4,444	192.9
1979	54,589	751.5	23,250	648.1	4,294	192.1
1980	55,520	783.8	21,647	713.2	4,402	199.2
1981	55,130	833.1	20,732	765.2	4,483	197.0
1982	59,900	950.3	20,841	791.3	4,120	205.1
1983	64,647	1,043.1	21,122	851.7	4,204	221.2
1984	68,332	1,122.8	19,026	818.7	4,148	197.1
1985	68,659	1,152.5	22,706	899.5	4,146	210.6
1986	71,306	1,148.8	21,081	886.2	3,790	183.4
1987	77,001	1,364.4	22,798	929.9	4,399	198.9
1988	84,127	1,422.4	23,127	1,028.2	6,884 [2]	258.5[2]
1989	83,515	1,344.5	22,863	1,112.5	5,410	239.6
1990	83,509	1,349.0	22,110	1,071.6	6,226	264.6
1991	89,133	1,372.3	22,133	1,258.8	6,050	316.8
1992	94,225	1,432.6	25,157	1,488.5	7,405	361.0
1993	96,902	1,428.9	25,956	1,595.2	6,114	322.1
1994	112,510	1,662.8	26,284	1,809.3	8,047	415.5
1995 E	124,722	1,846.7	30,428	2,092.0	9,691	513.7
2000 F	159,913	2,391.5	37,627	3,058.7	12,782	779.4
2005 F	182,773	2,910.4	44,160	4,138.9	15,032	986.1

Note: Value in manufacturers dollars

E = Estimate
F = Forecast

1 U.S. shipments minus exports plus imports
2 Includes imports of some garter belts prior to 1989

A 1995 *Market Profile: Women's Undergarments* cites the reasons for such dramatic increases in sales of shapewear and intimate apparel as it reports, "An aging baby boom population and weight-control problems in the adult population have resulted in growing demands for shapewear products" (SBI 1995, 3). So, it seems that the baby boomers have cornered the market on shapewear and are pushing the growth of these products to all time highs.

But, what does this trend mean? Does it signify the onset of girdling as an everyday occurrence once again, and just how did this all seem to happen overnight? The answers to these questions have much to do with the history of girdles. Patricia Braus notes "Girdles began to lose favor in the 1960s, as baby boomers entered young adulthood . . . The boomers' belief in sexual freedom, and a new emphasis on comfort, dealt a mortal blow to the [girdle] industry . . . [By the 1970s], girdles became a sign of age or prudery" (1995, 54). This explains the decline in girdle sales which many women I interviewed attributed to the practical invention of pantyhose (personal interviews). A 1989 article from The *Denver Post* also acknowledges the impact of pantyhose noting, "Women no longer needed garters [neither on garter belts nor on girdles] to hold up their stockings, so girdles weren't selling. And then, control-top pantyhose provided more freedom and comfort. That was the demise of the girdle" (Seipel 1989, 3). What this article also points out is the impact this decline had on traditional girdle sales. "Playtex's best girdle year was 1973, when $63.1 million worth were sold; last year, the figure was $30 million" (Seipel 1989, 3). So, the history of girdle sales makes clear that there really was a legitimate and powerful decline in girdle sales after 1973, and current sales figures confirm that contemporary shapewear sales are on the rise. The question then becomes do these two movements in undergarment history come from a common place? Is the push for contemporary shapewear really a resurrection of the girdle?

One reason for the current trend toward girdling via popular shapewear is a result of the fact that the same demographic group, baby boomers, who rejected girdles because they were too constraining are finding themselves bulging in their later years in ways they wish they didn't (Braus 1995, 55). The *Specialists in Business Information* comment in their recent *Market Profile: Women's Undergarments* that, "Some industry experts feel baby boomers are using undergarments to give them a psychological lift. Data indicate baby boomers are turning to shapewear as diet and exercise fail to limit the effects of aging" (1995, 4–5). Beyond this the *Specialists in Business Information* find that, "In fact, the percentage of the adult female population considered overweight has increased sharply over the past fifteen years. The percent of adult women who are overweight nearly doubles as one compares women in their twenties to women in their fifties" (1995, 5). The basis then for a resurgence of girdling in the form of contemporary shapewear is that the baby boomers are overweight, more overweight than their predecessors at this age. Hence, they are resorting to using shapewear to appear thinner.

But what is perhaps most intriguing about this resurgence is that no one including boomers and manufactures wants to label this advent of contemporary shapewear as girdling. Journalist Patricia Braus points out, "Baby boomers will accept control garments that masks their flab, but only if manufacturers choose their words carefully" (1995, 55). In other words, the g-word shouldn't be mentioned (1995, 55). The new shapewear is called all sorts of different things: slimmers, shapers, and smoothies among them; however, there is noticeable similarity in the form and function of contemporary shapewear and traditional girdles. As an article, "The Ultimate Squeeze Play," from a 1991 issue of *Newsweek* notes, "They've got euphemistic new names, of course—body slimmers, body shapers—but the constricting press of excess flesh is unmistakable, and no one is fooled. To paraphrase Gertrude Stein, a girdle is a girdle is a girdle . . . but the aging baby boomers who are wearing the new girdles and corsets have come up against one convincing reason: gravity" (Darnton 1991, 63).

However, I suggest that while women may not be fooled (in fact, they may recognize that these shapewear products are girdles in disguise), the fashion journals and trade presses are certainly sending out the message that wearing these garments, if not necessary, is strongly suggested for reasons of fashion. As Sarah Mower argues, "Granted the girdle's lengthy history requires quite a lot of getting past, but if we are gung ho about taking on spring's hourglass figure, a certain amount of underwear rearrangement is part of the bargain" (1995, 68). According to Sarah Mower it is a choice women face—to be in fashion or not; however, Vevlyn Wright suggests that women do have a choice and they are choosing to wear girdles for their own reasons. She writes, "In the 90s, women wear girdles for a variety of reasons that have nothing to do with concealing extra pounds. Some wear them to improve their posture. Others swear by them for alleviating low-back pain. And, some women wear them because they make them feel good" (1998, 16).

While it is satisfying to think that women have gained some ground in the girdling realm. They no longer are trained as young girls into the practice of girdling as a rite of passage to womanhood, nor are women habituated into the practice of girdling to the extent that it is assumed appropriate and standardized as a practice of womanhood; however, many women, and the number is growing, choose to engage in the practice of girdling even if the apparatuses are called by different names. Ten of the 40 women I interviewed[8] and 46 of the 267 women surveyed (17.23 percent)[9] acknowledged that they owned a contemporary shaper (slimmer, shaper, smoother) of some sort. One fifty-seven-year-old South Carolina native noted, "I only wear it under this really tight knit dress that I wear to parties or black-tie affairs (personal interview)." I sensed her defensiveness and wondered if my question—"What do you think about contemporary shapewear?"—seemed too invasive, but I think that what is really going on here is that women are struggling to make the choice whether or not to adhere to contemporary standards of the ideal feminine form. This form is one that is clearly indicated by fashion, as fashion writer Jody Shields points out foundationwear has again become a kind of outerwear. She notes:

> Fashion designers have borrowed the look of innerwear from the fifties—and made it into a whole new game. The provocative inspiration: the aptly titled foundation garments—Merry Widows, waist-cinchers, panty girdles, corsets, mystifiers, all-in-ones, and push-up brassieres. Each was deliberately unrevealing and never fashioned from wispy fabrics, policing the body with a heavy hand. Any kind of nude or natural look was unthinkable. As a result, women looked like Joan of Arc in elastic armor. Sure these undergarments could be taken off—but only after a struggle with cruelly finicky hooks and recalcitrant snaps and laces. This accessible/inaccessible character gave underwear a faintly fetishistic air. That fetishistic character is still part of the appeal today. Designers put innerwear details on outerwear: zigzag stitching, seams, stays, straps, gussets, grommets, and garters. (1990, 342)

What Shields suggests is a fashion phenomenon that sexualizes women and keeps them trapped in a male fantasy that conjures up the notion of chastity belts. This idea surfaced several times during my interviews, and a sixty-year-old from South Georgia commented that, "Her mother only let her wear heavy paneled girdles on dates because she thought the girdles would operate as chastity belts" (personal interview).

This idea of the sexuality of shapewear operates in new contemporary shapewear fashions where some girdles are actually designed with outer and inner appeal in mind. Fashion writer Sarah Mower explains that one category of girdles, "delivers functional figure improvements plus a look you wouldn't mind parading in front of your man" (1995, 68). This seems to me to be the most dangerous proposition of contemporary girdling. It is touted as a solution to both the 1) physical flaws of women's bodies—reminiscent of the built-in corrective features of girdles in the 1950s and 2) to the unappealing aesthetics of traditional girdles—which allow men to realize their fantasies of unveiling, uncovering, and revealing women's bodies. Nineties fashion designers congratulate themselves that they have solved the conundrum of how to make girdles that work and play. So, it seems that many women are being persuaded into girdles. They are making the choice to wear contemporary shapewear precisely because "These aren't your grandma's girdles" (Chandler & Palmer 1995, 37).

However, the discourse of comfort remains an issue even with the new shapewear. Several women I interviewed mentioned that they had tried contemporary shapewear fashions and that while they may not have been as uncomfortable as traditional heavy-paneled girdles, they were still constraining and after a few hours they wanted to get out of them. Journalist Susan Rittenhouse articulates this experience humorously in a recent article, "Girdles: Little Torture Chambers Made of Lycra" where she explains what happens after she manages to put on her modern-day girdle. She notes, "And ta-da, there I was—Smoothie Susan; completely lump free. But I couldn't move . . . When I was a kid, we had a phrase we'd say to one another when offering a choice. As a fifth-grader, I didn't know exactly what it meant except that it was some kind of ultimatum. We used to say 'you can like it or you can lump it.' With age comes understanding. I think I'll lump it" (1997, 5). What Rittenhouse describes is a choice in which women can decide to wear girdles and meet the standards of fashion or *not*. It is important to recall what happened to the women who did *not* listen to the prescriptives of girdling the first time around—the yanker, bulger, gauger, and groper group.

Still this does not seem such a simple choice. Contemporary girdling seems to have much less to do with fashion in terms of propriety than it has to do with presenting the ideal feminine body—a svelte, trimmed figure devoid of unnecessary fat or bulges. In other words, contemporary girdling is less concerned with making women's bodies appear more properly modest and more concerned with making them into appropriate sexualized objects. The real ultimatum from society is connected to the longstanding image of the ideal feminine body. The social message is that if you do not have an ideal body, and we have all been told that we don't, then we should aspire to one—either through a shaper, slimmer or smoother as was the case for a post-partum Gwyneth Paltrow or from the gym and 1,000 crunches per day work-out regimen—reported as the standard for maintaining washboard abs by Brittany Spears and Usher.

The choice then is to girdle externally or internally. Feminist philosopher Susan Bordo takes up this issue in her seminal feminist text, *Unbearable Weight*, where she argues, "as our bodily ideals have become firmer and more contained (we worship not merely slenderness but flablessness) any softness or bulge comes to be seen as unsightly—as disgusting, disorderly, 'fat'"(1993, 57). What Bordo suggests here is an internalized girdling, a process in which the gym-honed body evolves as the ideal. This argument finds support in contemporary public discourse where Valerie Steele maintains, "Women have been moving away from corsets by internalizing the discipline of corset-wear, exercising and bringing their bodies into the shape they would have otherwise obtained through foundationwear. But some women don't have that discipline. They have to be pushed into shape with undergarments" (qtd in Blumner 1997).

Hence, the fact that most women have not been wearing girdles since the late 1960s or 1970s is less an indication that women are comfortable with their bodies and letting it all hang out, than it is an indication that there has been an internalization of girdling. Valerie Steele comments further that, "For American women some kind of foundation wear has been part of women's fashion since the colonies" (qtd in Blumner 1997). The reality, historically speaking, is that women have almost always been held-in by some kind of confining undergarment, and the past thirty years have been something of an aberration. The resurgence of girdles is both an indicator of a return to constraint and restraint for women, and a return to external girdling because of failed attempts at internal girdling or because of a perceived failure in achieving the gym-honed body.

This notion is supported by fashion writer Vevlyn Wright who states, "But in recent years slim women have been relying on the foundation garments to achieve an uber-buff appearance. Supermodels wear them on the runway because of the smooth lines they create under form-fitting clothes" (1998, 15). So it seems that what's happening here in the realm of modern day girdling is that a choice to girdle is becoming less of a choice and more of a requirement as the ideal body is not just a thin body, but the muscular, shaped, and controlled body that Susan Bordo suggests. The fact that many women are choosing to girdle themselves in fashions of today's shapers, smoothers and slimmers is not merely a resurrection of the same habituated practice of traditional girdling. It is rather a practice of a new sort because it is a choice, albeit a limited one—like it or lump it. Women are choosing to shape their bodies in the 1990s body ideal that is so perfectly slender and honed that not an ounce of jiggle can be perceived. While women of the girdled eras were worried about jiggle, they were less concerned about slenderness. In fact the feminine body ideal is one that has changed over the decades, and girdling has always served to support and reinforce these feminine body ideals. It should therefore come as no surprise to find that women are choosing to girdle externally on top of an already precedented internal girdlization of a slender body ideal.

The history of girdling has revealed that this process was one of habituated practice filled with rituals regarding finding the right girdle and purchasing it, putting it on and wearing it correctly, and maintaining it as a most significant part of a lady's wardrobe. These practices were passed on and down for generations from mother to daughter to daughter since the inception of the girdle in the mid-1930s. Women wore girdles because they held them in and held stockings-up, and perhaps most importantly because their mothers told them to. What happened in the late 1960s was a social upheaval, a feminist movement, and a fashion coup. Girls in particular escaped dresses and girdles in honor of pants, pantyhose and mini-skirts, and many women flirted with the idea of wearing little or no underwear. The 1960s also signified a moment of social change in which the rules for everything from fashion to politics were broken. The decline of the girdle was part of this social change.

Similarly, the resurgence of the girdle in the form of shapewear signals a return to conservatism, a return to a sexual politics that is bound up—like that of a chastity belt. As Ruth P. Rubinstein, Professor of Sociology at the Fashion Institute of Technology notes, "We rode the wave of rebellion which included sloughing off the girdle. For a while we had the idea of letting everything hang out. We are now requiring more restraint" (qtd in Blumner 1997). What this signifies socially is a return to a femininity that is contained and controlled. This social pressure to control the extreme slender feminine body ideal—one that is so slender that it appears devoid of any bump or bulge— signals not only a shift in what women are wearing, but signals a shift in attitudes toward the feminine body. These attitudes articulated by rigid practices of femininity operating on the female body suggest the extent to which the female body continues to be used as a locus of social and cultural control.

NOTES

1. See popular magazine articles, trade journals and newspaper articles in bibliography.

2. See methodologies in introduction.

3. The resistance of women who took part in dress reform movements such as the one launched by Amelia Bloomer in 1851 in America is duly noted. For more on dress reform, see Ewing, *Dress and Undress,* 1978.

4. *Zona: The Girdle Zone* is a personal website that has been developed by a girdle enthusiast/fetishist, the Virginian; however, his site is well-researched and draws from Valerie Steele's analysis of corsetry and girdling. http://www.girdlezone.org

5. Audrey's comments are posted in the "You're asking Me" section of *The Girdle Zone* website.

6. Suzanne's comments are posted in the "You're asking Me" section of *The Girdle Zone* website. Certainly, there is always the threat of fraud with web postings, and I am not uncritical of the material on the Zona website. I leave it to the reader to assess the strength of these postings, but I include these accounts to broaden the scope of the project to include cyber discourse for the purposes of discourse analysis.

7. For a larger discussion of the role of women as consumers and their relationship to advertising in women's journals, see Damon-Moore and Scanlon.

8. See interview methods addressed in the introduction.

9. See telephone survey methods addressed in the introduction.

Chapter Two

Dress Codes:
Foundationwear Required

Bodies which do not conform, bodies which flout the conventions of their culture and go without the appropriate clothes are subversive of the most basic social codes and risk exclusion, scorn or ridicule.

Joanne Entwistle, *Body Dressing*

The subject of dress codes provides some of the richest evidence of women's responses in terms of both acceptance and resistance to the assertions of social and cultural control of women's bodies. In spite of the fact that this study investigated both claims concerning the fashioned body as a locus of social control and claims that fashion and beauty practices potentially facilitate women's resistance to social control, the notion of dress codes was not addressed in either the telephone questionnaire or the open-ended interviews.[1] However, during the in-depth interviews the term dress code was invariably used by interviewees with regard to women's social obligation to attire themselves suitably for various social, religious and professional occasions. The notion of dress codes similarly arose in terms of protocols for dress and appropriate feminine dress in women's magazines.

Although many women today feel free not to wear shaping garments on a daily basis, most agree that there are specific occasions that still call for the donning of foundationwear—weddings, proms, balls, funerals, high church, formals, bar or basmitzvahs among other significant social events. Fashion historian Valerie Steele maintains that foundation garments have been and will continue to be a requirement of women's dress for centuries even though some American women may only wear them for special occasions (1985, 224). Telephone survey data reveals that 50 percent of women currently wear some form of foundation garment everyday (including underwire and push-up bras); while 29 percent of respondents indicated that they wear shaping garments only on special occasions.[2] As Joanne Entwistle argues, "codes of dress come to be taken for granted and are routinely and unreflexively employed, although some occasions, generally formal ones (like weddings and funerals) which set tighter constraints around the body, lend themselves to more conscious reflection on dress" (2001, 47). It is important to point out the extent to which these special occasions are rituals of courtship and reassert traditional, religious and class definitions of gender roles.

Annette Lynch's account of a modern day African American debutante cotillion provides such an example of formal gendered dress codes. Lynch is careful to point out the extent to which these Waterloo, Iowa, debutantes, chosen for academic achievement and community service, confront "historical stereotypes depicting black women as promiscuous and lacking in intelligence and grace" (Lynch 1999, 92). These African American Iowa debutantes combat the stereotypes of race and class by embracing traditional and idealized femininity. Dressed in white, accompanied by escorts in black, they are led around the dance floor in idealized, ritualized, traditional and upper-class performances of femininity. Lynch cites ritualized excuses to dress for formal occasions as "public enactments contributing to the development of images of black women that challenged cultural stereotypes and helped women recognize their own potential and receive the respect of others" (Lynch 1999, 95). While Lynch emphasizes the agency of these African American women who participate in the ritual of the debutante ball, she understates the degree to which this ritual performance of gendered dress reinscribes traditional class and gender roles.[3] Lynch's ethnographic study of debutantes suggests that although race and class factor into ritual feminine dress, they are lesser factors than ideal femininity itself.

Women's attire at special occasions powerfully reflects the idea of shaping garments as a fashion requirement. Indeed as foundation garments shape women's breasts, waists, hips, buttocks and thighs, they produce heightened forms of femininity making women's bodies fit the image of the ideal feminine body. To the extent that women's bodies can be equated with ideal femininity—woman as body—then women who achieve the ideal feminine form embody ideal femininity and may be seen as such. Hence, these events, special occasions, and/or religious rituals celebrate ideal femininity, as they demand a stricter and more traditional adherence to the codes of gendered dress.

Breasts and Bras

During many of my in-depth interviews, women detailed their experiences of wearing foundation garments to satisfy rigorous social dress codes. Women used language such as "socially acceptable," "appropriate" and "required" to describe moments when they felt compelled to wear special or additional foundation garments to special events. Many women discussed at length their experiences regarding the presentation of their breasts at formal occasions. Several women described the need to wear strapless bras to proms under dresses that were themselves strapless or thinly strapped, as in the case of spaghetti straps or single shoulder styles. Women explained that not wearing a bra under such a dress was not an option in spite of the fact that strapless bras brought with them many problems. Strapless bras frequently needed to be stuffed; an eighty-eight-year-old from Chicago commented that, "I used Kleenex and Kotex to keep the thing up." Since strapless bras kept sliding down to their waists, some women had friends help them remember to pull them up throughout the prom. But, a sixty-two-year-old Italian woman laughingly recalled, "I watched in horror as my friend danced at senior prom with the boy of her dreams while her strapless bra actually worked its way around to the back of her dress." However, these stories are not limited to women over fifty. A twenty-something woman explained, "I felt like a mummy at my senior prom in a bra that went all the way down to my waist. It really didn't work for me." The fact that many women chose to wear strapless bras, in spite of the fact that these bras did not work for them, suggests the degree of social pressure to adhere to a dress code requiring strapless bras to be worn under formal dresses.

However, several women discussed their disappointment with strapless bras, long-line strapless bras and even contemporary bustiers. They commented that these foundations were "bulky, didn't fit right or moved around too much." Still others sought other options, blurring the lines between wearing and not wearing a bra by using paste-ons. Most women reported that breast size was a major consideration in this operation. One twenty-year-old from Virginia noted, "I wore the cups that stick to your chest right under your boobs to homecoming with a strapless dress. Luckily mine were small enough that the cups stayed on, but they were a pain to peel off." A thirty-five year-old from North Carolina commented that her breasts were a D cup, so she actually had to wear two paste-ons per breast, but she also noted they did work. Still, a third woman complained, "I tried the stick on bras, *they do not work*! If you are any larger than a C cup." Finally, an eighty-one-year-old from South Carolina explained, "After a dinner party I stood in the shower for 3 hours trying to get the things off and was left with two bullseyes on my chest." Many women who tried paste-ons considered them a viable option to strapless bras. In fact, for all their difficulty many women preferred wearing paste-ons to struggling with strapless bras, but this prompted me to question several women about the need to wear anything under these kinds of formal

dresses. After all, most formal dresses are lined and some even have cups
sewn into the lining, but every woman I talked to voiced her discomfort with
the idea of going without a bra or bra option—a slip with built in bra, paste-
on, bustier, or strapless (long-line or not)—under a formal dress. In fact, thirty
of the forty women I interviewed suggested that the codes of formal dress required formal foundations. Even in general survey questions which refer-
enced women's everyday wearing habits, 62 percent of women reported that
wearing shaping garments makes them feel feminine and 38 percent of
women feel exposed without these garments.[4] Additionally when I consulted
Woman's Day "Shoptalk Bra Survey" of 906 women across the United States,
67.6 percent of the respondents agreed that they would buy a bra for a special
occasion.[5]

The survey numbers combined with the interview responses reinforce the
significance of gendered dress codes as means of social control of women's
bodies as they relate to gender performance and gender roles in society. In
Fashion and Its Social Agendas social historian Diana Crane documents the
historical pattern of establishing gender hegemonies through gender dress
codes. Crane maintains, "For women, clothes were in the nineteenth century,
and are still, powerful expressions of gender hegemonies" (2000, 237). Indeed the standardization of bra cup size in 1935 marks such a moment of gendered hegemony as Warner produced the first Type A-D cup brassieres
(Fields 1997, 145). However, Crane also expresses the significant part fashion has played in society by allowing women an avenue for resistance against
constraining gender roles. She comments, "Clothing has performed important
roles in maintaining the visibility of alternative discourses about gender
roles" (2000, 237). While the embedded femininity in foundation garments
may make them appear less likely to be the site of contested cultural meanings, a twenty-year-old from Virginia relayed this experience concerning her
best friend's prom attire. "For our senior prom her mother bought her this
pimped out, black, lacy, corset to wear with her dress. I thought it was hilarious because it looked like a stereotypical hooker outfit piece, and she's this
little Gap, J Crew, happy girl. She wore it once, for that night, and then gave
it to me. It remains in my bedroom at home for a decoration and a laugh. I
love that thing!" This anecdote conveys the message of the stereotypical virgin-whore dichotomy that is so often critiqued by feminist scholars, but it also
pokes fun at the ridiculousness of this often-practiced dichotomy of ideal
femininity. As the friend wears the stereotypical foundation garments of the
whore, she also wears the stereotypical persona and most probably the dress
of a virgin. Now the garment hangs alone after being worn only once in a play
of ideal femininity that is laughable in the days of post-prom. In a similarly

humorous scenario, another undergraduate details her experience with a push-up bra. She explains, "I bought a push-up bra, and when I got home I tried it on. I hated the way it looked so unnatural, so I returned it and never wore it. I showed it to my boyfriend, and he cracked up; we named it the *rocket bra!*"

The experiences of these women demonstrate the complex contradictions embedded in the practice of choosing and wearing bras that present their breasts in ways that are at once socially acceptable, attractive and fashionable, yet leave space for play within the confines of ideal femininity. In choosing a bra, women negotiate the social meanings of the breast in terms of desire, sexuality, eroticism, and fecundity as well as changing notions of ideal shape and size. While it is extremely difficult to discern exactly how such determinations are made, to answer the question—How do women choose bras? or perhaps more specifically, How does a woman choose a bra for an occasion?—certain historical changes in the ideal feminine silhouette affect women's choices. Fashion historian Jill Fields agrees and notes, "It [the bra] plays a critical part in the history of twentieth-century American women's clothing, since the shaping of women's breasts is an important component in the changing contours of the fashionable silhouette" (1997, 122). Hence, bras and the presentation of breasts follow the cycle of fashion, and as fashion theorist Susan Kaiser points out, "Neither the cultural dope nor the celebratory models of fashion subjectivity capture how many if not most people describe their process of minding appearance" (Kaiser 2001, 83). The previous case of the *rocket bra* demonstrates one woman's conscious negotiation of 2002 fashion as this bra fails to meet her ideas of the natural appearance of breasts.

In contrast, women in the late 1940s and 1950s embraced the conical shaping of the breast (perhaps synonymous with the *rocket bra*). While technology in the form of foam rubber continued to contribute to bra padding, the use of wire and underwire to achieve conical breast shape intensified.[6] In their seminal fashion history of the bra, *Uplift: The Bra in America*, Jane Farrell-Beck and Colleen Gau explain the significant role of wire in shaping ideal 1950s style breasts:

> Wire became an essential component in the brassiere industry. With the war over, chromium plated wire was again available, and manufacturers promoted the efficacy of flexible spiral, flat, and round wires. An emphasis on rigidity hit a new peak with advertising of 1950s underwire brassieres. These were marketed primarily to large-breasted customers at first, but were soon discovered to thrust and uplift smaller bosoms to new heights. The numerous configurations of heavy wire separating the breasts, spiral wire under the breasts, flexible wire over the breasts, branching and circular wires used by designers in every company were a torturer's tour de force. (2002, 126)

The case of 1950s style wire-enhanced conical bras reinforces the question of agency and negotiation of the bra market as it begs the question—What is being styled? The Breast or the Fashion Silhouette? The Body or the Clothes? Anne Hollander and Fred Davis support the notion that the ideal body of woman in a given historical period demonstrates fashion's ideal silhouette of the day (Hollander 1978; Davis 1992, 81). Hence the ideal feminine body (and the ideal breast shape) is always a fashioned body constructed in the process of fashion played out in social dressing, fashioned identity, and gendered dress. Davis explains, "As a process it [fashion] is sustained through some complex amalgamation of inspiration, imitation, and institutionalization, all of which seem necessary, even though the nature and degree of their fusion is, as we can infer from fashion history, quite variable" (1992, 123).

In fact, fashion's changing ideal of breast shape fluctuates with shifting social, cultural and particularly economic factors, as in the case of the availability of wire after World War II. Colonialism provides another example. Anthropologist Londa Shiebinger explains:

> Colonial relations also affected perceptions of the breast. Late nineteenth-century anthropologists classified breasts by beauty in the same way that they measured skulls for intelligence. The ideal breast—for all races—was once again young and virginal. Europeans preferred the compact "hemispherical" type, found, it was said, only among whites and Asians. The much maligned breasts of African (especially Hottentot) women were dismissed as flabby and pendulous, similar to the udders of goats. When women of African descent were portrayed sympathetically, they were shown having firm, spherical breasts. (1993, 64)

Although Shiebinger's example comes courtesy of a 1936 historical and gynecological compendium, the case of privileging breast shape and size continues to be a function of contemporary fashion and codes of dress. I found an article in *In Style Magazine* listed under a column titled "Asset Management: Tips on making the most of your figure" with the subtitle, "Learning Curve" which supported Shiebinger's example of privileging certain types of breasts. The play on words actually supports the analysis of the work of bras in shaping the breasts while reinforcing the understanding that the breast can never exist in culture as *unfashioned*. The text of the article reads:

> Women have tried many a fad to help create the ideal silhouette up top. The latest innovation from Jockey achieves the goal without water, gel or unwanted bulk. In stores now, the new Smooth Contours bra is made of a light, soft foam that responds to the heat of your body, comfortably molding to your curves without a gap to be found. Smaller-size women, in particular will appreciate the slight enhancement of the cup (you'll look bigger, but not inordinately so). And

the seamless surface looks smooth under a fitted cotton T-shirt. (*In Style*, June 2003, 106)

The cultural production of the fitted T-shirt and the need for women to look smooth underneath it, produced a bra to wear with the T-shirt. The T-shirt is itself imbued with all kinds of significance—American rebellion, patriotism, sexuality, youthfulness and so on. This bra and the work it does of shaping breasts, particularly those of "smaller-size" women, proffers a normalizing option as it helps to "create the ideal silhouette up top" for June 2003. Not surprisingly and perhaps not coincidentally the shape of the bra replicates the colonial breast ideal detailed by Shiebinger.[7]

This same ideal shape, what Shiebinger's sources deem "hemispherical" is discussed by Iris Marion Young in her landmark essay, "Breasted Experience." Young examines the evaluation of women's breasts within a phallocentric culture. Like Shiebinger, Young finds U.S. culture to be smitten with a particular type of breast but points out, "Some other cultures venerate the woman with wrinkled, sagging breasts; they are signs of much mothering and the wisdom of experience" (1990, 192). She articulates the status of breasts in U.S. culture as being subject to a "Capitalist, patriarchal American media-dominated culture [that] objectifies breasts before a distancing gaze that freezes and masters" (Young 1990, 191). Such objectification might be thought to be thwarted by what my mother would call, "a good bra," which to her mind means one that adequately supports and covers the breasts, while preventing the movement or jiggle (and by all means conceals the nipples). However, sociologist Murray Wax argues that bras may make breasts even more apparent so that, "even beneath several layers of clothing, the onlooker can appreciate the feminine form" (Wax 1957, 589). Nipples aside, what Wax suggests is the erotic nature of bras and breasts. Whether women wear bras or not, their chests are seen as erotic.

However, when interviewed, most women declared that they would feel naked and exposed without a bra in public. I spoke to three women who claimed to always wear a bra—even in bed at night. Additionally, when I asked women about their early experience with bras most noted that they had a difficult time adjusting to wearing bras, even training bras, yet many also pointed out that they really wanted to wear bras because they made them feel feminine and grown-up. While most women recognized that they had been trained to wear a bra, that the reason that they felt more comfortable wearing a bra in public was because they were socially conditioned to do so, most women saw no reason to stop wearing a bra. A twenty-year-old undergraduate stated, "Without a bra in public, I feel naked because I do not get the proper support. I guess that they also wouldn't be the exact same shape if I did not wear a bra, and maybe that's what makes me uncomfortable or feel naked." A forty-year-old homemaker from South Carolina agreed and noted, "I feel really uncomfortable not wearing a bra like I'm naked, not dressed." Similarly, Jane Farrell-Beck and Colleen Gau report, "In our informal survey of women over fifty years of age, respondents gave several reasons for wearing their first brassiere, including the desire to achieve a fashionable look, submission to peer or maternal pressure, or the need for support. Only a small number of women mentioned comfort as an inducement to start wearing a brassiere" (Farrell-Beck and Gau 2002, 71). What is striking about these responses is precisely that women are conscious of desiring to feel feminine by wearing a bra and feeling exposed or subject to violation without one. In other words, women recognize that they have been trained to wear bras and now as one thirty-two-year-old office manager noted, "it would feel funny not to wear a bra."

While Iris Young suggests that a woman's breasted experience is in large part mediated by the male gaze (1990, 191), I would add that based on the above accounts a woman's decision to wear a bra is similarly mediated by the male gaze. That women feel exposed if they do not wear a bra—even though according to Wax, wearing a bra makes breasts more apparent—suggests that bras offer a layer of protection[8] against unwanted touching. However, bras cannot and do not dissuade evaluation of the breasts. Young asserts:

> What matters is the look of them, how they measure up before the normalizing gaze. There is one perfect shape and proportion for breasts: round, sitting high on the chest, large but not bulbous, with the look of firmness. The norm is contradictory, of course. If breasts are large, their weight will tend to pull them down; if they are large and round, they will tend to be floppy rather than firm. In its image of the solid object this norm suppresses the fleshy materiality of breasts, this least muscular, softest body part. (1990, 191)

Young's description of this evaluation of the stigma and praise ascribed to breasts in U.S. culture provides an understanding of the extent of objectifying standards for breasts, but Young also points out that "Without a bra, a woman's breasts are also deobjectified, desubstantialized. Without a bra, most women's breasts do not have the high, hard, pointy look that phallic culture posits as the norm" (Young 1990, 195). Certainly, the norm of perky B and C cup breasts appears in magazines everywhere, but as Young notes, our breasts without our bras rarely fit this ideal shape and size.

Although during my interviews, most women did not comment on the shape of their breasts, seventy-five percent of women indicated that they felt their breasts were either too large or too small. As it turns out, size does matter to women. I was surprised to find that women who considered themselves to be large breasted were equally as critical of their figures as women who thought themselves to be small breasted. In fact, of the forty women I interviewed, over half noted that they wore bras that either maximized or minimized their breasts. A thirty-five-year-old physical therapist remembered being embarrassed at an early age by the size of her breasts when she went looking for a prom dress. "When I tried on my prom dress, a sales lady put her hand down my bra and pulled my breasts up to be more 'perky.' As she did this she said, 'Such a little girl, such big boobies.' Needless to say, I wanted to run back to the changing room as fast as I could!" With this kind of treatment, it is not surprising that some larger-breasted women actually wear bras that are several sizes too small. A fifty-six-year-old homemaker from Philadelphia recalled, "I actually had a friend in high school who went to the doctor because she was having chest pains; she thought she was having a heart attack. It turned out that being well-endowed, her bra was too small." Five women, all under the age of forty, explained that they wear smaller bras mainly because larger bras are unattractive. A thirty-year-old hotel manager explained, "The larger the bra, the fewer decorations, flowers, and other pretty stuff. Larger bras look more like some kind of contraption or apparatus, you know, like that Bette Midler piece from the film, *Beaches*, about Otto's Titsling and Phillippe DeBrassiere's Brassiere."[9]

Victoria's Big Secret

A twenty-one-year-old undergraduate explained, "I don't really like Victoria's Secret bras anymore because they don't offer as much support as Maidenform, though they are cuter." While women may criticize the lack of support offered by Victoria's Secret bras, most in-depth interviewees (ranging in age from their teens to their late thirties) reported that they had purchased and worn a Victoria's Secret bra at one time or another. Sales data from *Women's Wear Daily* confirms that bras comprised almost 20 percent of Victoria's Secret sales in 1997 and were said to be a major factor in repeat purchases (Monget 1997, 48, "Little Nothings Are Big Business"). In fact, according to a 1995 article from *Women's Wear Daily*, Victoria's Secret is number 4 on the list of top foundationwear companies beating out long-standing and famous competitors Maidenform, Bali and Vanity Fair (Monget 1995, 44, "Intimate Apparel/ Sleepwear").[10] In in-depth interviews, many women reported that they thought Victoria's Secret bras were "prettier and lacier." Some women even explained that shopping at Victoria's Secret made them feel "more feminine."

In-depth interview responses, popular women's magazines, and trade journals all link Victoria's Secret's recent success to the way in which its corporate marketing strategies use the trope of woman as the virgin-whore to structure

and restructure ideal femininity. In a 1991 article for *Working Woman* magazine, Sue Woodman describes how Victoria's Secret capitalizes on "unabashed
femininity" by emphasizing the fusion of woman as both sultry and demure
(Woodman 1991, 77). Victoria's Secret unabashedly proffers stereotypical
femininity in the form of the virgin-whore dichotomy. In spite of the fact that
the "core business" of Victoria's Secret comprises women in the 18-to-30
range, its marketing campaigns geared toward women from 18 to 49 have resulted in an increase in sales in the bra mall market, so that in 1999 Victoria's
Secret bra sales make up 42 percent of bra mall market sales (Woodman 1991,
77; Monget 1995, 44, "Intimate Apparel/Sleepwear").[11] As fashion writer
Mimi Swartz finds out in her undercover visit for *Mademoiselle* to a Victoria's
Secret store, "Pretty is a word you hear over and over again when women talk
about Victoria's Secret"(Swartz 1990, 238). Swartz also points out that
"pretty" and "sexy" are used interchangeably by women visiting the store.
She explains, "Women want to be really sexy—as long as they aren't made to
feel cheap about it. Keeping that secret is, in fact, Victoria's Secret's secret"
(1990, 238).

   Swartz and others identify the unique combination of Victoriana and femininity sold by Victoria's Secret as a combination which works on women regardless of age, race or class (Swartz 1990; Woodman 1991; Workman 1996;
Valdivia 1997; Faludi 1991, 190). Victoria's Secret effectively conjures notions of the reign of Queen Victoria and its upper-class attributes: sexual repression, unrequited romantic love, purity, piety, and virginity, to successfully
market intimate apparel and foundation garments.[12] As Feminist Media Studies expert Angharad Valdivia explains, that while Victoriana certainly functions as a signifier for Victoria's Secret, even Frederick's of Hollywood,
noted for its working-class roots, changed it's marketing strategy in order to
keep up with the times (Valdivia 1997, 233). While Valdivia's comparison of
class in the catalogs of Victoria's Secret and Frederick's of Hollywood supports Swartz's observation of the proffering of a simultaneously sultry and
demure femininity in Victoria's Secret catalog, Valdivia cites Frederick's use
of Victoriana to be mainly for background appeal while still presenting
women who appear more sexually empowered. She maintains, "While
middle-class sexuality [as represented in Victoria's Secret Catalog] may be
more opulent and leisurely, there is a troublesome component of passivity. . .
In contrast, Frederick's women may not function in as lush a setting, but they
look more in control of their sexuality, in terms of when it happens and with
whom" (Valdivia 1997, 247). Hence, class functions in these catalogs to dis-
tinguish class-based forms of femininity and sexuality. Noting the significance of class in the marketing of these catalogs, it seems important to point
out that although Frederick's markets to a working-class audience, many of

its items are more expensive than those available at Victoria's Secret. However, the consumer may so identify with Frederick's image of femininity and sexuality that she may not bother to shop the competition if it does not meet these identifications.

Furthermore, Valdivia raises the question of agency for women as consumers of both catalogs. She notes, "Both catalogs suggest that part of women's work is to encourage sex with male partners. This then, becomes an additional component of domestic work, one that has always has been there but now has the twist of Victorian sexiness" (Valdivia 1997, 247). But Cultural Studies practitioner, Jane Juffer argues that Victoria's Secret's catalog encourages a certain type of sexual agency for women within the sanctity of their own homes—sexual agency inside the domestic sphere. Juffer maintains that Victoria's Secret so successfully markets the virgin-whore dichotomy of femininity that it actually provides an empowering pornography for women. She declares, "The images [from the catalog] draw out the contradictory nature of my own existence, counter-posing the erotic with the everyday, the naughty with the nice" (Juffer 1996, 28). She articulates the pitfalls of this agency particularly in terms of race and class. She explains that the labor of underpaid hourly workers who produce the garments are rendered invisible by the markings of high British culture in spite of the fact that Victoria's Secret is headquartered in Columbus, Ohio. Additionally Juffer notes the minimal use of women of color as models in the catalog as reflecting a white femininity.

> The kind of feminine sexuality that can be located within this nostalgic representation of England as home is almost always white—with occasional light-skinned black models advertising swimwear and apparel, but rarely lingerie. The racism is particularly obvious in the 1994 "Christmas Dreams" issue of the catalog, where black models are featured more prominently than in other catalogs but only to situate them more clearly as exotic Others. (1996, 36)

In this way Juffer recognizes that there are serious limitations and challenges to the agency she envisions for women consumers of Victoria's Secret catalogs. Nonetheless, Juffer argues that some women are able to reappropriate the proffered Victorian femininity into an empowered and self-fulfilling sexuality. She notes, "This mixture of power and vulnerability foregrounds the constructedness of gender by playing different representations of femininity off against each other, perhaps enabling some kind of awareness of the gaps of these images (Juffer 1996, 41). Perhaps, as Juffer suggests, some women successfully negotiate the images of Victoria Secret and rearticulate a femininity that fulfills their own desire for themselves. Juffer troubles the notion that women can only desire themselves via the linchpin of the male gaze.

She openly raises the question of femininity for the pleasure and fulfillment of woman's desire.

Bras, Fashion and Desire

Iris Young also questions the pleasure that women take from looking at fashion magazines and catalogs in her essay "Women Recovering Our Clothes." Young is concerned that in occupying the subject position of the male gaze, women objectify themselves and other women hence we participate in the reinscription of our own objectification (1990, 180). However, Young like Juffer is quick to point out that women have access to different means of community via clothing, which I argue may be supported by the communal experience of women choosing and wearing foundation garments. Young explains:

> We can mine traditionally female social practices and experiences and find in them specific ways that we as women relate to one another and to ourselves, female specific intrinsic values. There is no question that there are race, class and sexuality differences in women's relations to one another, and in this women's culture women most often relate to women of the same race or class identification as themselves. Still, I have often found it easiest to bridge such difference between myself and another woman by talking about elements of women's culture—often clothes. (1990, 181)

In fact, during in-depth interviews women frequently discussed the experience of buying first bras in the context of a rite of passage. The experience of buying a bra with their mothers, grandmothers, girlfriends or sisters signaled a rite of passage into womanhood and the shared culture of femininity. Hence, among the many different interviewees, there resonated a commonality of experience through the experience of wearing bras. This commonality supports Young's assertion that women can come together in the places of women's culture, fashion and beauty culture, the culture of femininity—where bras are an important part of this culture.

Today, perhaps, no single contemporary feminine foundation begs the question of why women wear it, more than the bra. Better than half of the women I interviewed specifically mentioned the need to wear bras which maximized their breasts under dresses at formal occasions. Water-bras, padded bras, and renditions of the push-up bra—Victoria's Secret's Miracle Bra and Sara Lee's Wonderbra— were among the most popular. In the telephone survey, 30 percent of women confirmed that they have worn push-up bras at one time or another.[13] A twenty-three-year-old undergraduate commented, "A lot of people wear push-up bras, but I generally think it is most frequent among people who dress up. I never dress up, so I have no need to wear them." As if in answer to her classmate, a twenty-year-old undergraduate commented, "I've worn a Wonderbra. I wouldn't wear one all the time, but if I'm in a dress that might need an extra boost, I'll wear one." In fact, women frequently raised their concerns about cleavage suggesting a parallel between dressing up and cleavage, known by the upper-class name as décolletage. A thirty-five-year-old Georgian noted, "If I was looking for a push-up bra, then I would want a bra that would create cleavage that I don't have." Another twenty-year-old student recalled, "This past Halloween I was a vampire with a low cut dress, so I got a push-up bra that has air in it. My bust definitely increased a few sizes that night. It's funny because I look back at the pictures taken and I have cleavage in every one. When I see them, I say WOW! Where did those come from?" Each of these responses indicates the social desire of women to fit into the image of the ideal feminine body, which certainly includes ideal breasts. In her landmark essay titled "Breasted Experience" Iris Young explains, "Cleavage is good—the more, the better" (1990, 196). Hence, women's donning of cleavage-enhancing bras allows women to appear more desirable, more quintessentially feminine, by mirroring an ideal shape that accentuates the unique attributes of women, the breasts.

However, certainly dress reform in its many forms and especially the removal of bras by women protesters at the 1968 and 1969 Miss America Beauty Pageants demonstrates an active resistance to wearing bras for the purpose of producing an ideal breast shape and size as a necessary practice of femininity. Historians Vicki Howard, Kathy Peiss and Lois Banner concur and argue that pursuing fashion has not resulted in the monolithic oppression or victimization of women (Howard 2001, 198; Peiss 1998, 261; Banner 1983, 86). Iris Young shares an example of such resistance in her own embodied account of shedding her bras during the second wave of feminism.[14] She declares, "I was no feminist when, young and impetuous, I shoved the bras back in the drawer and dared to step outside with nothing on my chest but a shirt" (Young 1990, 195). Young's account expresses her sense of excitement, daring, and freedom, but she is quick to note, "I never threw the bras away: they were there to be worn on occasions when propriety and delicacy required them" (Young 1990, 195). While Young's experience of shedding her bras frees her, she reports, like most of the women I interviewed, that special occasions dictate the donning of some kind of foundation garments. Although this information is surprising as it comes from the lived experience of noted feminist pioneer Iris Young,[15] it reinforces the significance of social dress codes for women where foundation garments are concerned—even for feminists.

Panty Hose

While from 1910 onward brassieres molded breasts to fit ideal fashion standards, panty hose covered millions of legs by 1969. Jane Farrell-Beck and

Colleen Gau explain, "Being sheer, panty hose were dressy enough to go everywhere, sometimes accompanied by panty girdles but often providing the only figure shaping below the waist" (2002, 143). In this way, panty hose replaced girdles, garters and stockings and became a new article of femininity, a new requirement of social and professional dress codes. As revealed in telephone survey data, 60 percent of respondents have worn control-top panty hose, a contemporary shaping cousin of the original panty hose.[16] In in-depth interviews, many women reported wearing panty hose on a regular basis in the work place although some women noted that they only wore them for special occasions. One twenty-five-year-old woman from Chicago commented, "Employees must wear hose to fly free with the airlines." She assumed that it was clear she was speaking of female employees. I wondered if there were similar requirements for male employees—boxers or briefs, socks or no socks, belt or no belt, tie or no tie? Other interviewees noted that their offices required women in skirts or dresses to wear panty hose while it was appropriate to wear socks with pants.

Connected with the 1980s notion of "power dressing," women in business have taken up the practice of wearing smart suits, matching pumps and of course, panty hose. British fashion sociologist Joanne Entwistle discusses the significance of the impact of power dressing on the construction of the career woman. She asserts, "So prominent a part has this discourse on 'power dressing' played in the construction of the career woman that it would be hard for any professional or business woman today to escape its notice even if they chose not to wear the garb" (1997, 312). Entwistle suggests that written codes of dress, as in the case of the airline policy requiring female employees to wear panty hose when flying for free, are no longer required since the construction of the career woman. She explains, "Companies expect their professional female workers to have internalised the codes of dress required by the job. Rather than send her home, a company is more likely to suggest, or even purchase, the services of an image consultant to work with the woman" (Entwistle 1997, 319). This is perhaps no better evidenced than in the 1980s when the Ladies Professional Golf Association (LPGA) hired a fashion consultant to promote heterosexual femininity for golfers on the tour (Hargreaves 2000; Festle 1996; Burton-Nelson 1991).

This internalization of professional feminine dress codes resonates with Foucauldian notions of the management of the self. Power, for Foucault, is not a possession, nor is it centralized or exercised from above (Foucault 1995). Susan Bordo explains how this power, disguised in the form of self-management, circulates throughout the body politic, where it regulates "the most intimate and minute elements of the construction of space, time, desire and embodiment" (Bordo 1993, 27). All subjectivities including gendered subjectivities are constituted through individual self-surveillance and obedience to norms that arise out of knowledge—power discourses. Beauvoir's myth of woman then follows Foucault's model as normalized femininity circulates throughout the culture with women performing self-surveillance at every turn.

In this way, written dress codes are unnecessary to subjugate women, just a look is satisfactory. The male gaze works to objectify woman, keeping her in her place. The notion of the look or the gaze runs through the theories of Beauvoir and Sartre; however, Foucault historicizes the gaze and adds to its workings a very minute analysis of the specific ways in which power gains control of subjectivities (Foucault 1995). Drawing on Jeremy Bentham's notion of the panopticon, Foucault conveys the image of a self-policing society. Sandra Bartky moves one step further, describing the beauty regimens women willingly take up and the critical eyes they focus on themselves in the rearview mirror (Bartky 1990). Hence as Entwistle concludes, "Once an individual has internalised the concept of a career as a project of the self, fewer external management constraints are required" (Entwistle 1997, 319).

In response to Entwistle's theory of internalized dress codes, it is most striking that many interviewees discussed their strategies for masking figure flaws and described the process of choosing foundation garments as an act of making themselves more attractive. A twenty-one-year-old undergraduate stated, "I wear the control-top panty hose because they seem to flatten my stomach when I'm in a tight dress, which makes me feel confident." A thirty-year-old mother of two explained, "Both I and my sister wore what we called skinny minnies in college. I mean, I know we aren't fat, but we looked better with a little support." Similarly, a sixty-year-old schoolteacher stated, "I wear a push-up bra and a girdle to special events. They're not that comfortable, but they accomplish what I want them to do. I look and feel better about myself when I wear them." Not surprisingly, data from the telephone survey revealed that 84 percent of women agreed that women wear foundation garments to mask figure flaws.[17] Additionally, 60 percent of the women surveyed agreed that shaping garments were a fashion requirement (most noted bras as the reason for this choice).[18]

However, several women also ridiculed the imposition of dress codes, internalized or otherwise. One student declared, "A lot of clothes women are wearing now are tighter and more fitted to show off the body. Women feel it's necessary to wear shaping garments. I think this is because they feel insecure about their bodies or they are trying to fit a certain body image." The notion that women can resist but choose not to is definitely in circulation in youth culture, but as another student notes, sometimes we are fooled. She stated, "I didn't like the idea of control-top hose, so I didn't buy them. But, my mom did, so I never knew the difference until my mother announced in front of my aunts, uncles, second cousins and grandparents, that the reason I was paid a compliment about my figure at a family wedding was because I was wearing control-tops. I was really embarrassed!" Embarrassment regarding pantyhose frequently emerged during in-depth interviews. I think every woman has a story about tucking the back of her dress into her panty hose or putting her panty hose on all twisted and being unable to walk. Perhaps these, too, are rites of passage for women in America. At a minimum, they represent some kind of urban legend. An eighteen-year-old freshman remembered being required to wear panty hose under dresses as part of a high school sorority dress code. She recalled being told by the president of the sorority to wear panty hose, "Otherwise our behinds would end up looking like two cats wrestling in a bag—suggesting that our behinds would jiggle. I thought it was absolutely hilarious and burst out laughing, only to be lectured later." It is possible this anecdote may be the result of a cultural reference to a scene from the popular 1980s film, *Steel Magnolias*.[19] The scene opens with Janice Van Meter, the new mayor's wife, dancing in a beautiful dress without a girdle at Shelby's wedding. Clairee Belcher comments to Truvy, "Looks like two pigs fightin' under a blanket."[20] Whether this performance is described as two pigs fighting under a blanket or two cats wrestling in a bag, the dress code for women revolves around the social stigma of jiggle.

For many women younger than forty, limiting jiggle is equated with wearing control-top panty hose rather than wearing girdles. This is not to say that contemporary shaping garments are not worn by younger women, but many women under forty can remember their mothers and grandmothers wearing girdles every day. A thirty-seven-year-old administrative assistant recalled seeing her mother wear long-line girdles. "They came up high, well above the waist and had boy legs that went all the way down the thighs. They had garters for stockings and left little waffle pattern's on my mother's skin." Similarly, a nineteen-year-old student responded to my interview question about memorable experiences with shaping garments by exclaiming, "Yeah, seeing my mom run around the house half-dressed in those damn control-top panty hose!" Like these women, I have 1970s memories of my own mother walking around the house with her blouse tucked into her support hose with a long white girdle over top. Seeing our mothers wearing these foundation garments allowed us to make the connection between womanhood and femininity, between what women wore and what women were supposed to look like. That these images of our mothers still stand out so vividly in our memories is a testament to the significance of shaping garments in the construction of ideal feminity and the ideal feminine body.

NOTES

1. For a complete discussion of telephone survey and in-depth, open-ended interview methods, consult the introduction. To view telephone survey data, see Appendix A.

2. See appendix A, variable v11.

3. See Willis and Williams (2002) for a photographic history of the black female body.

4. See appendix A, variables v22 and v23 respectively.

5. See Market Research, Kalish 1995. Questionnaires were mailed to 1,250 members of Woman's Day Shoptalk Panel. There was a response rate of 73.7 percent. The panel, which represents a cross-section of the adult female population, is balanced by age and geographic region to U.S. Census Data, so that it accurately reflects the national composition of females 18+. The tabulations and summary results in this report are based on an analysis of 906 respondents.

6. It comes as little surprise that the Wonderbra and the Merry Widow were produced out of the same 1950s obsession with wiring.

7. What is perhaps interesting is that there is little commentary in Shiebinger's example on the conical breast, which as aforementioned was the hit of the 1950s. See Shiebinger 1993, 65 (Fig 2.6).

8. The idea of foundation garments as protection is taken up in more depth in chapter 6.

9. "Otto's Titsling." Soundtrack from *Beaches*. Film directed by Garry Marshall. Buena Vista Entertainment, 1988. Soundtrack released November 1988 by Atlantic Records, recorded by Georges Delerue and Bette Midler.

10. The top three in descending order are: Hanes Her Way, Fruit of the Loom and Playtex.

11. Statistics come from Victoria's Secret Strategic View of the Line 2001, Foundations, December 1999.

12. For a detailed discussion of sexual repression and sexual agency concerning the corset, see Fields 1999; Finch 1991; Roberts 1977; Kunzle 1977, 1982; Steele 2001.

13. See appendix A, variable v6.

14. On a historical note, Young (like so many feminists) debunks the myth of bra burning in the 1960s.

15. Like so many feminist theorists, I am indebted to the work of Iris Marion Young who died of cancer on August 1, 2006 prior to the publication of this book.

16. See appendix A, variable v8.

17. See appendix A, variable v36.

18. See appendix A, variable v40.

19. Herbert Ross dir. 1989 *Steel Magnolias*. United States. Sony Pictures.

20. Clairee Belcher is played by Olympia Dukakis, and Truvy is played by Dolly Parton.

Chapter Three

Boomers and X-ers:
Mothers and Daughters

What we wore everyday—cinched waists, smoothed out curves and bumps, and constrained our movements. What relief to unhook brassieres, unzip girdles, and step out of the cage of Jackie Kennedy box suits. Letting our hair down, we proclaimed Our bodies, Ourselves.

Shari Benstock and Suzanne Ferriss, *On Fashion*

How does the female body become the site of contested meaning as it takes up wearing shaping garments as a practice of the discipline of femininity? In *Unbearable Weight*, Susan Bordo discusses a primary practice of contemporary femininity in the United States in terms of a desire to achieve the slender body. Bordo describes how middle and upper-class women have become enculturated into a quest for the ideal slender body (1993, 204). Bordo argues that the pursuit of this ideal centers around contemporary notions of femininity that emerged from the women's movement of the 1960s where the maternal, domestic and reproductive body was rejected and replaced by a slender ideal embodying white masculine qualities—"detachment, self-containment, self-mastery, control—which are highly valued in our culture" (1993, 209). In studying foundation garments from the 1930s to the present, I have found a variety of ideal bodies to be in evidence during different periods. Bordo supports this notion of shifting feminine body ideals, but articulates the rise of the slender body as coinciding with the backlash against feminism and women's roles in the public sphere. Bordo notes, "The era of the cinch belt, the pushup bra, and Marilyn Monroe could be viewed for the body, as an era of 'resurgent Victorianism.' It was also the last coercively normalizing body-ideal to reign before boyish slenderness began its ascendancy in the mid-60s" (1993, 208). Bordo provides point of departure in the 1960s where the discipline of femininity, of enculturated feminine desire,

moves away from a maternal and domestic location and takes up the empowerment traditions of masculinity embodying them in the ideal feminine form, the
slender body.

While Bordo discusses the forces which operate on the body to facilitate
the achievement of this ideal through diet, exercise, chemicals and surgery,
she is largely concerned with the damage that this ideal has on female bodies:
anorexia, bulimia, surgical scarring, psychological dysfunction and death
(Bordo 1993, 166). I am likewise concerned about the harms caused by the
severe disciplining involved in the pursuit of the slender body. Consequently,
my discussion here operates in concert with Bordo's concerns as I examine
the cultural phenomenon of girdle resurgence in the context of the production
of shapewear commodities designed to feed the desire of middle-class women
striving to achieve the slenderness ideal.

Bordo suggests that the slenderness ideal is predicated on a class habitus as
well as a feminine habitus; however, she is also careful to point out the extent
to which this ideal knows no age boundaries (1993, 26 and 193). This notion
is borne out in my own research where I find that foundations manufacturers
are marketing shapewear products to both baby boomers and generation x-
ers.[1] My evidence comes from a variety of sources including market surveys
and reports, trade journals, newspaper articles, popular magazine articles and
mail order catalogs. Each of these contributes to my understanding of girdle
resurgence as a cultural phenomenon and as a marketing strategy. My purpose
in conducting this research is to demonstrate how Bordo's slender body ideal
is perpetuated as a mandate of femininity between generations while it is
simultaneously commodified by foundationwear manufacturers. I examine
how this commodification perpetuates the cycle of desire for a growing audience of women who seek to achieve an "image of ideal slenderness [that] has
grown thinner and thinner throughout the 1980s and 1990s" (Bordo 1993,
191). In exploring girdle resurgence as a phenomenon, I hope to understand
how the slender body ideal intersects these marketing strategies operating at
the level of the feminine body in fashion.

What underpins these marketing strategies in terms of consumption and
desire is at the center of this analysis. As sociologist Gail Faurschou points
out, "Postmodernity then is no longer an age in which bodies produce
commodities, but where commodities produce bodies: . . . bodies for fashion"
(Faurschou 1987, 72). What Faurschou explains is the cycle of desire and the
production of commodities that produce bodies. She argues, "It is no longer
an economy seeking to fulfill the needs of a modernizing society but a society driven to create a perpetual desire for need, a need for novelty, for endless
difference and instant satisfaction" (1987, 72). Certainly the notions of
commodity fetishism and the production of desire in the marketplace are not

new ideas. However, following the circuit of this desire historically and culturally, through two generations, baby boomers and generation x-ers, linked at least potentially as mothers and daughters provides a better understanding of the hegemonic role of the fashioned body, the slender body, the (re)shaped body.

The popularity of contemporary shapewear operates as a cultural articulation of American women's relationships to their bodies. A fashion writer from a local newspaper in Quincy, Massachusetts, notes, "In recent years slim women have been relying on the foundation garments to achieve an uber-buff appearance. Supermodels wear them on the runway because of the smooth lines they create under form-fitting clothes" (Wright 1998, 15). Certainly designers and their models have been at the fore of the girdle resurgence, demonstrating how women can achieve and maintain a slender and seamless appearance regardless of the changing external fashions. Fashion writer Sarah Mower from *Harper's Bazaar* responds with chagrin to girdle resurgence. She exclaims, "Why—and how—the girdle should have shown up so conspicuously at the [1995] spring collections . . . [since] the repulsive part is the hard-to-shake association with ugly, unhealthy pre-feminist industrial strength underwear for which the term unmentionable must have been coined" (1995, 68). Additionally, *Business Week* described girdle resurgence as an already legitimized practice of the fashion world. Chandler and Palmer note, "Designer Karl Lagerfeld presented corsets under suits instead of blouses in his 1994 couture showing. Additionally, the December issue of *Vogue* featured super model Cindy Crawford in a one-piece girdle by Isaac Mizrahi"(1995, 37). Hence, girdle-like garments, shapers, slimmers and smoothers, leap to the fashion stage in the mid-late 1990s. The role of these garments is to mask flab, to eliminate bulges and to facilitate the achievement of the ideal slender body.

The desire to achieve such a flabless slender body pervades the market research of foundationwear manufacturers who cite the needs of baby boomers and generation x-ers as the driving force in the current foundationwear market. A 1995 article from *American Demographics* claims that baby boomers ages 31–49 are "fueling the market for products that flatter the hips, breasts, eyelids, and other parts of the body that sag with age" (Braus 1995, 50). These aging boomers appear to be responsible for much of the market increase in shapewear according to an independent *Market Profile: Women's Undergarment* from July 1995. The report argues, "Historically women increase spending on undergarments as they age, peaking when they enter the 45–to–54-year-old age group. As a result, the U.S. women's undergarment market has been strengthening as members of the huge baby boom population approach their peak purchasing years" (SBI 1995, 4). What the report suggests is that as baby boomers age, they "are turning to shapewear as diet and exercise fail to limit the effects of aging" (SBI 1995, 5), but this is only half of the phenomenon driving the women's foundation garment market. The other half is related to the interest of younger women, "Who are developing a growing interest in intimate apparel. Since 1991, women under age 35 have increased their spending on undergarments at the strongest rate. This age group has also been a trend setter in undergarment fashions, since women under age 35 are most likely to use push-up bras, use daywear as outerwear, and are the most tolerant to sacrifice comfort for appearance" (SBI 1995, 5). The report claims that these two demographic groups are directly responsible for the increased consumption figures for new foundations.

The relationship between boomers and x-ers is potentially one of mother and daughter. What is perhaps most significant about this possible relationship is that these women, separated by a generation, aged 46–64 and 27–44 (in 2006), are proffered the same image of the ideal female body.[2] This slender ideal body is illustrated in Figures 3.1–3.3. Figure 3.1 taken from Victoria's Secret (VSS) *Christmas Specials* 2000 Catalogue depicts the slender ideal body of a young woman wearing a Body By Victoria bra and panty set. Body By Victoria (BBV) is made from a light control microfiber–nylon/Lycra spandex. Below this image is a hang-tag[3] from a Nancy Ganz BodySlimmers product, the Bustshaping Bodyslip (Figure 3.2). While Ganz notes that younger women use her products, aging boomers are the primary targets for Ganz's BodySlimmers line which was recently purchased by Warnaco, one of the Big Four shapewear giants (Monget "Warnaco and BodySlimmers" 1996, 14). In observing each of these representations, I see no difference in the bodies. Both are slender, trimmed to the bone with evident musculature—most notable by the taut abdominal muscles of the VSS image and the arms and thighs of the BodySlimmers image. What is also evident is that the face of the BodySlimmers image is missing. Perhaps this is so we cannot see the age of the model used in the hang-tag for a product that is marketed to baby boomers. In fact, the same comparison may be made to the Hanes Her Way hang-tag (Figure 3.3 features a Sara Lee Brand product—also a Big Four corporation).[4] In spite of the fact that the Hanes Shaping Slip is marketed to a boomer demographic, the image on this hang-tag is a slender ideal body identical to the VSS body in Figure 3.1. I can make out a mouth and chin and part of a nose on the Hanes hang-tag, but I cannot tell the age of the model in the image. Signs of age are absent or erased by both Hanes and Bodyslimmers hang-tags. These hang-tags suggest by the absence of the model's face the prevailing and pervasive reality that the slender ideal body applies to women of all ages.

Figure 3.1. Body by Victoria
VSS Christmas Specials 2000

Figure 3.2.   BodySlimmers Hang-tag. December 2000

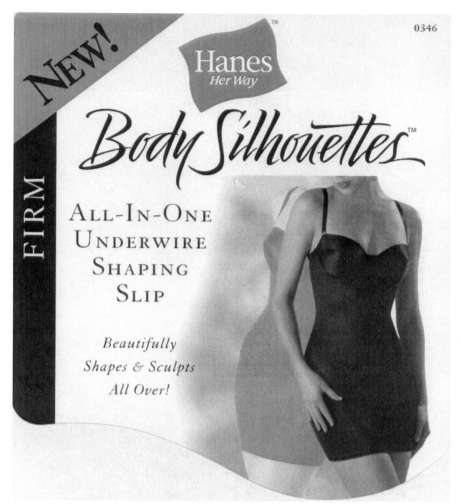

Figure 3.3.   Hanes Her Way Hang-tag. December 2000

Foundations manufacturers do not find this concept unusual as they are rushing to market foundations to both generational groups in order to fulfill this desire in both groups, to meet the needs of both groups. In 1995 the annual report of Intimate Brands, Victoria's Secret's parent company noted that, "among the operational strategies for this year is the introduction of sexy-looking shapewear items for fall, aimed at an aging consumer" (Monget "Shapewear Defines Its Targets" 1996, 8); however, by 1996 the target shifted for Victoria's Secret to include much younger customers. In 1996, John Caleo, vice president of merchandising and design for the Olga Company expressed no surprise when he heard that Victoria's Secret was developing a sexy controlwear targeted at a younger customer ("The Shape of Things to Come" 1996, 16). He explained, "We had a customer but were not really getting anyone new . . . through research we found that not only is there a customer in the baby boomer, but also that Generation X would like control, so we had to rethink our product" ("The Shape of Things to Come" 1996, 16). With this rethinking underway, women's foundations manufacturers have been going wild since the late 1980s and early 1990s trying to expand their markets. Caleo suggests that it is at the middle of the decade that the market really expands to include boomers and their daughters in the foundations frenzy, also known in the fashion industry as "girdle resurgence."

This should indeed come as little surprise since mothers have traditionally taken their daughters shopping for their first foundation purchase, the training bra. Even after their initial trip to the mall to buy their first bra with their mothers, according to a *Seventeen* magazine survey from August of 1995, "teenage girls are most likely to go bra shopping with their moms (64%), but they also shop for bras with friends (21%) and by themselves (15%)" ("70% of Women do not Enjoy Bra Shopping" 1996, 2). Women's foundations manufacturers target new consumers not only boomers, but to their daughters, generation x-ers, via trendy new designs and by encouraging mothers to introduce their daughters to all kinds of foundations. Nancy K. Brennick, director of merchandising for Wonderbra and Bali, noted the Un-d's consumer target is, "most likely the daughter of an established Bali customer. We already own the Bali customer. We now want to continue to reinforce loyalty to a Sara Lee Brand" (qtd in Monget "Sizing up Sales" 1995, 9). Brennick's notion of owning the customer underscores the way in which these boomers and x-ers are disciplined by their consumption.

Although mothers and daughters shopping for bras and other foundation garments may seem an insignificant and normal cultural phenomenon, I contend that this experience operates as a training exercise disciplining daughters in the ways of the feminine habitus. Simone de Beauvoir explains the process in which mothers train their daughters in the ways of femininity. "The mother is at once overweeningly affectionate and hostile toward her daughter; she saddles her child with her own destiny: a way of proudly laying claim to her own femininity and a way of revenging herself for it" (Beauvoir 1989, 281). The mother experiences her own femininity as a burden and a weakness, but she desires to pass on the discipline of femininity to her daughter to facilitate her daughter's operation in a masculine world as a feminine body. Beauvoir similarly expresses the way in which daughters experience this initiation into femininity, what I call a feminine habitus. Beauvoir explains, "the treasures of feminine wisdom are poured into her ears, feminine virtues are urged upon her, she is taught cooking, sewing, housekeeping, along with care of her person, charm, and modesty; she is dressed in inconvenient and frilly clothes of which she has to be careful, her hair is done up in fancy style, she is given rules of deportment: Stand up straight, don't walk like a duck" (1989, 282). My use of the term feminine habitus here and previously comes from Bourdieu's concept of the habitus. In *Outline of a Theory of Practice*, Bourdieu articulates, not unlike Beauvoir, how the experience of habitus becomes embodied through practice.

> The principles em-bodied in this way are placed beyond the grasp of consciousness, and hence cannot be touched by voluntary, deliberate transformation, cannot even be made explicit; nothing seems more ineffable, more incommunicable, more inimitable, and, therefore, more precious, than the values given body, *made* body by the transubstantiation achieved by the hidden persuasion of an implicit pedagogy, capable of instilling a whole cosmology, an ethic, a metaphysic, a political philosophy, through injunctions as insignificant as "stand up straight" or "don't hold your knife in your left hand." (1977, 94)

Bourdieu and Beauvoir both focus on the method of discipline, the way in the body takes up the disciplines of the habitus through practice. The training of the body occurs at the level of the body where "seemingly insignificant details of dress, bearing, physical and verbal manners" are practiced (Bourdieu 1977, 94).

In spite of the fact that Bourdieu does not specifically mention a feminine habitus, he points out that, "It is not hard to imagine the weight that must be brought to bear on the construction of self-image and world-image by the opposition between masculinity and femininity when it constitutes the fundamental principle of the division of the social and symbolic world" (1977, 93). Bourdieu largely focuses his discussion on social habitus, but he recognizes the ways in which certain properties are socially valued.

> In a class society, all the products given an agent, by an essential *overdetermination*, speak inseparably of his class—or, more precisely, his position in the social structure and his rising of falling trajectory—and of his (or her) body—or, more precisely, all the properties, always socially qualified, of which he or she is the bearer—sexual properties of course, but also physical properties, praised, like strength or beauty, or stigmatized. (1977, 87)

Bourdieu suggests that these qualities are gendered, but does not concern himself with the unique embodiment of these qualities in terms of gender; however, Bordo and Beauvoir point out the extent to which these qualities in the case of young girls and women are entrenched in the disciplines of femininity. Beauvoir similarly expresses femininity as a discipline thus pointing to the possibility of a feminine habitus in Bourdieu's sense of the term. "The little girl, on the contrary, in order to change into a grown-up person, must be confined within the limits imposed upon her by her femininity" (Beauvoir 1989, 315). I maintain that the properties named by Bourdieu limit the young girl in terms of social praise or stigma and as a function of discipline within the feminine habitus.

Both Beauvoir and Bourdieu suggest the existence of a feminine habitus as they recognize the power embedded in the disciplines of masculinity and femininity. Finally, both point to the significance of the child's relationship with the mother and father. For Bourdieu this means parental relationships "which by their dissymmetry in antagonistic complementarity constitute one of the opportunities to internalize, inseparably, the schemes of the sexual division of labour and the division of sexual labour" (1977, 89). For Beauvoir this means the girl child's recognition that "she was to become one day a woman like her all-powerful mother—she will never be the sovereign father; the bond attaching her to her mother was an active emulation—from her father she can but passively await an expression of approval" (1989, 287). In this way, Bourdieu and Beauvoir lay out the terms of a feminine habitus, which I argue is in operation as mothers train their daughters to take up the practices of femininity. These feminine practices stand at the core of my argument since they discipline the body in terms of enculturated gestures, bearing and dressage, what Bourdieu describes as bodily hexis. "Bodily hexis is political mythology realized, em-bodied, turned into a permanent disposition, a durable manner of standing, speaking, and thereby feeling and thinking" (Bourdieu 1977, 93).

Foucault similarly raises the issues of disciplining what he calls docile bodies in *Discipline and Punish*. Foucault explains how normalization operates at the crux of the mechanisms of discipline in society. Foucault explains, "The judges of normality are present everywhere. We are in the society of the teacher–judge, the doctor–judge, the educator–judge, the social worker–judge; it is on them that the universal reign of the normative is based; and each individual, wherever he may find himself, subjects to it his body, his gestures, his behaviour, his aptitudes, his achievements" (1995, 304). As the philosopher David Couzens Hoy argues, "Foucault is interested not only in how individuals get programmed by the social institutions in which they find themselves, but also why they accept being programmed" (1999, 8). Foucault and Hoy suggest that the complicity of the subject to willingly take up the disciplining of the body comes from the power of normalization. Hoy argues that although the theories of Bourdieu and Foucault are distinct, "[they] can profitably be put on the same spectrum insofar as Bourdieu can be read as deepening

Foucault's account of how subjectivity is constructed through power relations by providing a much more detailed sociological theory of this process" (Hoy 1999, 11). Norms operate for Foucault as the habitus operates for Bourdieu. For Bourdieu stigma and praise facilitate social habitus, while punishment and discipline support normalization for Foucault.

Behind normalization and habitus lies the training of the body. Bourdieu discusses training in terms of bodily hexis wherein "children are particularly attentive to the gestures and postures which, in their eyes, express everything that goes to make an accomplished adult" (1977, 87). Foucault articulates the importance of training as a discipline of normalization. He explains how soldiers are trained through a system of signals and practices to embody the physical bearing of the soldier. "Place the bodies in a world of signals to each of which is attached a single, obligatory response: it is a technique of training, of dressage" (Foucault 1995, 166). Bourdieu and Foucault each express ways in which the docile body becomes the habituated and disciplined body. Susan Bordo conveys how the female docile body becomes trained. "Through the pursuit of an ever-changing, homogenizing, elusive ideal of femininity— a pursuit without a terminus, requiring that women constantly attend to minute and often whimsical changes in fashion—female bodies become docile bodies" (1993,166).

Bourdieu, Beauvoir, Foucault and Bordo each contribute to this project through their insistence on the significance of the training of the body as a mechanism of control of the subject. Ladelle McWhorter describes Foucault's argument concerning the shift in the exercise of power over the mind to a disciplinary power over the body. She writes, "Power in the institutions that developed through the nineteenth century tended to act not so much on the mind and its representations as on the body and its gestures, not so much on the reasoning as on doing" (McWhorter 1999, 73). Nancy Fraser reads Foucault similarly as she notes, "Foucault dramatizes this point by claiming that power is in our bodies not in our heads. Put less paradoxically, he means that practices are more fundamental than belief systems when it comes to understanding the hold that power has on us" (Fraser 1981, 279). This shift is manifested in the discussions of each of these thinkers who recognize that control of the body is linked to control of the subject and who suggest that much of this training occurs during childhood and adolescence. Thus, the training of the young girl in the ways of femininity cannot be discounted nor should the role of the mother in such training be overlooked. Mothers bring their daughters into the world of the femininity where, "make-up, false hair, girdles, and 're-inforced' brassieres are all lies" (Beauvoir 1989, 357).

Manufacturers of foundation garments exploit this facet of the mother–daughter relationship, a conditioning of the ideal slender body, as they proffer shaping garments to both mothers and daughters. While marketing to mothers and daughters means using different marketing strategies to engage these divergent audiences, the socialized and manufactured desire for the slender ideal body remains the same for boomers and x-ers. Patricia Braus notes, "Marketers and designers must work carefully when offering anti-aging and anti-fat goods to baby boomers. . . One way to ease their discomfort is by careful redesign and relabeling products such as the move from girdles to body shapers" (1995, 54). Every foundation garment in women's lingerie bears a new and improved name; Slimmers, Underwonder, Undertones, BodySlimmers, Body Touches, Body Silhouettes are all examples of the newly redesigned and relabled shaping garments available for consumption by baby boomers at their local malls and department stores. These relabeled and redesigned foundations are marketed to boomers in terms of comfort, fit, and fashion. Comfort means lighter control garments with more spot control. According to Nancy Ganz, BodySlimmers designer, "Not everybody wants firm control . . . more women are coming into intimate apparel departments these days because of the fashion exposure lingerie has received" (qtd in Monget "Microfiber for the Millennium" 1998, 11).

This means that manufacturers have made the move to microfiber materials in order to capture boomers' notions of comfort. The new fabrics known as microfibers are very high-tech fabrics in midweight bright nylons that exude almost satin luster. They are branded Silky Touch and Microtouch by BASF and Tactel nylon and Lycra and Micromattique polyester and Lycra by DuPont (Corwin 1995, 51 and Monget "Micro for Mill" 1998, 8). These fabrics work for manufacturers as innovations of technology, which allow for facile redesign and relabeling of the old g-word. With old notions of girdles pushed out of their minds by new satiny, glamorous, silky fabrics that promise light to moderate control, boomers have been out in force purchasing spot control shapers particularly light control bottoms and control panties. Ganz for BodySlimmers argues that these products are not only for large women since "every woman has a body part that bothers her" (qtd in Monget "Shapewear Defines" 1996, 8). BodySlimmers introduced a new collection of feminine Shapewear in August of 2000 which advertises the technology of new fibers in shaping garments noting, "The light but powerful lace and clean lines make the group ideal under delicate knits and fine fabrics that can show every bump and line" ("Smooth Move" 2000, 6).

In other words, the object of the game of fashion for foundations manufacturers has become one in which the seamless foundations through new fabric technologies create the illusion of a flabless body. This new kind of girdling experience is what is being proffered to boomers under new names and labels accentuating the extent to which these garments produce slimming, smoothing results in a revolutionized garment—not your grandma's girdle. Ganz and her BodySlimmers continue to market to boomers in terms of presenting a product that is innovative, comfortable, and fashionable, but they are not denying its marketability to younger demographic segments. In fact the recent success of control bottoms, sold as shaping panties has BodySlimmers and other shapewear manufacturers hoping to expand their markets. As Ganz points out, "My products are attracting younger consumers into the stores, and I'm addressing that with pretty stretch laces and firm-control nylon and Lycra products, because there's a lot of sheer looks still going on in ready to wear" (qtd in Monget "BodySlimmers Stretching" 1996, 12).

What is being marketed and sold to younger consumers, mainly generation x-ers, is the assumption that shaping and control is something they need and want. Ganz's suggestion that all women are dissatisfied with their bodies makes the commodification of this control of x-ers' bodies all the more significant. This shaping and control in terms of seamless foundations is being masked by frills, lace, silky fabrics and other "feminine" frippery. While, "Shapewear has become one of the fastest-growing apparel categories in two channels: specialty chains and discounters, [and] shapewear sales at specialty chains, most notably Victoria's Secret, more than doubled to $35 million resulting in a five point share gain since 1996," the target market for panty shapers and control bottoms has shifted to include younger consumers (Monget "New Direction" 1999, 12). Strategies for expanding the shapewear market to include generation x-ers means transforming "the appearance of shapers, giving an updated, contemporary look or a look of feminine lace embellishments" and aiming "control briefs—high-cut, long-leg, and thong-back styles at young consumers" (Monget "New Direction" 1999, 12). Dispelling myths about old control items is less of an issue for younger customers who have not been around long enough to remember old-style girdles. In fact, teens are "looking for control-top panties and girdles to wear under prom and graduation outfits" (Chandler and Palmer 1995, 37). The newness of shaping panties, cleavage enhancing bras, bustiers and power-slips is not lost on generation-x. The marketing strategies behind specialty stores like Victoria's Secret and Cacique "showcase cotton/Lycra and nylon/Lycra panties with pretty accents like lace trim in a palette of basic and fashion colors" ("Go Figure" 1996, A20).

The difference between marketing strategies to boomers and x-ers hinges on notions of femininity. Boomers carry baggage. They remember traditional girdles. They are a sensible and practical group who wants to look and feel young without sacrificing comfort. X-ers are being treated by manufacturers as girls, girls that just want to have fun and enjoy being girly, flirty, sexy and maybe a bit glamorous. The question becomes what is really going on here. I would suggest that manufacturers market to x-ers as the daughters of boomers, those that are caught up historically in a period of feminist backlash.[5] This means that the enculturated desire for slenderness is a given for the x-ers. For Victoria's Secret, marketing to x-ers means marketing to 17–34 year olds. This has as previously noted not always been the target marketing audience for VSS.[6] Original targets in 1989 and 1991 were "upper-income women from 18–49" (Woodman 1991, 77). The shift in targets comes in the mid 1990s after successful marketing has captured the "thirty and forty-something customer, who may come into the shop with her daughter but doesn't think of buying something for herself" (Strom 1993, 10). After capturing the boomer market, in the early 1990s, VSS and other foundations manufacturers are after a new market, the daughters of boomers.

The quest to expand the market of foundationwear, its fabric technologies, and its potential into bras and panties is at the fore of VSS's marketing plan for 2000 and 2001. According to the 1999 Market Patterning for total bras and total panties VSS opportunity to claim space is dwindling since the VSS bra share is at 51 percent in target age (17–34) and VSS panty share is at 67 percent in the target age (17–34). In order to expand foundationwear positioning for panties in the marketplace VSS plans to extend dominance in glamour, seamless, color and pattern dominance, thongs, v-strings and bikinis and to invest in existing, powerful subrands: Body By Victoria, Body Bare, and Signature Cotton. In order to increase bra sales, VSS Key Bra Principles for 2000 are to extend dominance in glamour, demi-bras, cleavage enhancing bras, strapless bras and color dominance and to invest in existing powerful subrands: Body By Victoria, Body Bare, Signature Cotton and Miracle Bras. These foundations are viewed as the keys to expanding VSS markets. Cotton bras and panties that have long been big sellers will still be around, but new Lycra/cotton blends as demonstrated in the Signature Cotton line bring light control to daily wear foundations. Indeed, VSS recognizes that Cotton blends are outpacing market growth for target customers in the 17–44 age group wherein growth from 1998 to 1999 was noted at 37.8 percent and the volume of the market that was cornered by Cotton blends was 63.1 percent according to Victoria's Secret's Panty Fabrication Chart (Table 3.1).[7]

The VSS marketing strategy is based on consumer research in the target market. They have shifted their target within the market to that group of consumers who seem to be buying at the highest rate; however, VSS also uses trends to plan its marketing campaign within its target market. VSS assesses these trends in terms of marketplace competition and what products seem to be generating interest according to the Total Bra and Panty Competitive Intelligence Chart (Table 3.2).[8] The first trend observed in this report is named as "Overt Femininity—Curves and Augmentation." VSS

TABLE 3.1. PANTY FABRICATION TYPE BY AGE GROUP (I)

Cotton Dominant Panty Growth Outpacing Market in Target Customer Segment

Age group	All panties		Cotton dominant panties					
			Total		100% cotton		Cotton blends	
	1998-1999 growth	% of $ volume	1998-1999 growth	% of $ volume	1998-1999 growth	% of $ volume	1998-1999 growth	% of $ volume
10-16	22.1%	4.7%	19.4%	6.0%	10.6%	5.9%	190.7%	6.7%
17-44	6.1%	52.3%	10.7%	57.0%	7.9%	56.3%	37.8%	63.1%
45-54	7.1%	19.4%	0.9%	17.6%	-3.8%	17.4%	59.2%	19.5%
55-64	8.5%	11.3%	-2.6%	8.9%	-1.3%	9.2%	-16.4%	6.2%
65+	10.2%	12.4%	18.8%	10.6%	21.6%	11.3%	-19.0%	4.6%
		100%		100%		100%		100%

Cotton blends outpacing market growth for target customer

TABLE 3.2. TOTAL BRA AND PANTY COMPETITIVE INTELLIGENCE

Trend observed	Competitor/place observed	Implications for VSS
Overt Femininity - Curves and augmentation" reign eternal"	Market "buzzing" around the next evolution in lighter, more natural cleavage enhancing bras.	Obligation to be first to market with innovation that delivers cleavage in the most modern way.
Increased interest in "high tech" foundations	Triumph Europe "ultra-sonic" bra sold out in Paris and generating client interest in VSS internal shop test.	Clients very curious about "next" and what they have not seen before.
CUSTOMIZATION TREND in all arenas.	Fabrics and components that mold or conform to the individual are "winning" - BBV strapless, "X-bra," comfort wires, and stretch linings.	Continue to distort resources to the development of new products with maximum adjustability. Could be first with Memory Foam.
SOFTNESS is a "non-negotiable"	Microfibre now dominant in all channels of distribution and clearly marketed to the customer. "Meryl" is key in Europe not yet dominate in the U.S. Market.	We mustdifferentiate ourselves from the pack and vault into the future with ultra-soft fabrics that do not put "restrictions" on print and color expansion
Thongs, thongs, thongs.	Competitors dedicating more floor space and "pages" to thongs - great example Saks spring intimate book.	We must defend our market dominance through stronger in shop positioning of thongs and continued distortion within panty assortment.

notes that an implication for its marketing is to be the first to bring lighter and more natural cleavage enhancing bras to its customers. What is defined here in this report is a trend in which femininity, overt femininity, is constituted strictly as curves and augmentation. The rationale behind cleavage enhancing bras, smoothing, shaping, stretch-cotton/Lycra panties and other control garments is to give the generation x-er a curvaceous form, a feminine form. Femininity is what is distinctively and definitely for sale here. Femininity for the x-er means the slender ideal body with breasts. Since breasts are an unlikely complement to a slim-figured teen, augmentation vis-à-vis a push-up bra produces the ideal. If the bra is seamless, made from microfiber fabric, the augmentation may be undetectable. Similarly a young slender body would lack the curves of hips and waist. Shaping panties can accentuate hips, buttocks and waists. VSS even makes a high-waisted thong that gives the illusion of a defined waistline. The description from the VSS catalog of Body By Victoria is "A modern concept in seamless lingerie. Designed in high-tech soft microfiber that conforms to your shape, so all you see is curves. Panties: Imported Tactel microdenier nylon/Lycra spandex" (Spring 2000, 9). What the catalog description does not say is that these are shaping panties which offer light to moderate control. VSS is selling curves as femininity to the 17-34 year old age group who according to VSS are motivated by Style, Fit and Price in that order (Table 3.3).[9] This suggests that unlike boomers, the primary concern is style, then fit and comfort. What x-ers are buying is a notion of femininity as curvaceous, sexy, flirty, soft, colorful and in many cases lacy. Thus, it would seem that control garments, shaping panties, and cleavage-enhancing bras may indeed be controlling and augmenting the slender body, but they are being sold not as garments which proffer control to generation x-ers, but foundation garments which offer feminine curves.

In contrast to marketing to boomers, which proffers some other kind of femininity, one that is flabless and smooth, and somewhat comfortable, marketing to generation x-ers means creating curves in the right spots. The suggestion seems to be that of the Miracle bra—some curves you just can't get from working out. Young generation x-ers are not likely to be flabby, bulgy or bumpy. They are likely to lack any curves at all. They are told that to achieve shape, to achieve curves, they need foundations that create the ideal feminine form. Meanwhile, their mothers who have curves in the wrong spots are eliminating bulges and smoothing out bumps with relabled girdles in high-tech fabrics. Both groups are buying products fashioned in the new Micromattique fibers, but levels of control and shaping are varying from light and moderate to firm and super control. The markets for everyday shapers and control briefs may well be the same in terms of colors and patterns, because boomers remember old girdles only came in white or beige, but the strategies to sell to these markets are still somewhat different.

I am not sure that we are entrenched enough in a girdle resurgence that would rekindle the girdling rituals practiced and passed on from mothers to daughters in the 1940s and 1950s, but I think I can see this coming. The slender body ideal seems to be maintaining its dominance as a desired and commodified form. I suggest that this ideal remains precisely because it is virtually unachievable for most women without some form of augmentation. Wearing foundation garments allows for such augmentation with minimal physical health risk; however, the desire to achieve a slender ideal body through the wearing of foundations poses a risk to feminine subjectivity, to the feminine lived body. I express this risk as one in which boomers and x-ers, mothers and daughters, have become bound by an ideal which augments not only their bodies but limits, shapes, molds and defines the boundaries of feminine subjectivity. Bordo reminds us that such preoccupation with the achievement of a slender body ideal "may function as one of the most powerful normalizing mechanisms of our century, insuring the production of self-monitoring and self-disciplining 'docile bodies' sensitive to any departure from social norms and habituated to self-improvement and self-transformation in the service of those norms" (1993,187). How long will it be before we all accept the necessity of shapewear—and no longer laugh at Truvy's response

TABLE 3.3. PANTY PURCHASE MOTIVATED BY STYLE, FIT AND PRICE
Target Customer (Age 17–34)

Key influence on purchase decision	All panties	Non cotton	Cotton
Style / colour	32%	38%	28%
Fit / comfort	25%	23%	27%
Price	23%	21%	25%
Brand reputation	9%	8%	9%
Quality / durability	3%	2%	5%
Other	8%	8%	5%
Total	100%	100%	100%

to Janice Van Meter's ungirdled performance in *Steel Magnolias* when Truvy comments, "I haven't left the house without Lycra on these thighs since I was fourteen." Clairee responds, "Well, you were brought up right."[10] What does that mean for the rest of us?

NOTES

1. For a discussion of generation-xers, consumption and ideology see Heywood and Drake 1997.
2. The Specialists in Business Information Industry Reports are independent market researchers.
3. This BodySlimmers hang-tag came from the lingerie department at JC Penney.
4. This Hanes Her Way hang-tag came from the lingerie department at Kohl's.
5. For a discussion of backlash, see Faludi 1991.
6. See Victoria's Secret Market Research.
7. See Victoria's Secret. *Strategic View of the Line 2001: Foundations.* Dec. 1999: 66.
8. See Victoria's Secret. *1999 Market Patterning: Total Bras.* Apr. 20, 2000: 38.
9. See Victoria's Secret. *1999 Market Patterning: Total Bras.* Apr. 20, 2000: 25.
10. Herbert Ross dir. 1989 *Steel Magnolias.* United States. Sony Pictures. Clairee is played by Olympia Dukakis, and Truvy is played by Dolly Parton.

Chapter Four

The Myths of Freedom and Control: Constructing the Ideal Feminine Form in Advertising

... the magazines now not only reflect endlessly upon the reader, upon who she is, what she does, what she wants, and what she thinks, but also invite the reader to be more self-reflexive about her relation to fashion, cosmetics, and beauty, and to reflect upon her body in a new detailed way—as object of her own creativity and control, as instrument of her own social power, and at the same time, as target of men's violence and oppression in a society where gender is still a very lopsided power structure.

Leslie Rabine, "A Woman's Two Bodies"

"Need control? Want freedom?" These questions stand at the center of the controversy concerning representations of women's bodies in foundationwear advertising. Although the advertisement from Figure 4.1 explicitly proffers freedom and control, this language both trivializes and complicates women's relationships to their own bodies as mediated by foundation garments and the social necessity for wearing them. The ad presents a paradox: Can a woman's body be both controlled and free at the same time? Foundation garments are posed as the answer to this question as they offer woman the power to transform her flawed body into what Barthes terms "fashion's ideal body" (1983, 260). Fashion's ideal body has been manipulated through advertisements for decades in an effort to entice the average woman to purchase garments that are designed to transform her body into the ideal body. Foundation garments— corsets, corselettes, girdles, panty girdles, all-in-ones, body briefers, flattener bras, sweater bras, push-up bras, power slips and more—form the base for this transformation. They construct the shape of the feminine form by altering the real body where it conflicts with the ideal body. Since foundations provide the base for fashion, the term foundationwear can be easily substituted for fashion in Barthes statement that, "Fashion [foundationwear] transforms the real body

Figure 4.1. Need Control? Want Freedom? *Montgomery Ward Catalog* 1966

and succeeds in making it signify fashion's ideal body: to lengthen, fill out, reduce, enlarge, take in, refine" whatever figure flaws present themselves (1983, 260).

In this manner foundationwear works to reshape the ideal body in order to meet whatever demands are made upon the feminine form in any historical moment. Certainly, Roland Barthes' conception of fashion's ideal body is a mythologized body—a body that exists only as an ideal and not in the real, but a body nonetheless that will be sought after even as it changes shape thereby illustrating its elusiveness. The transient and elusive elements of fashion produce and reproduce the ideal body in fashion history. As Georg Simmel points out, "As soon as an example has been universally adopted, that is, as soon as anything that was originally done only by a few has really come to be practiced by all, we no longer speak of fashion" (1971, 302). Fashion in Simmel's terms ceases to be "in fashion" the moment it is taken up by the dominant culture. In this same way, fashion's ideal body does not remain the same for any determinable period, but rather shifts and changes with the historical and material demands of culture. The consequence of the shifting action for this ideal construction of the feminine form is as Susan Bordo posits, "an ever-changing, homogenizing elusive ideal of femininity—a pursuit without terminus, requiring that women constantly attend to minute and often whimsical changes in fashion" (1993, 166).

The whimsical changes surrounding the construction of fashion's ideal body are demonstrated perhaps most clearly in advertisements and catalogs for foundation garments. These advertisements depict foundation garments whose purposes are to control and shape the real body, the flawed body, in order to transform it into fashion's ideal body. However, what is perhaps most significant about these advertisements is not only that they demonstrate the point of the elusiveness of fashion as it applies to the female body, but that they make use of language and representations which suggest that some kind of freedom is being sold along with the controlling undergarment. What follows here is a detailed analysis of selected advertisements, catalogs and articles focusing on foundationwear from the late 1930s to the present which draws on the work of scholars in the fields of semiotics, advertising, sociology, feminist theory, history and of course some undergarment specialists and fetishists.

Through this analysis I explain how representations of foundation garments in advertising demonstrate the elusiveness of the ideal feminine form, how they convey the message that these garments can be used by women to transform their flawed bodies into ideal ones by controlling and shaping them, and how the advertisements employ language and images that proffer some kind of freedom. This freedom can sometimes be referred to in merely a bodily sense, wherein a garment may be said to be less constricting than its predecessor; however, quite often there seems to be some kind of socio-political freedom being proffered in these advertisements. Roland Marchand suggests that this mixed social messaging that is so prominent in advertising is most likely a mistake on the part of the reader of the ad. Marchand explains that there is frequently a conflation of consumer and sociopolitical freedoms found in the provocative expression of advertisements (1986, 186). What Marchand suggests is that advertisements promote the freedom to consume, but often consumers read the ads as indicating a promotion of social and political freedom.

This certainly seems to be the case of a 1937 *Life Magazine* article titled, "A Good Figure Costs American Women $65,000,000 A Year." This article looks very much like an advertisement for Warner Brothers and an invitation to women to continue to spend and possibly increase their spending on the latest innovations in the foundationwear industry. The article points out the significance in the improvement of the newest corset and touts its ability to offer women control and freedom as it "flattens out obtrusive hips" and "approaches the breasts, separating them properly" (*Life* 1937, 66). The article credits Warner Brothers with the important invention of the streamlined Lastex corset which "although containing no bones, still performs its major function of thigh and bust control" (*Life* 60). The article argues for the value in such an invention and confirms that "Today U.S. women are spending $65,000,000 a year to keep their figures under control—and Warner Brothers gets the lion's share of this business" (*Life* 60). Thus, the messages that are iterated and reiterated with each image in the article are that Lastex will solve the problem body, women need new foundation garments, and finally women should spare no expense in choosing the latest in foundation fashions to shape their figures into the ideal form.

Figure 4.2 illustrates what is newest and best about this Warner Brothers innovation in technology. Here, we see a woman in a Lastex net slipover. The foundation garment itself looks particularly uncomfortable; however it is made with a revolutionary new material called Lastex. Lastex was rubber elastic thread that could be produced in the same lengths and with similar degrees of fineness to other threads and was developed by the Dunlop Rubber Company (Ewing 1978, 146). While this material would seem to promote only sweating by today's standards, "it meant a new concept of corsetry because figure control no longer depended upon boning, lacing and the imposition of a rigid kind of cage on the figure" (Ewing 1978, 147). The result is that in 1937 it is not indeed surprising that we should see this young woman tap dancing in the black Veil of Youth net slipover and demonstrating her garment's fluidity.

Tap dancing to prove her garment's fluidity, a Warner model demonstrates the black "Veil of Youth," a boneless Lastex net slipover which permits complete freedom of action, can be folded in a purse.

Figure 4.2. Tap Dancing "A Good Figure Costs American Women $65,000,000" *Life Magazine* 1937

However, having acknowledged the significance of the technology in the production of such a garment for women, it is important to consider the power of
this representation in advertising. This article appears in *Life*, an extremely popular magazine that is providing publicity for Warner's who is putting on a fashion show that has attracted some 1,100 buyers from department stores (*Life* 62).
This article points out what women spend "to keep their figures under control"
while simultaneously depicting an image of a woman "tap dancing to prove her
garments fluidity" (*Life* 60, 63). There can be no question that this article proffers the freedom to consume foundationwear and the freedom of bodily movement even as it calls for continued "compression of the female waist" (Life 60).
Thus, the article illustrates the paradox of freedom and control while presenting
a new ideal body to its readers. The image of the young woman tap dancing in
the black "Veil of Youth" provides what Barthes describes as the third solution,
the third way in which "Fashion resolves the passage from the abstract body to
the real body of its readers" (1983, 258). The representation of this young
woman wearing the Lastex net slipover "transforms the real body and succeeds
in making it signify Fashion's ideal body: imperatively feminine, absolutely
young, endowed with a strong identity [at least strong enough to dance around
in her underwear] and yet with a contradictory personality" (Barthes 1983, 260).
Finally, the image of the girl tap dancing depicts the foundation garment as having only positive effects on the girl's freedom.

This theme of freedom is repeated in the same article in Figure 4.3. The caption to Figure 4.3 reads, "Informally gathered in the dressing room, these models range from the slender type at left to the stylish stout at right." (*Life* 64). Here
we see women dressed in one-piece corselettes. What is conveyed both in the
posture and in the language is that these women are not aware that they are being photographed since they are "informally gathered" and some of the women
are not looking at the camera. However, these women all have their heads canted
to one side or the other and most of the woman have their knees bent. Erving
Goffman reads "the bashful knee-bend as a foregoing of full effort to be prepared
and on the ready in the current situation" (1979, 45). Goffman suggests that in
having a person posed in this manner, the photographer is facilitating a reading
of the models as more natural (1979, 45). The knee bending in this picture speaks
to me in the same manner. These women are aware of the camera, and they are
posing with knees bent so as not to appear posed.

As for the head canting, Goffman notes that "the head is lowered relative
to that of others, including, indirectly, the viewer of the picture. The resulting
configurations can be read as an acceptance of subordination, an expression
of ingratiation, submissiveness, and appeasement" (1979, 46). While the
ladies in the picture appear to be engaged in delighted and expressive conversations in which their heads are canted to imply listening to one another,

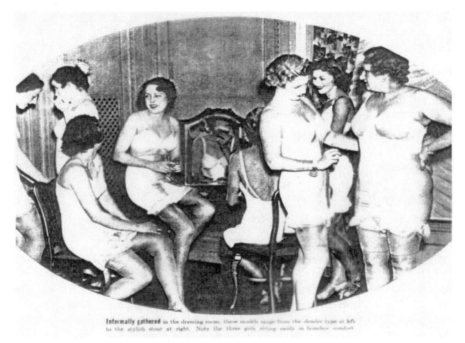

Informally gathered in the dressing room, these models range from the slender type at left to the stylish stout at right. Note the three girls sitting easily in boneless comfort.

Figure 4.3. Informally Gathered "A Good Figure Costs American Women $65,000,000" *Life Magazine* 1937

what is actually being conveyed is the quintessential virtues of feminine posture—ingratiation, submissiveness, and appeasement. The picture actually seems to signify that these women are posed to appear in the manner that would suggest their acquiescence to a photographer, who is trying to depict them as "informally gathered." The significance of this is that the caption also reads, "Note the three girls sitting easily in boneless comfort" (*Life* 64); however, they probably were never seated until the photographer asked them to do so for the photo. Thus, the creation of the image of easy comfort and freedom of movement is one that is conjured by the photographer and the models, and is represented to the reader as a freeing quality of the garment. Having said this, it seems important to note that the caption also refers to a range of model body types "from the slender type at left to the stylish stout at right." This seems to signify an acceptance of a range of body types that is not evidenced in later foundationwear advertising.

Hence, the size and shape of the model at right is worth noting since she is considered to be "the stylish stout." If we were to take this model out of 1937 and place her in the present, she would be considered quite large. This is worthy of consideration particularly with regard to historical arguments that seem

to arise around the issue of overweight women today. What today seems striking about this image is the fact that she does embody a figure that would have
been acceptable in her day. Historian Ann Beth Presley notes, "The silhouette
of the 30s emphasized the natural form of the woman's body with clearly defined curves, and women tried diligently to maintain this ideal" (1998, 320).
But, what of the woman who has no curves? Is her lack of curves in the 1930s
just as problematic as being overweight is today? This idea that there is an
ideal body for each historical material moment is supported not only by
Barthes who points to "Fashion's ideal body" but also by anthropologist
Margaret Lock, who claims that "culture can be dominant, and nature, including the body, is then redefined and reified largely in terms of culturally
determined categories" (1993, 136). Hence, what we end up with is a 1937
model who may serve as "Fashion's ideal body" only within the context of
her historical and material conditions, conditions which in the 1930s embraced a more voluptuous feminine form.

The size of models from the 1940s varies little from that of the 1930s, and
in fact, the figure type seems quite similar. As we look at Figure 4.4, a buxom
woman stands for an ad that simply reads BESTFORM, thus touting her perfect 1940s figure. What is worth noting in terms of the historicity of foundationwear is the effect that World War II had on the corsetry industry. "Miss
Mary Anderson, director of the Women's Bureau of the Department of Labor
declared corsets to be essential to the performance of women's tasks in the
war effort, pointing out that fatigue was the main reason why women frequently left their war jobs" (Ewing 1978, 156). However, this ad like many
BESTFORM ads of post-war days signifies patriotism through the use of flag
stripes in the backing of the ad. Hence it is both patriotic for women to put
forth their BESTFORM and to support U.S. companies during the post-war
period.

Figure 4.4 is indicative of the more conservative look of post-war days
which is reflection of Christian Dior's New Look (Presley 1998, 322). When
the New Look appeared in 1947 Dior was quoted as saying, "Without foundations there can be no fashion" (Presley 1998, 322). This is most significant
when we consider that the BESTFORM ad is maintaining that there can be
"No finer fit at any price." What emerges here is another ideal body image
calling for women to try this garment that promises "to curb your curves from
waist to hip. Made of flexible, airy nylon this is a girdle to control your
pounds, extoll your curves. Giving you hips you'll hooray, a waist worth buying a belt for. All at a purse-easy price—with money [left] over for the matching bra." This advertising language speaks of the necessity of containing the
female post-war form in a matching girdle and bra set. As historian Ann Beth
Presley suggests there is a need to recover the femininity of pre-war days in
a celebration of freedom and post-war days (1998, 322). This BESTFORM

curbs your
curves from
waist to hip

Made of flexible, airy nylon,
this is a girdle to control your
pounds, extoll your curves. Giving
you hips you'll hooray, a waist worth
buying a belt for. All at a purse-easy
price—with money over for the
matching bra. ■ Style 5452—14" sizes
25 to 32. ■ Style 5652—16" sizes 26 to 36.
White and pink. **$5.00** ■ Matching
nylon bra—style 6094. **$1.50**

BESTFORM

no finer fit at any price

Figure 4.4.   Bestform. Advertisement. "No Finer Fit at Any Price," 1940s

advertisement sends the message that purchasing a BESTFORM girdle and bra will fulfill the patriotic duty of the American woman consumer to (re)shape her body into the new post-war ideal body, Dior's New Look.

The girdle and bra represented in the BESTFORM ad are indicative of the New Look launched in February of 1947. As fashion historian Rebecca

Arnold asserts, "Women may have shown independence and valor during the war but they were expected to slip softly back into the domestic realm, clad in the dramatically feminine sculpting of New Look fashion" (2001, 101). This high-waisted girdle represents the new style known as the cincher. Dior articulates the desired look is for "flower-like women, with rounded shoulders, full, feminine busts, and hand-span waists" (qtd in Ewing 1992, 155). The return to femininity is manifested in this advertisement in terms of the tulip embellishments on the girdle panels suggestive of ovaries, a hand-span waist, and a bountiful bosom. The ad maintains that "no finer fit [can be found] at any price." All of this language suggests that controlling the body can be a freeing experience. Historian Catherine Williamson explores the repetition of this concept in post-war advertising. She notes:

> Post-war culture experienced an explosion in commodities designed to control [the female] body. Girdles and bras promised to reconstruct the female body into the desired form, treating it as so much clay to be molded and shaped. Consumer culture hammered home the message that placing the female body under the controlling influence of industry would free women to experience a kind of pleasure that they had never known. (1996, 7)

What Williamson expresses is represented in both the language of the ad, "BESTFORM: no finer fit at any price" and in the pleasure of the model's face. Her coy smile conveys the notion that she finds something secretly pleasurable, and then again there is the repeated signifier of freedom in the flag stripes backing the ad.

However, at least the BESTFORM ad shows the model's face. In Figure 4.5, the Slack-ees girl is portrayed as a mystery girl or is she? The advertisement conveys her as Fashion's ideal body without ever showing us her face, but it seems clear that we are meant to know who she is. Everyone knows someone like her. She is what Barthes describes as "this monster we obviously recognize [as] the permanent compromise which marks the relation between mass culture and its consumers: the Woman of Fashion" (261). This ad ran in the now famous trade journal, *Corset and Underwear Review*, in February of 1947. The text appeals to men—"who are in charge of departments"—to identify this "Woman of Fashion" as the ideal, and through men's desire to see this image, the demand will be placed on women to become her—to say "Slack-ees, please." Hence, the language of the advertisement is directed toward those men who have the power to create the need for this elusive "Woman of Fashion." These managers can give women the freedom to choose to be—the faceless Slack-ees dream girl with "her dramatic pose, her lovely [and] lissome lines." We can actually imagine her drumming up business for these men and their departments. After all she's free because "she sells Slack-ees." Even the name Slack-ees—conveys the freedom of movement, the ease of wearing

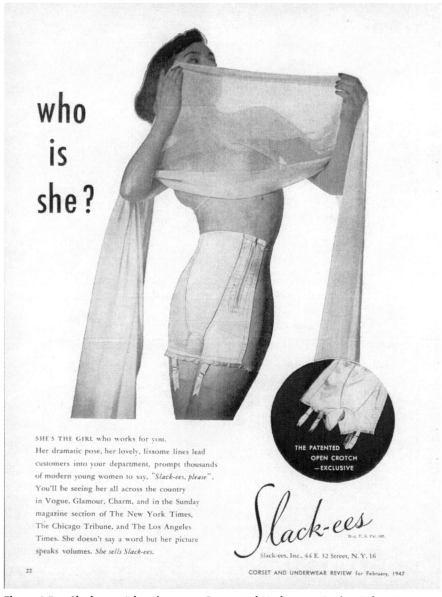

who
is
she?

SHE'S THE GIRL who works for you.
Her dramatic pose, her lovely, lissome lines lead
customers into your department, prompt thousands
of modern young women to say, *"Slack-ees, please"*.
You'll be seeing her all across the country
in Vogue, Glamour, Charm, and in the Sunday
magazine section of The New York Times,
The Chicago Tribune, and The Los Angeles
Times. She doesn't say a word but her picture
speaks volumes. *She sells Slack-ees.*

THE PATENTED
OPEN CROTCH
—EXCLUSIVE

Slack-ees
Reg. U. S. Pat. Off.

Slack-ees, Inc., 44 E. 32 Street, N. Y. 16

CORSET AND UNDERWEAR REVIEW for February, 1947

Figure 4.5. Slack-ees. Advertisement. *Corset and Underwear Review* Feb. 1947

Slack-ees. It may indeed be easy to wear Slack-ees, but to "speak volumes" without a face is an impossibility that will undoubtedly leave this girl not only hidden behind her veil, but constrained within her girdle and contained within an ideal body that has been constructed by men (who probably wrote the ad) for men (who own and operate the department stores).

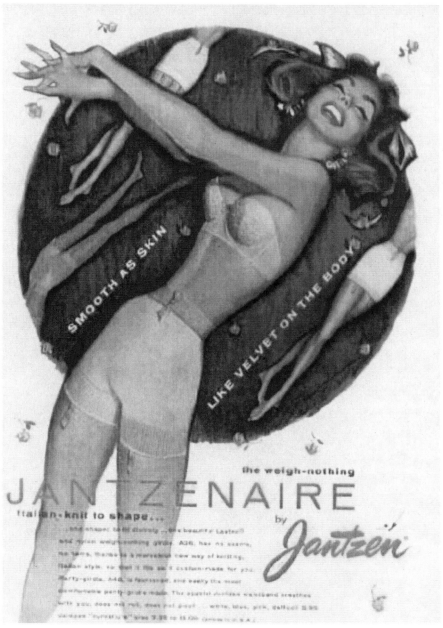

Figure 4.6.   Jantzen. Advertisement. "The weigh-nothing Jantzenaire" 1950s

The signifiers of freedom in Figure 4.6, the free-floating bodies and "the weigh-nothing Jantzenaire" might have been more compelling to teenage girls, the primary audience for this advertisement than the faceless Slack-ees girl. The ideal teen body proffered in this ad is reminiscent of the boyish body of the 1920s liberated flapper. This ideal resurfaces in the Twiggy body typology of the late 1950s. Advertising scholars Stuart and Elizabeth Ewen describe this ideal teen body as "The young, agile, long-limbed girl, whose naturally shaped body is well suited to the working requirements and mobility of the modern world" (1982, 150). In Figure 4.6 the girl is set free as she dons a girdle that is "smooth as skin" and feels "like velvet on the body." The significations of femininity and fun, freedom vis-á-vis weightlessness surround the young, teenage girl who wears the smile of ecstasy. Indeed, she is free to pursue her youthful femininity through the beautiful and uplifting experience of "the weigh-nothing Jantzenaire." The Jantzenaire advertisement indicates that she will be transformed bodily and socially by wearing this girdle. All she must do to experience this transformation is to give over to the social conventions of the 1950s that require even teenage girls to wear girdles. Sociologist Georg Simmel argues, "Whenever we imitate, we transfer . . . the responsibility for the action from ourselves to another. Thus the individual is freed from the worry of choosing and appears simply as a creature of the group, as a vessel of the social contents" (1971, 295). In the act of wearing this girdle, the 1950s teenage girl becomes socially identifiable as "a creature of the group" of fashionable young girls. What's more the language of the advertisement even inherent in the brand name Jantzen*aire* signifies walking on air, weightlessness and free-floating in space and time which may allow the reader of the ad to see herself being freed through the experience of purchasing and ultimately wearing this magical girdle.

The magic of girdles continued in the 1950s as is shown by Figure 4.7. Here an advertisement for Flexees Coolaire girdle and strapless bra illustrates the height of fashion for this decade. The strapless bra came into and remained in vogue because of its pairing with strapless dresses (Ewing 1978, 163). Girdles continued to be produced using nylon and elastic nets that still made them fairly heavy, and women of the fifties continued wearing them primarily because they "controlled curves and trimmed outlines under fashions that were much more formal and figure-fitting" (Ewing 1978, 164). "The Flexees Figure" conveys this figure-fitting moment in fashion as the model shown here seems hardly able to separate her legs for all the apparatus hemming her in. She is represented as having "an entrancing silhouette," a smooth silhouette devoid of unsightly bumps or bulges, but her power of movement seems arrested. In this manner the woman depicted here is subject to the limitations of what Bakhtin refers to as "the classical body." Cultural studies practitioner Laura Kipnis describes this classical

THE

flexees

FIGURE

For a cool, cool Summer just your size... choose a *Coolaire* foundation, by *Flexees!* This breeze of a fabric ... of open weave Nyralon*... gives you an entrancing silhouette, with the comfort you love! Be fitted now to *Coolaire*, by *Flexees*, at your favorite store!

Coolaire Bras: $2.00
Coolaire Girdles: $7.95

Figure 4.7.   Flexees. Advertisement. "The Flexees Figure" 1950s

body as "a refined, orifice-less, laminated surface—[one that] is homologous to the forms of official high culture which legitimate their authority by reference to the values—the highness—inherent in this classical body" (1992, 376). This is indeed the body of high culture, a 1950s embodiment of Dior's New Look which is illustrated by "sharply defined breasts, narrow torso, sloping hips, and long legs that the style produced. Although still slender, the waist was less extreme than in the 1940s" (Bressler 1997, 132). This glamorous ideal body of the 1950s is one that would have been coveted by women of all classes. It represents what is perhaps most enticing about many foundationwear ads as it conveys not only an ideal, but also the freedom and hope for achieving this ideal. This ad signifies the freedom for the potential of social mobility and is at least partially attributable to the suggestion of summer leisure time, which would be the privilege of middle- and upper-class women who were not obligated to work outside the home. The text of the ad reads, "For a cool, cool Summer just your size . . . choose a Coolaire foundation, by Flexees." The underlying social message seems to be—if you can achieve this look, you will achieve the status that is ascribed to it. This of course, for many women is impossible, but the message is there all the same. The control in this advertisement for Flexees stems both from the language that promises an "entrancing silhouette" and the representation of the female body here in the form of "the classical body." The oppositional language which connotes freedom is manifested in the "ees" of Flexees, the "aire" of Coolaire, and finally in the phrase "with comfort that you love." Hence, the advertisement maintains the mixed social messaging that gives the reader a contradictory notion of bodily control and social freedom.

Freedom is also foregrounded in the Playtex girdle advertisement in Figure 4.8 where we see young women leaping in their girdles across this page, which appeared in *Seventeen* magazine in 1950. The language of the ad artfully suggests just how freeing the experience of wearing this girdle can be as it calls on the young teen to college age female consumer to "Imagine a girdle that slims and trims you so comfortably, moulds you with such freedom of action that you can wear it from the first class till last goodnight and forget you have it on." This language reinforces the representation of young women leaping so uninhibitedly that the reader can only be drawn to one conclusion—that trimming her body can actually free her in a way that she can never know otherwise. In fact, the introduction to the ad claims to be able to "Solve ALL your girdle problems with [the] Invisible Playtex Girdle." However, the fine print suggests that Playtex can solve other problems too as it "slims you gently, whittles away at waist, hips and thighs." The reader can imagine how improving her figure can improve her life. She will be given more than freedom of action; she will be freed on a whole new level—a social level.

Famous designers

of campus clothes

solve ALL your

girdle problems with

Invisible Playtex® Girdle

STANLEY WYLLINS, creator of this slim party-goer: "If you're wearing a Playtex, then you've no problem. For Playtex slims and moulds your figure at waist, hips and thighs."

Imagine a girdle without a single seam, stitch or bone — so perfectly fitting, so smoothly slimming that it's completely invisible — even under the most clinging of your new clothes.

Imagine a girdle that slims and trims you so comfortably, moulds you with such freedom of action that you can wear it from first class till last goodnight and forget you have it on.

Imagine a girdle that washes dainty in ten seconds, pats completely dry with a towel

in just seconds more — ready to wear again right away.

Imagine a girdle that even to the touch feels like no girdle at all, yet so effective that it shapes your silhouette *naturally* from waist to thighs. No need to imagine such a girdle, here it is! The Invisible Playtex Girdle!

No wonder it's praised by designers as no other girdle ever before. See it, buy it at your favorite department store, or better specialty shops everywhere.

FRANK PERRULO offers this black faille with a word of advice: "Playtex slims you gently, whittles away at waist, hips and thighs — fits invisibly even under a sheath-like dress."

Figure-slimming secret of Playtex is its all-way action-stretch. Made of pure latex, this sensational girdle fits and feels like a second skin, actually trims away inches from those problem bulges, to give you a slender, supple silhouette in the most complete comfort.

SYD RAPPI calls this her favorite for cocktails, says: "If you're wearing a Playtex, you've no problem when it comes to newest fall clothes. It gives you new smoothness, trimness."

In **SLIM**, silvery tubes,
PLAYTEX LIVING® GIRDLES. . . $3.50 to $3.95
In **SLIM**, shimmering pink tubes,
PLAYTEX PINK-ICE GIRDLES . . $3.95 to $4.95
In **SLIM**, golden tubes,
PLAYTEX FAB-LINED GIRDLES . $4.95 to $5.95
— Fabric next to your skin —
(All prices slightly higher in Canada and Foreign Countries)
Sizes: extra-small, small, medium, large;
Extra-large size slightly higher
At all department stores and better specialty shops everywhere.

INTERNATIONAL LATEX CORPORATION
Playtex Park ©1950 **Dover Del.**

Figure 4.8.   Playtex. Advertisement. "Invisible Playtex Girdle" *Seventeen* **Dec. 1950**

Figure 4.9.   Warner's. Advertisement. "Even the Smartest Girls are taken in" 1961

The social sophistication of the girdle began to fall apart with younger women in the 1960s although "those over the age of 30 still clung to stockings, suspenders, and supportive panty girdles" (Bressler 1997, 135). The undergarment industry continued to produce foundations for this older group of women, but "rejected the curves of the 1950s and turned to the tall, thin, willowy frame that epitomized the decade" (Bressler 134). Figure 4.9 represents this turn to a willowy upper-class body ideal as long and lean figures walk with glamour and grace in their girdles through this ad. Social class is signified in the ad by using the word smart in the caption, but also in the name of the girdles being advertised, "Warner's new Royale Highness" girdles. The language in the ad reads, "Slight of hand! Warner's original 'Royale Highness' in lightweight power net and rayon satin elastic (it made slimming so easy, a whole family gets into the act). The front and back panels pat you sleek and smooth, give just enough pull to firm where nature's released." Thus, Warner's is proffering a royal garment made using the latest technology in fabrics—power net and rayon satin elastic—to control the unruly feminine form. The association of technology and smartness, progress and social mobility are all implied in the language and visual signifiers in the ad. Clearly, the smartest girls stand erect with grace and poise as if they are royalty, and the "Royale Highness" girdle collection facilitates the proper comportment of the ideal feminine body.

Although social class seems clearly signified, it is important to note that the ad is directed at young women, quite probably college women, whom Warner's hopes to win over and keep in girdles. The language of the ad is a play on words—"Even the smartest girls are taken in—and love it!" The play on words is an indication that girls could be tricked somehow by this ad and by the product; however, what is also conveyed is that being taken in or being taken advantage of is not always a bad thing. In fact, the logic being used here is that if the smartest (either the most intelligent or the best dressed) girls are allowing themselves to be taken in, slimmed, and trimmed by girdles, then perhaps other girls should do the same. Thus, the ad seems to operate on much the same level as Simmel's conception of imitation as mentioned earlier wherein the act of imitation frees the individual from direct responsibility and labels her as the member of a group. What better group to be a part of than that of the smartest girls?!!!

And, the smartest girls in the late 1960s would surely have worn Lycra as used in the making of the bra and girdle depicted in Figure 4.10. DuPont again creates a new man-made fabric made from spandex fiber that is used extensively in swimwear and foundationwear (Ewing 1992, 224). "Three times as powerful as natural rubber, Lycra could make a girdle with real control" (Melinkoff 1984, 150). What is unusual about this advertisement is that

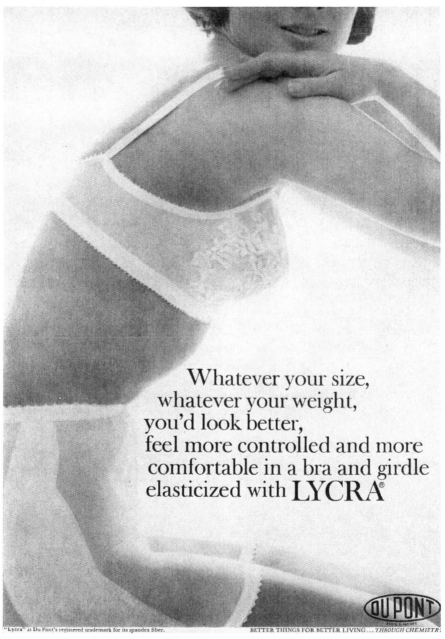

Whatever your size,
whatever your weight,
you'd look better,
feel more controlled and more
comfortable in a bra and girdle
elasticized with LYCRA®

Figure 4.10.   DuPont's Lycra. Advertisement. "Whatever your size" 1960s

it is not an advertisement for a particular brand of bra and girdle, but rather it is an ad for foundations made of Lycra. DuPont becomes a peddler of women's undergarments through technology, through new fabrics, through the textile industry and the fashion-industrial complex. What is more, DuPont advocates girdles and bras by zooming in on the model's body and eliminating her face from view. What then becomes important is not the model or her celebrity image, but her body. The anonymous body comes to be recognized as the ideal body. Roland Barthes explains, "The cover girl's body is no one's body, it is a pure form, which possesses no attribute" (1983, 259). It is not identifiable as anyone/thing other than the ideal body. Having noted such anonymity, we must consider how this anonymity allows DuPont to appeal to any woman. The ad reads, "Whatever your size, whatever your weight, you'd look better, feel more controlled and more comfortable in a bra and girdle elasticized with LYCRA." DuPont is able to speak to the collective "you" of all women—regardless of size or weight—and assure us that Lycra will give us the power to look better, to control our bodies, and to be more comfortable. In this way, DuPont, a textile manufacturer prescribes Lycra to fix the naturally flawed bodies of all women. Through the use of Lycra, a modern man-made technology, women are offered to chance to tame their unruly bodies and achieve the ideal body of fashion.

However, according to the advertisement in Figure 4.11, "What you feel in a Warner's—isn't the girdle." Thus, a woman wearing a Warner's girdle will feel differently from a woman wearing some other brand of girdle even if they are both Lycra. The difference is that this panty girdle seems to offer some kind of privilege. The representations shown here rely on the seduction of orientalism as they indicate a life of exotic luxury. The bountiful platter of luscious fruit—mangoes, grapes, pineapples, pomegranates, the model lounging on large silken pillows laid atop Persian rugs while leaning against colorfully cushioned walls—all fit together to conjure up notions of the opulence of a royal palace in the Far East. The message is a provocative and seductive one conveyed in the model's direct stare. Indeed, as feminist media studies practitioner Angharad Valdivia points out in "The Secret of My Desire: Gender, Class and Sexuality in Lingerie Catalogs" when models engage the camera, and therefore the implied viewer, directly, they are granted a much more powerful stance (1997, 241). Here, the model is represented in a position of power. She is centered in the advertisement. She seems in control of the objects that circle around her. This is especially evident in the way she alluringly caresses the grapes that gently rest in an abundant bunch on her palm in order to effect what Erving Goffman refers to as a " just barely touching of the kind that might be significant between two electrically charged bodies"

What you feel in a Warner's—isn't the girdle.

What do you feel in this girdle whose name is Delilah™? Like Delilah, naturally. Decorative and dangerous. The sophisticated lace tummy panel provides the decor. The double derrière panel and unique Warner's® construction supply the figure that makes any woman feel dangerous.

Incidentally, you don't feel the girdle because it's made with nylon and uncovered Lycra® spandex—the lightest, most weightless girdle fabric of all.

Wrap up the Delilah feeling with Warner's Delilah bra—lace top, Shapeliner® undercups, 5.00. Pantie 8.95, girdle 7.95. Nylon and Lycra spandex bra and girdle in canteloupe, blue mist, blueberry, primrose, swiss pink, blonde, black and white.

**Figure 4.11.   Warner's. Advertisement. "What you feel in a Warner's—isn't the girdle"
1964**

(1979, 29). The senses of sexuality, power, and control are virtually palpable here. The advertisement suggests that wearing a Warner's can make a woman feel freed in a sensual way while maintaining control of her body and her surroundings. Constraint as idea has been silenced in this ad, in spite of the fact that we can see the panty girdle and bra as huge white apparatuses covering most of the model, controlling and shaping her body.

In contrast, Warner's "The Riddle" in Figure 4.12 focuses on the ideas of confinement and constraint. This advertisement zooms in on the waist, hips and thighs that wear the girdle thereby containing what is seen. This kind of imaging is known as "body cropping" which has been heavily criticized within feminist scholarship as evidence of the objectification of women (Valdivia 1997, 240). What is seen in the ad has already been constrained, confined, limited; this part of the body is objectified as it is reduced. The language of the ad describes how using nylon and Lycra spandex enables the girdle to "get rid of those tell-tale panels—but keep the power." In this ad, the girdle has power. The wearer can gain access to the power by "feel[ing] it. No bumps. No lumps. Nothing to pinch you. Nothing to poke through your most clinging dress. Just smooth stretch nylon and Lycra spandex." "The Riddle" is claimed to be invisible and pinch-free and smooth because of its secret fabric; however, we can see at close range how tightly it adheres to the body. This girdle may not pinch, but it certainly does constrain even if it does give the wearer the freedom to trick the public by eliminating those "tell-tale panels."

While Warner's is busy trying to get rid of the tell-tale panels of its girdles, Maidenform has models wearing their bras out in public. The Maidenform "I dreamed" campaign ran from 1949 to 1971. According to a *New York Times* article from March of 1997, the original Maidenform "I dreamed" campaign depicted women, "clad in foundation garments, enacting fantasies of accomplishment and purpose" (Elliot 1997, 2). These fantasies of accomplishment and purpose provide the keys to understanding the power of representation in foundationwear advertising.

Perhaps one of the most noteworthy examples of the rich fantasy life of Maidenform women appears in the "I dreamed" campaign as Cleopatra (Figure 4.13). The title reads "I dreamed I barged down the Nile in my Maidenform Bra," and there is a Cleopatra with a golden headdress, reminiscent of a blonde wig, barging down the Nile in her Maidenform bra. The signs of her privileged social class, her questionably fair skin, indeed her whiteness, reappropriate the power of the Cleopatra as the quintessential signifier of the exotic feminine other. The fantasy of Cleopatra as an exotic other is co-opted by this seemingly fair-haired, fair-skinned, Anglicized version of her. Clearly, this representation of Cleopatra is conflicted in terms of racial signification, but it is also conflicted through the image of wealth dripping from her body

Here is the first girdle to get rid of those tell-tale panels— but keep the power. Where does it get the power without panels? That is The Riddle™ by Warner's®

See those innocent-looking flowers? They're set into the fabric by a secret new Warner process. And that's what makes The Riddle perform like a paneled girdle—but without the panels. Feel it. No lumps. No bumps. Nothing to pinch you. Nothing to poke through your most clinging dress. Just smooth smooth nylon and Lycra®spandex. The Riddle by Warner's is the greatest riddle since the Sphinx. Pantie girdle shown 10.95. Other Riddles from 8.95.

24

Figure. 4.12.   Warner's. Advertisement. "The Riddle" 1964

I dreamed
I barged down the Nile in my *maidenform* **bra**

Sweet Music*...Maidenform dream bra...features spoke-stitched cups for Cleopatra curves! All-elastic band for freedom of fit;
reinforced undercups for everlasting uplift. White in A, B, C cups. This and seven other enchanting Sweet Music styles, from 2.50.
*REG. U.S. PAT. OFF. ©1962 BY MAIDENFORM, INC., MAKERS OF BRAS, GIRDLES AND SWIMSUITS

Figure 4.13.   Maidenform Bra. Advertisement. "I dreamed I barged down the Nile" 1962

and the co-optation of political, social, economic and military power that is
not often associated with women in mainstream U.S. culture. In this way,
Cleopatra's image in this ad is co-opted for the empowerment of American female consumers, but it is also simultaneously devalued as it is literally
bleached of its authenticity. bell hooks explains how otherness is often reap-

propriated by mainstream culture and in this way images are also distorted and conflicted. hooks maintains, "The commodification of Otherness has been so successful because it is offered as a new delight, more intense, more satisfying than normal ways of doing and feeling. Within commodity culture, ethnicity becomes spice, seasoning that can liven up the dull dish that is mainstream white culture" (1992, 21). We have seen this in contemporary U.S. culture through the evolution of blues, rock, and hip-hop music, but we should remember this is not a new phenomenon nor is it limited to music, but rather cultural significations frequently appropriate and reappropriate the signs of the exotic other into the dominant culture. The repeated Anglicized image of Cleopatra in the fantasy ads of the Maidenform "I dreamed" campaign underscores the turbulent nature of the ad campaign as it sought to empower women while drawing on images that were frequently fraught with orientalism, sexism, and classicism. The canvas of fantasy life for women was in many ways opened up by this revolutionary ad campaign, but it also broke open Pandora's box of stereotypes and misrepresentations associated with race, class, gender and sexuality that have plagued women in advertisements ever since.

It is important to note that this is an articulation of a fantasy from 1964 when women were only beginning to come to consciousness about the sexual revolution. Women simply did not wear their underwear as outerwear at this time, so in many ways this campaign was ground breaking and outrageous. It gave women a sense that while their bras may have seemed physically restrictive, they did not preclude empowerment. In fact, the campaign suggested that wearing a Maidenform bra could incite women to do things that they never imagined possible. By wearing a Maidenform bra women could live out their dreams; however, sadly many of these dreams are focused on women living out the lives of exotic others as opposed to living their own lives in more freeing and satisfying ways.

This is also apparent in Figure 4.14 where a female version of Ben Hur commandeers a royal gold chariot with eagle insignia in the coliseum complete with bronzed helmet, golden lapels, armored wrist plates, red feathered plume and red velvet cape while wearing her white Maidenform Counterpoint Bra (Figure 4.14). Once again the dream here is set off by escaping reality and becoming someone else (in this case by becoming a man). Photojournalist Carol Squiers comments that the "I dreamed bra campaign showed women attired in exotic outfits with only a bra as a top (beating Madonna by about 30 years), who 'dreamed' they did wonderful things" (1995, 3). Recognizing the feminist argument that women must also draw on the male imaginary and traffic in the male symbolic, I argue that this image of a woman as Ben Hur is predicated on the key

COUNTERPOINT*...new Maidenform bra made with super-strong Spandex—new, non-rubber elastic that weighs almost nothing at all yet lasts (and <u>controls</u> you) far longer than ordinary elastic. Exclusive "butterfly insert" adjusts size and fit of each cup as it uplifts and separates! Cotton or Spandex back. White. From 2.00.

*REG. U. S. PAT. OFF. ©1961 BY MAIDENFORM, INC.—MAKER OF BRAS, GIRDLES AND SWIMSUITS   All Cotton Broadcloth, Acetate, Cotton, Vyrene (Spandex) Elastic.

Figure 4.14.   Maidenform Bra. Advertisement. "I dreamed I drove them wild" 1961

concept of male domination. While depicting a woman in this position of power, privilege and authority does upset traditional gender roles, it also replicates a domination model of power, one in which women, most often white women, take up the position of the traditional patriarch or master.[1]

This is not to say that nothing positive emerges from the Maidenform "I dreamed" campaign. In fact, the Maidenform campaign quite possibly provides the first glimpse of women's sexual empowerment in advertising. The caption of the Ben Hur "I dreamed" ad reads, "I dreamed I drove them wild in my Maidenform Bra." The question is who is driven wild? Who is the audience here? It is implicitly men, or at least the male gaze that even women take up as they imagine themselves in the ad.[2] Women are encouraged in the "I dreamed" campaign to imagine themselves as empowered and sexual beings. In this way there seems to be some access gained to sexual power as women in the Maidenform ads venture out into the world with their bras exposed. Feminist cultural studies practitioner Emily Salus discusses how women are empowered by wearing undergarments as outerwear. "The overt presentation of lingerie as fashion addresses women's femininity. By wearing an object that is strictly feminine and signifies sexual availability, women gain power publicly" (Salus 1992, 145). The women represented in these Maidenform bra ads seem to be confronting cultural stereotypes that depicted women as weak, helpless and domesticated. By wearing their bras in public, they seem to gain some kind of access to sexual and possibly social and political freedom as they assume here the identities of those who are recognized as strong, capable, and worldly. However, it remains unclear how far this freedom extends since many of the Maidenform "I dreamed" campaign ads have to do with assuming the identity of the other. Thus, the paradox continues as the Maidenform ads[3] describe their bras as those that provide control "for longer than ordinary elastic," while they still proffer some kind of sexual, political and social freedom.

Women's social and political freedom became contested terrain during the sexual revolution and into the Women's Movement, and from the late 1960s to the early 1970s objectification of the female body stood as central issue in this contestation. Susan Bordo comments, "All the cultural paraphernalia of femininity, of learning to please visually and sexually through the practices of the body—media imagery, beauty pageants, high heels, girdles, makeup, simulated orgasm—were seen as crucial in maintaining gender domination" (1993, 182). What women wore under their clothes became as important as what they were wearing on the outside. Girdles and especially bras became symbols of repression and constriction to the growing militant wing of the Women's Movement (Bressler 1997, 136). According to cultural anthropologists Roger Lancaster and Micaela Di Leonardo second-wave feminists strove to expose "the entirely social—and male-dominant—ideologies of women's sexual passivity . . . and notions of universally 'correct' feminine body types, bodily self-presentation, and body grooming and adornment" (1997, 30). However, the Women's Movement failed to abolish bras and girdles from the fashion scene. While the younger generation rejected traditional corsetry, they became increasingly body, diet, and exercise and health conscious and chose to don dancewear, leotards and tights which were worn as both inner and outerwear (Bressler 1997, 137).

Meanwhile the over-thirty generation continued its relationship with more serious foundations; however, even these garments were affected by the health-conscious dancewear fashions as they served the purpose of creating a slimmer silhouette. But, by the end of the decade, cleavage was making a comeback (Bressler 1997, 137). The "body briefer" from J.C. Penney Catalog 1976 (not pictured) demonstrates a return to cleavage and portrays the newest trends in panty girdles and bras in an all-in-one. The body briefer provides smooth control without many lines. The body briefer as the name implies enables women to present a reduced version of their bodies—one that is firmer and smoother than their real body. Thus the fashioned body is transformed by the body briefer into an ideal body that is privileged to lounge around with other women in her foundationwear as is typical of the representations of women in lingerie catalogs.[4]

However, if the body briefer didn't provide enough control for a woman in the 1970s, she could always turn to the J.C. Penney's "B-Thin" (not pictured). This foundation garment demonstrates the move in the 1970s toward thinner bodies engaged in dieting and exercising with the idea of reducing figures to fit the ideal. The slogan for the "B-Thin" reads, "Designed to smooth you now, then shape down with you as you reduce." The emphasis is no longer on a body that is merely constrained, but rather the 1970s ideal body must be in a state of change. The ideal body of the 1970s was always moving toward a better a body, a thinner body, a body that could be reduced and reshaped both by its practices of diet and exercise and by its foundationwear. The freedom offered by the Penney's "B-Thin" ad was the freedom to become something that the wearer was not already—*thin*.

In contrast, the 1980s feminine ideal was a female professional who wore elegant short skirts with severely padded jackets, but whose gym-honed body was supported by a well-cut contoured bra and/or other lace and silk underclothes (Bressler 1997, 138). The strapless support corselet and briefer from a 1982 Montgomery Ward's Catalog (not pictured) indicate that support and contouring can still be lacy. In this way femininity was worn under the business suits and structured outerwear of the 1980s. The strapless but supportive corselet and briefer contour the body giving it the desired feminine lines. Fashion historian Nancy Workman articulates the harm she sees these kinds of representations causing as they illustrate femininity to be something that is done during a woman's off-hours. Workman argues, "Reinscribing the sexual stereotype, the ads imply that women reveal their true natures *after* work; that a woman cannot be thought feminine while competent or business-like" (Workman 1996, 71).

Workman articulates a contemporary problem with the duality of the Cartesian mind/body split that is alive and well in the twentieth century and seems to apply particularly well to the 1980s fashion conundrum for women when being fashionable on the outside meant becoming more austere, serious and structured while wearing lace and frills underneath. In other words, a woman can really be free to be feminine only under her business attire. The idea that these garments are at all constricting or confining is not at issue here. The 1980s foundationwear ads are meant only to convey the elements of lacy and lovely femininity, a femininity which conflicts with the 1980s ideal "Woman of Fashion"—the businesswoman.

Similarly, the "Less Exaggeration minimizing bra with firm support and just the right understatement" from the same 1982 Montgomery Ward's Catalog (not pictured) suggests that the overt femininity signified by large breasts conflicts with the 1980s ideal body. The catalog page explains that this bra is made to keep large breasts from appearing too large. Apparently in the 1980s breasts that were too large also had to be controlled and contained. This fits in well with the idea that women of the 1980s were to be feminine underneath, but on the outside they were supposed to be virtually unsexed. Nancy Workman suggests how lingerie advertising facilitates this notion of private femininity. She notes," Thus to remain feminine, it was necessary for women to privately wear undergarments which associated them with the old traditional divisions between the sexes" (Workman 1996, 71). The minimizing bra supports this idea of de-emphasized external appearance of femininity as it illustrates the reducing qualities of these bras from side views. Thus, we are shown how the minimizing bra reduces the appearance of the size of the breasts.

Reducing the appearance of the size of the breasts also may be tied in with the 1980s ideal of a more slender figure. A woman with large breasts may have looked heavier than the ideal body should have in the 1980s. As Terry Poulton points out, a survey published in 1984 by *Glamour* magazine "found that a huge majority of the 33,000 female respondents declared they would rather lose ten to fifteen pounds than achieve any other goal in life, despite the fact that only 25 percent were overweight and another 25 percent were underweight" (Poulton 1997, 63). This information supports the notion that by the 1980s the ideal female body was becoming thinner and thinner as even large breasts were being provided means of being minimized. Thus, the paradox of freedom and control is conveyed in terms of what is proffered by the ad—the ability to camouflage femininity by minimizing and controlling the breasts.

This trend of minimization continues through the1980s and by the 1990s, as Valdivia explains, "It is nearly impossible not to notice that women as represented in popular culture have gotten thinner and thinner" (1997, 227). The ideal 1990s body is terrifyingly thin, worked-out, toned and flabless, yet still the fashion calls for reduction of hips and thighs while dramatically exaggerating the bustline. The "Power Slimmer" from Frederick's of Hollywood demonstrates this 1990s body ideal (not pictured).[5] The description for this undergarment promises that "This Power Slip delivers a flat tummy, slender hips, and bust-out cleavage"; however, what this advertisement offers is just not a real and achievable possibility for many women—especially plus-sized women to whom this garment is also marketed. The ad proffers a transformed and reshaped version of the real body that is a virtual impossibility for most women. Control and shaping are the primary concerns in this ad although a sense of freedom is implicit in terms of the power that the wearer of this foundation will be granted. The ad paradoxically proffers the freedom to control the body in amazingly constraining and powerful ways. In this way the ad supports Workman's point that even in the 1990s "women's bodies need to be shaped to be seen as desirable" (Workman 1996, 70).

The notion that reshaping is as important as slenderness is supported both by the evolution of ideal body images and by foundation garment consumption figures. Thus contemporary foundationwear known as shapewear like that shown have been re-conjured into existence by the undergarment industry which describes this resurgence of containment to be a result of baby boomers' concerns about their weight. A 1995 SBI *Market Profile: Women's Undergarments* reports that "An aging baby boom population and weight-control problems in the adult population have resulted in growing demand for shapewear products" (SBI 1995, 3). This source also reports that the women's undergarment sector has become a strong and growing sector of the U.S. women's apparel market (SBI 1995, 4), and that another driving force behind this growth is "a renewed fixation with the bustline in fashion, which cause demand for push-up bras and underwire bras to soar" (SBI 1995, 4).

Thus, it should come as no surprise that "The Everything Briefer" from Frederick's of Hollywood (not pictured)[6] "has angled boning that whittles the waist, smoothes hips and urges breasts upward." "The Everything Briefer" as described here performs exactly the body-shaping techniques that are required to create a body that seems flabless and a bustline that seems bounteous. In this manner, the ad seems to promise everything by providing a consumer the power (freedom) via "The Everything Briefer" to transform (control) the real body into the ideal body thus completing the paradox of freedom and control. At the same time there is something more than a little bit scary about this ad's description as it seems to foreshadow a return to Victoriana. The briefer is described as a "Victorian style power lace corset-slip." The description of what the briefer does taken together with the description of what it is supports Nancy Workman's critique of 1990s advertisers and producers of undergarments. She states, "commercial forces continue to replace the social and moral ones in determining what is appropriate wear for contemporary women. As well as being victims of a moral order that insists the body be confined to be desirable, women are increasingly victimized by a culture which saturates the marketplace with items that are manufactured needs" (Workman 1996, 69). In addition, Workman cites the cultural resurgence of a 1990s post-modern Victoriana to be behind much of the confining moves in body shaping and foundationwear (1996, 68).

What seems most relevant to this analysis about the move to a resurgence of Victoriana is just how visible this move has become in the language and images of foundationwear advertising. The "Dreamy Curves" corset from Frederick's of Hollywood (not pictured)[7] promises that "Life can be a dream come true." The implied dream is one of Victorian bliss, and one in which there can be a return to femininity and certainly a return to a curvier body (albeit thinner). This corset "nips you in, and urges over-the-top cleavage . . . all around boning plus a built in torso tamer . . . There's nothing this garment doesn't have." The description suggests that the corset will perform a shaping miracle, and that this miracle will make the wearer's Victorian dreams come true. Freedom is proffered here as a dream culminating in the moment of transformation when the wearer of this garment becomes recognized as fashion's ideal body for the 1990s.

Another example of such proffered freedom is evident in Figure 4.15 where Victoria's Secret introduces yet another ideal body—"Body by Victoria." This ad confirms that this foundationwear functions as both underwear and/or outerwear, "alone or layered . . . the possibilities are endless." The possibilities listed—"It's a bra. It's a skirt. It's a top. It's a dress"—imply its limitlessness. But, what is it exactly? From the ad, it seems to be one of two things either "The Body Bandeau with a merrowed hem" or merely "The Bandeau" which "can be worn as a top or a skirt." The insinuation is that *IT* can be anything you want it to be, and furthermore that the wearer can be transformed and shaped by the unlimited possibilities of *IT* because it represents "something new for the body."

But, we must ask, which body? Whose body? The ad answers implicitly. Since it is produced in only "One size," it must be for made for the ideal body. The ideal body as depicted here is the "Body by Victoria," and it becomes virtually impossible to imagine any other body in these garments. So, the message that is conveyed by the ad is that the consumer may be freed through the experience of wearing these Bandeaux made of "Domestic nylon/Lycra spandex" which can transform a real body into the "Body by Victoria."

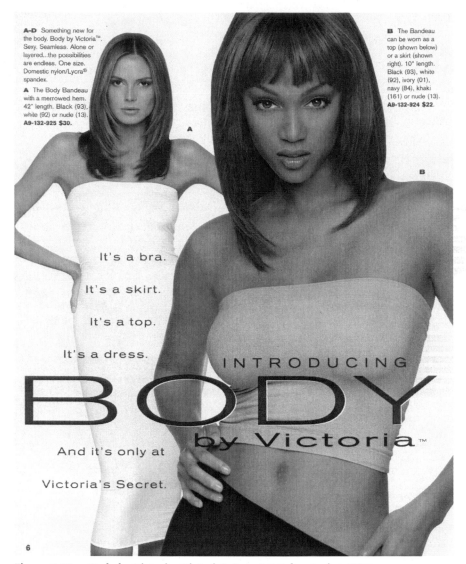

Figure 4.15.   Body by Victoria. *Victoria's Secret Catalog.* Spring 1999

But, what is really happening here is that the ad assumes some social control has already been put into action. The real body has already been reduced to one size. While it may still need to be shaped by the Bandeaux, its dimensions have been socially controlled by fashion. In other words, in the 1990s there has been an internalization of girdles. Women control their own bodily dimensions via the tools of diet and exercise, so that the only task left to perform is that of shaping. Constraint has therefore become less of an external requirement and more an internal one. Thus the "Body by Victoria" proffers the freedom not to constrain but to shape and contour the body into the ideal feminine form because the body is already under the social controls of vigorous diet and exercise.

In contrast, if an ideal body in the 1990s can be assumed to be one size, all breasts cannot. The 1990s brought with it an absolute fixation on the bustline, and younger women have become the most affected by this fixation. "Since 1991, women under age 35 have increased their spending on undergarments at the strongest rate . . . are most likely to use push-up bras, use daywear as outerwear, and are the most tolerant to sacrifice comfort for appearance" (SBI 1995, 5). Thus, younger women have been targeted by the push-up bra market since "the successful introduction of Sara Lee's Wonderbra." (SBI 1995, 4). The Wonderbra and its push-up counterparts, unlike The Body by Victoria seem to signify a very dramatic return to traditional foundation garments whose primary function may be described in terms of a mechanical apparatus which shapes and controls the body. The Wonderbra itself has been described in such terms by Carol Squiers. She comments, "The Wonderbra is a marvel of a contraption, a suspension bridge for the breasts that pushes up and plunges at the same time, like some kind of movie special effect" (1995, 6). In this way, the Wonderbra along with other push-up bras come to be the controlling and constraining foundations for the 1990s as they construct the mandatory bustline for the decade.

"The Miracle Bra" represents Victoria's Secret's stab at the push-up bra market. In spring of 1999, Victoria's Secret Catalog carries text which describes the one version of "The Miracle Bra" as "Top Secrets, designed for a flawlessly smooth finish" (not pictured). The idea behind the bras depicted here is that no one will know that they are being worn, since there are no seems to be seen through clothes. The text reads, "in seamless satin [The Miracle Bra] has cleverly angled, underwire cups with removable push-up pads for enhanced décolleté" (13). According to the language in the ad, the masking is completed by the bra that creates breasts by shaping and contouring, yet its seamless design allows the bra to be incognito. Thus, what is proffered is a "Top Secret" transformation of the breasts.

Similarly in Figure 4.16 the text from the Victoria's Secret spring specials catalog in 1999 explains that "The Miracle Bra" can create "World renowned shaping with cleverly angled underwire cups and removable pads [because] *some curves you just can't get from working out* [my emphasis]"(A2). The language of the ad implies that even the ideal 1990s body may need some help when it comes to breasts because the ideal body works out to get rid of fat, and breasts are largely comprised of fat. This caption provides the perfect

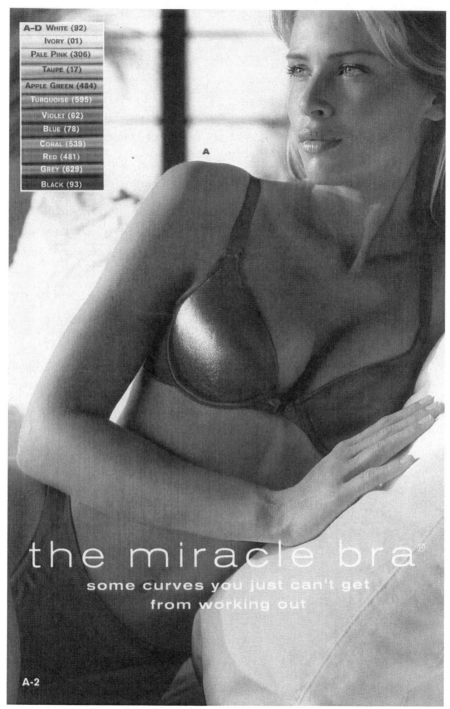

the miracle bra®

some curves you just can't get
from working out

A-D White (92)
Ivory (01)
Pale Pink (306)
Taupe (17)
Apple Green (484)
Turquoise (595)
Violet (62)
Blue (78)
Coral (539)
Red (481)
Grey (629)
Black (93)

A

A-2

Figure 4.16.   The Miracle Bra. *Victoria's Secret Catalog.* **Spring 1999**

example for Bordo's critique of the flabless gym-honed body and internalized girdling as this language underscores the fact that the breast is a curve that cannot be created by working out. Thus, "The Miracle Bra" and other push-up bras have become the primary means for ideally thin women to create the illusion of larger breasts and enhanced décolleté. Freedom is proffered in terms of the consumer's ability to get the curves you just can't get from working out. This has been particularly the case since as a 1995 Market Profile points out, "some in the industry also feel that the fear of implants has given a boost to padded bras" (SBI 1995, 62). The result is that padded push-up bras like the "Wonderbra" and "The Miracle Bra" have come to be recognized as the foundation garments for the 1990s precisely because of their amazing pushing and plunging power to transform the breasts.

However, as has been noted before, this transformation is transient, elusive, fleeting. Even if the shaping capacity of a foundation garment is actualized on a body that fits the dimensional requirements of its historical moment, the ideal body will most certainly be altered by fashion in a manner that requires the body to resume its quest to satisfy what will become the new ideal body. What seems clear at this point is that through an analysis of foundationwear advertisements spanning from the late 1930s to the late 1990s, we can recognize this elusiveness as it constructs and reconstructs, constitutes and reconstitutes, shapes and reshapes the ideal feminine form. We can also understand that it is this elusiveness which facilitates the advertisements' proffering of a freeing experience that is almost always bound up with the experience of being free to claim or capture via consumption that physical ideal which is mostly newly available for sale. Bodily freedom also appears frequently as a manifestation of the paradoxical elements proffered as freedom and control in the ads as they illustrate how foundations can control and shape the body through a transformation of the real body into the newest ideal body.

Susan Bordo explains how this continued search to achieve the newest body ideal poses a threat to women's social autonomy and may lead to a perpetual form of social control. Bordo maintains, "Female bodies become docile bodies—bodies whose forces and energies are habituated to external regulation, subjection, transformation, improvement" (1993, 166). Bordo describes how it is that fashion can socially control women through its elusive requirements of habitual improvement of the self and the body. Under the terms of gendered dress codes, rituals of heterosexual courtship, social conventions of femininity, restrictive gender roles, and stereotypical media representations of women, a woman's power and her physical autonomy may be overcome by external forces of regulation. In this way fashion's power seems, as Georg Simmel points out, to exceed itself. He notes, "It may almost be considered a sign of the increased power of fashion, that it has overstepped the bounds of its original domain, which comprised only personal externals, and has acquired an increasing influence over taste, over theoretical convictions, and even over the moral foundations of life" (1971, 304). Hence, fashion under late capitalism has become a force that controls those elements of life that should be beyond its realm, but by virtue of its power, and its elusive self-perpetuity, fashion continues as a force that in many ways determines our politics, genders, sexualities, societies, classes, ethnicities, and cultures. Barthes argues that fashion and its system function in this manner to preserve the myth of life. He posits, "But, in our society, what is new in Fashion seems to have a well-defined anthropological function, one which derives from its ambiguity; simultaneously unpredictable and systematic, regular and unknown, aleatory and structured, it fantastically conjoins the intelligible without which men could not live and the unpredictability attached to the myth of life" (Barthes 1983, 300). Barthes confirms then that fashion exists as that which is necessary as a paradoxical system connected to "the myth of life." He views fashion as that which is precipitated by the conditions of capitalism and the myths it perpetuates. Bordo, Simmel and Barthes all converge at the moment when fashion exceeds itself and becomes a form of social control which mediates the lives of those who seek to achieve its elusive ideal.

NOTES

1. See Irigaray 1985a for a discussion of the male imaginary and male symbolic. See also Lorde 1984 for a discussion of the using the master's tools to dismantle the master's house. See also Bourdieu 2001 for a description of masculine domination.

2. See Young 1990 "Recovering our Clothes."

3. For further discussion of the Maidenform "I dreamed" campaign, consult chapter 5.

4. See Valdivia 1997 for a complete discussion of representations in lingerie catalogs.

5. Frederick's of Hollywood. Online. 17 April 1999.

6. Ibid.

7. Ibid.

Chapter Five

Under Cover Agency?

To the extent that people inevitably style or dress their bodies in some way, using the resources available and affordable to them, and few individuals are immune to fashion in contemporary society, some kind of conceptual, reflexive space is needed between these cultural dope and celebratory models of style and fashion.

Susan Kaiser "Minding Appearances: Style, Truth and Subjectivity"

Fashion's ever changing and elusive feminine body ideal unremittingly begs the question of agency. In previous chapters, I have discussed the historical and material systems of power operating on and around women's bodies and the meanings and practices of wearing foundation garments in terms of protocols, prescriptives, dress codes, and requirements of femininity articulated and rearticulated in popular women's magazines, advertisements, trade journals, and fashion. This chapter demonstrates how the history of practices and meanings of wearing foundationwear have produced the contested terrain of both the symbolic and social practices of wearing foundation garments. As women choose different foundationwear to meet the historical and material demands of fashion, the rationales for wearing these garments and the meaning(s) of their practices are also in flux. Furthermore, as women wear foundations they negotiate the meanings of their bodies in the social world; they contribute to both the construction of individual and group subjectivities. It should then come as little surprise that the practices and meanings of wearing foundation garments function simultaneously as structures of domination and as spaces for resistance.

The telephone survey data and in-depth interviews conducted for this study concerning the practices and meanings of wearing foundation garments support a model of limited agency. As has been discussed in previous chapters, descriptions of women's bodies as flawed or problematic have led to "Fashion 101" and "Fashion Emergency" type programs and advice columns which articulate women's bodies as problems to be solved. This perception of women's bodies is validated by telephone survey data[1] where 44 percent of respondents strongly agreed and 40 percent of respondents somewhat agreed with the statement "Women wear shaping garments to mask figure flaws." Thus, 84 percent of women consider that wearing shaping garments is a response to body problems.[2] Additionally, 17 percent of respondents strongly agreed and 46 percent of respondents somewhat agreed with the statement "Shaping garments enable women to achieve the body that nature did not give them"—implying that for many U.S. women, the natural body equals the problem body.[3] When juxtaposed with the mythical ideal body—the problem body, as a way thinking about the inherently flawed natural bodies of U.S. women—becomes a powerful structure of domination.

In fact, during in-depth interviews many women discussed their bodies in terms of flawed parts, "sagging breasts, pot bellies, small breasts, big butts, large hips, cellulite, big boobs, thick waists, flabby thighs" and so on. Wearing foundation garments seems to solve many of these "body problems" as foundationwear makes women look better in their clothes. Forty-seven percent of survey respondents strongly agreed and 35 percent somewhat agreed with the statement "My clothes look better when I wear shaping garments."[4] In addition, 54 percent of respondents agreed that "People find me more attractive when I wear shaping garments,"[5] and 45 percent of respondents agreed that "All women look better when they wear shaping garments."[6] These survey results which focus on improving the appearance of women's bodies emphasize the position of women in society as objects of beauty, subject to criticism, and eligible to be made over and improved upon. This is not to suggest that the structure of domination may be isolated in the beauty-fashion complex, patriarchy or capitalism, but rather that the structure of domination is itself the ideology of the flawed body which circulates throughout our social institutions and discourses producing subjects who are self-policing. As Sandra Bartky points out:

> The woman who checks her makeup half a dozen times a day to see if her foundation has caked or her mascara has run, who worries that the wind or the rain may spoil her hairdo, who looks frequently to see if her stockings have bagged at the ankle or who, feeling fat, monitors everything she eats, has become, just as surely as the inmate of the Panopticon, a self-policing subject, self committed to a relentless self-surveillance. (1988, 78)

This notion of self-surveillance of the body certainly is confirmed by telephone survey research; however, women's agency is also evidenced in the survey as shown in the way women have taken control of their bodies and how they feel about their bodies in foundationwear. For example, 53 percent of women surveyed agreed with the statement, "When I wear shaping garments, I feel sexy."[7] Also, 51 percent of respondents agreed that "Shaping garments make women sexier."[8] While these statements bear striking resemblance to one another, the first attempts to assess how an individual woman feels, how she measures her own feelings of sexuality when she wears shaping garments. The second attempts to have women evaluate other women and themselves (taking up the position of the gazer) in terms of the effect shaping garments have on the sexual appeal of women's bodies.

As I have noted, foundation garments layered over the meanings of the female body not only complicate those meanings, but also transform the meanings of the body as constructed by foundation garments and the meanings the garments themselves carry. As embodiment and fashion theorist Joanne Entwistle argues, "It [dress] is a practical negotiation between the fashion system as a structured system, the social conditions of everyday life such as class, gender and the like, as well as the 'rules' or norms governing particular social situations" (2001, 52). Thus, we must recognize the difficulty in attempting to assess the difference between how an individual woman experiences herself wearing foundation garments versus how women see them themselves and other women wearing foundation garments. Although as Entwistle points out, the process of dressing (and I am sure foundation garments which form the foundation of dress constitute a significant part of this process—at least for women) always involves a negotiation between the individual and the social body. The responses to these survey questions do indicate that while women may wear shaping garments in order to appear sexier, women may also be sexually empowered by the way they feel in their chosen foundation garments. This is to say that although women's agency in wearing foundation garments is difficult to measure, nonetheless notice must be taken of the fact that women can and do exercise agency in terms of their choice to wear or not wear foundations as well as their choice of type, kind, color, cut and/or style of foundations.

In interviews, many women were quick to point out that although they certainly followed fashion, they did not consider themselves slaves to fashion. Many women expressed the extent to which they negotiated between comfort, personal style, fit and fashion. A sixty-two-year-old New Yorker explains, "I like to wear a two-way stretch. I don't know what it's called today. I call it a two-way stretch. It may seem old-fashioned and out of sync with what young women wear today, but it makes me feel better because my back feels supported and my belly does not stick out. I wear it because I like it, not because I have to." Similarly, a twenty-year-old college woman comments,

"I always wear a bra, not because of social acceptability, but because of the support and comfort it gives me. I am not into wearing things to please others." Another college student states, "I still don't understand why some women feel the need to wear some shaping garments like girdles or shapers to feel more comfortable with themselves and their bodies. However, I do think some shaping garments are necessary, like bras, and are not necessarily just used for physical appearance but actual support." In each of these cases, women clearly argue that they recognize the social conventions they are up against. Still they actively and consciously choose to negotiate the realms of social acceptance and their own desires for comfort and support.

Recognizing women's agency within institutions of femininity and fashion legitimizes and in some ways celebrates personal style, fashion and to some extent consumption; however, it is important not to lose sight of the ongoing negotiations that women must engage in as they confront such powerful institutions. A nineteen-year-old college athlete maintains, "Without a bra in public I would feel naked because I wouldn't get the proper support. I guess, they [my breasts] wouldn't be the exact same shape if I did not wear a bra and maybe that's what makes me feel uncomfortable and naked." A fifty-nine-year-old from Oklahoma also confirms, "Certain outfits call for a shaper. When I wear it, I look better and feel better as long as it accomplishes what I want it to do." Both of these women wear shaping garments to simultaneously satisfy fashion and to make themselves feel comfortable. Their comfort is bound up with the way they look; the way they feel is tied to how they imagine they are being read by others and of course how they see themselves—through the lenses of the institutions of fashion and femininity.

Again this is significant since women must confront these power dynamics in everyday life. Two college women explain how they negotiate requirements of fashion and femininity in the public and private spheres. The first states, "I feel confined and restricted when I am wearing a bra. I also feel very safe. I feel everything is where it is supposed to be and that is very comforting, but I feel natural and insecure without one." The second notes, "When I don't have a bra on, I feel loose and free. This feels great! When I am sitting around the house, I never wear a bra. When I go out, I wear a bra everyday, and they [bras] make me feel normal. I feel as though every other woman wears them." Certainly wearing foundations cannot be reduced to a binary argument of coercion or resistance. These women express the myriad of intersecting pressures exerted on their bodies spanning from ideologies of womanhood to current fashion ideals—dress versus undress, tropes of the Victorian woman (loose and wanton versus corseted and chaste), the virgin-whore dichotomy and the objectification of women (as women must be always concerned about how they are seen), and of course, the current ideal body.

Such social conditioning is demonstrated in telephone survey data where 21 percent of respondents strongly agreed and 25 percent of respondents somewhat agreed with the statement, "All women look better with shaping garments."[9] Also, 14 percent of respondents strongly agreed and 17 percent somewhat agreed with the statement "All women need to wear shaping garments."[10] Additionally, in response to the statement "Most women should wear shaping garments" 18 percent of women strongly agreed and 26 percent somewhat agreed.[11] Thus with 46 percent, 31 percent and 44 percent agreement respectively, women surveyed were willing to take up the position of the gazer and to prescribe the wearing of shaping garments for the improvement of the bodies of *all* and/or *most* women.

However, this is not to suggest that women surveyed were not conscious of the affects of social conditioning. When asked to respond to the statement, "Shaping garments are yet another fashion requirement," 17 percent of women strongly agreed and 43 percent somewhat agreed.[12] Women responded similarly to the statement, "Shaping garments help women keep up with the demands of fashion" with 22 percent in strong agreement and 55 percent somewhat in agreement.[13] Although these numbers 60 percent and 77 percent respectively indicate that quite a large number of women recognize the role of shaping garments in the perpetuation of women's fashion, the fact that 76 percent of women strongly agreed and 15 percent of women somewhat agreed with the statement, "The fashion industry places unrealistic demands on women's bodies" conveys the powerful fact that most women in this survey, indeed 91 percent, understand how the female body in U.S. culture operates as a locus of social control.[14]

Therefore, the cultural dupes or dopes theory that has been so long expounded upon by cultural studies practitioners since it first appeared in Adorno and Horkheimer's seminal work, "The Culture Industry," does not quite fit as a theoretical model for U.S. women's lived experiences with their foundation garments. However, as feminist cultural studies practitioner Angela McRobbie points out, "The emphasis in the new consumerist studies is on what women and girls do with consumer goods with how commodities give rise to meaning-making processes which are frequently at odds with the intended meaning or usage" (1999, 34). These newer models of consumption are largely celebratory and point to ways in which women subvert traditional meanings of cultural objects like foundation garments using them to engage in their own fantasies or play thus providing them with unintended pleasures.[15]

While my own research does not specifically address or query how women may use foundation garments to subvert intended meaning or usage, several women I interviewed described wearing foundation garments for special occasions like the prom as a parody of womanhood[16] attesting to the social conventions and ritual practices of prom, but recognizing and critiquing many of the practices of traditional femininity. These young women acknowledge their participation in the ritual of prom, but they are quick to point out that they are playing dress up, playing prom queen, playing at traditional femininity, and foundation garments constitute a part of this play. Additionally, several women pointed out that they wear certain foundations strictly for themselves. One twenty-year-old student explained, "I have a couple of fairly padded bras, but I wear them more for my sake than anybody else's. It's nice to have boobs sometimes." Another student noted, "When I wear my sports bras, I feel active and like there are many more important things to be ready to do than spending time having to think about where my breasts are." A sixty year-old from Oklahoma argued, "I feel more confident and more put together when I wear my shaper. I wear it for me." Some women claim that wearing foundation garments for themselves is equivalent to not wearing them to conform but to satisfy the desires of the self, the individual. This may be construed as subversive where these practices conflict with ritualized or social practices, especially if wearing foundation garments makes a woman feel sexually empowered. The sexual empowerment of women almost always signals some kind of resistance or agency. However, as cultural studies practitioner Paul Smith comments, "It is always a given that any act of agency is both constrained and free. At the point where the subject expresses agency, this is immediately caught up in the reactions of the surroundings" (lecture 09/24/96). Smith provides an understanding that all agency is limited. These women's accounts underscore the extent to which the act of donning foundationwear may be an expression of agency, of their own pleasure; however, this agency is likely to be co-opted by the dominant culture through fashion's ideal body.

However, as with the cultural dupe theories, consumerist models celebrating women's subversive consumption do not adequately explain the complex negotiations that women engage in as they choose and wear foundation garments. In "The Production of Glamour: A Social History of Intimate Apparel, 1909-1952," cultural historian Jill Fields argues for the use of a cultural hegemony model of analysis since it allows for "the contested nature of cultural meanings and the contradictions they pose" (1997, 72). She suggests that as the corset operated as a locus for a number of competing significations, so do modern day foundations (1997, 72). Drawing on the theoretical framework of Antonio Gramsci's hegemony,[17] Fields maintains "Fashions in dress are particularly useful for hegemonic analysis because a central defining element of fashion is change" (1997, 73). In fact, Fields cites a significant shift in fashion regarding the corset. She explains that women's rejection of heavy corsets in the 1920s and 1930s influenced manufacturers to produce new lighter support garments, like the girdle. However, manufacturers and retailers also found new ways to use fashion institutions—women's magazines, trade journals, and department stores—to gain a firmer grip on women's future fashion selections (Fields 1997, 110). Fields concludes by noting, "Women's spontaneous consent to wearing these garments was an ongoing and contested process which served fashion industry needs for continual purchase. Innovations in dress which supported women's desires for comfort would continue because industrialists sought not to end women's desires for fashion change, but to contain them" (1997, 110). Fields's use of Gramsci's hegemonic theory is particularly persuasive as it focuses on fashion as both a system of signification and a set of regulatory practices thereby underscoring the intense struggle over social meaning pervading the arena of women's foundation garments (1997, 74). In this way, Fields successfully leaves space for women's limited agency within the sphere of fashion while recognizing the power of cultural institutions and practices to monitor how women present and shape their bodies.

Similarly, Vicki Howard's essay, "'At the Curve Exchange' Postwar Beauty Culture and Working Women at Maidenform," supports the argument that women's relationships to beauty and fashion cultures have involved complex systems of consent and resistance. Using evidence collected primarily from Maidenform's company newsletter for employees, *The Maiden Forum*, Howard argues that women working at Maidenform in the post–World War II era, found solidarity in a women's culture within the Maidenform workplace. She maintains, "While beauty culture was a means of forging solidarity among those at Maidenform, its gender norms and beauty standards were not swallowed whole" (Howard 2001, 211). Howard notes in particular that the company newsletter simultaneously presented idealized notions of feminine beauty while providing alternative images of women at play and at work.

Howard discusses at length the portrayal of employee Pin-Ups with many references to class and gender significations. Howard highlights one case in which the 1946 Pin-Up of Helen Miskura of the designing department appears in *The Maiden Forum* in two contrasting photographs, "one that overturned the beauty standard and one that conformed to the ideal of a well-groomed woman" (Howard 2001, 206). In the first photograph Helen wears her uncle's work clothes—pants which bag horribly on her, his work boots which are ridiculously large, his work shirt and hat that although they appear to fit seem completely out of place on her body, and for good measure, she holds his pipe in her tight-lipped and unsmiling mouth. The humor in the image is palpable; Helen seems to literally be playing with gender although the caption claims that Helen thought "she was being very patriotic in her (uncle's) war working clothes" (Howard 2001, 206). However, in the second image, Helen has the air of polish and refinement with hair, makeup and dress conveying a woman of great beauty and taste. The caption of the second photo reads, "As we glance at the other picture we notice the 'real' Helen. A slender grey-eyed blonde, Helen adorns the Designing Department" (2001, 206). The two images and the accompanying text compellingly support Howard's argument that the beauty standards surrounding women at Maidenform both fostered a women's subculture and promoted solidarity among women employees that enabled a certain amount of parody and fun-poking at gendered norms.

Howard also provocatively suggests that although "Postwar commercial beauty culture was increasingly depoliticized and was no longer the source of workplace radicalism it had been in the early twentieth century," an ethnically diverse pool of working women at Maidenform managed to challenge middle-class images of feminine beauty (2001 198, 210). Through shared experiences, interests and values, these working women bridged ethnic and cultural differences as they worked, talked, laughed and read *The Maiden Forum* side-by-side.

The unique workplace environment of women working to produce fashion and beauty products with women consumers in mind seems to foster women's agency within the Maidenform Corporation. Howard explains that the women working at Maidenform also experienced themselves as consumers. In fact, "From 1944 through the 1950s, every Christmas the ILGWU Maryland-Virginia district office staff members sent a list of their brassiere sizes and choice of style to the Bayonne, New Jersey Plant" (2001, 210). These union members who annually received the bras as Christmas gifts were not troubled by taking gifts from the corporation from whom they sought to protect workers, but rather they provided feedback to Maidenform managers and even told their friends about Maidenform bras. In this way, Howard explains the relationship between women as producers and consumers to be one in which Maidenform workers found solidarity and agency.

While Howard does not argue that this form of agency is unique to Maidenform, I submit that Maidenform as a family-owned and-operated company (by William and Ida Rosenthal) from 1922 to 1997 provides a strong case for a woman-centered business. Women's contributions to the success of fashion and beauty industries are well documented in cultural history texts.[18] In fact, women's business success is accepted in fashion and beauty cultures because it is considered appropriate for women to produce and sell these products to other women. The public sphere of business is opened up to women through the avenues of fashion and beauty culture. Fashion historians Jane Farrell-Beck and Colleen Gau note in their book, *Uplift: The Bra in America*, "Women held almost half of the more than 1,230 U.S. patents awarded for breast supporters between 1863 and 1969" (2002, xii). This suggests that many women were designing breast supporters based on their own conceptions of what their bodies needed or what other women said their bodies needed. Farrell-Beck and Gau also provide a description of the successful origins of Maidenform [originally Maiden Form] which centers on satisfying the needs of a customer. "An actress-customer of Enid Bisset and Ida Rosenthal hated the binders [of the 1920s] and insisted on a breast supporter that would allow her chest to expand and create a flattering bustline. The name Maiden Form, taken as a product trademark in 1924, offered a direct contrast and challenge to the Boyshform [sic]" (Farrell-Beck & Gau 2002, 41). Thus, Maidenform began as a company predicated on the specific demands of female consumers.

This relationship between production and consumption is demonstrated in numerous surveys and marketing projects evidenced in Maidenform's market research files.[19] A 1957 marketing strategy report for Maiden Form by Alderson & Sessions indicates a strong connection between girdle and bra buyers. "It would appear that girdles are the most closely linked product to brassieres that the Company can market. In most instances girdles are sold to the same buyer as brassieres which simplifies the sales call."[20] While this strategy provides a way to increase overall Maidenform sales, the report asserts the advantages to men who comprise the sales force to retail outlets. "Therefore, if girdles are successful, as we believe they will be (despite their somewhat erratic introduction),[21] they offer an opportunity for more volume and therefore earnings to the men, as well as to the Company, which is important at this time."

What is not discussed is how girdles and bras are actually later marketed to consumers together. A "Teen-Age Market Study" from 1959 attempts to unite bra wearing patterns and girdle choice patterns in one survey.[22] A national mail survey was conducted with a sample size of 1,003 girls (1). The age distribution for the sample follows: 14 years and younger = 9%, 15 years =18%, 16 years = 29%, 17 years = 24% and 18 years and older = 20%. Ninety percent of the girls interviewed started wearing bras that were unpadded, but the survey shows an increase in use of a padded bra as the first one in the past three years (4). The study summary indicates that this increase in padded bra usage by younger women may be attributable to their desire to appear "physically mature" (1). Interestingly the girdle segment of the questionnaire indicates a steady increase in girdle wearing from the 14-year-old age group to the 18-year-old age group (5).

Thus, while younger girls wish to appear more physically mature, older girls feel the need to girdle their physically mature figures.

Creating New Needs

Like many other foundationwear corporations, Maidenform found that targeting young women or juniors provided them with a much-needed market for both bras and girdles. As Jill Fields notes, "Making lighter and more flexible girdles in junior sizes was one means of keeping young women in foundation garments" (1997, 107). However, as the "Teen-Age Market Study" indicates, 167 girls did not wear girdles (5). When they were asked why, their responses were as follows: Don't need it = 106 respondents, Uncomfortable = 17 respondents and I'm too thin = 13 respondents.[23] While these non-girdle wearing junior respondents make up only a small percentage of those who responded to the survey, it is clear that Maidenform took their responses seriously.

By asking what women wore and what women liked or disliked about their foundation garments, Maidenform hoped to be able to produce bras and girdles that would satisfy its consumers. In 1962, wear tests of 44 bras and 21 girdles were conducted.[24] The report notes that while before 1960 only 48 percent of wear tests for bras were "acceptable," the recent estimates showed a marked improvement in which 80 percent of wear tests for bras were "acceptable." Similarly, prior to 1960 only 64 percent of wear tests for girdles were satisfactory. After 1960, 80 percent of wear tests for girdles were "satisfactory." The evaluation concludes, "As in the case of brassieres, the girdle estimates were improved with time." I highlight these surveys, wear tests and evaluations to point out the lengths that Maidenform was willing to go to find out what women really thought of their products. While Maidenform certainly benefited from knowing and listening to its consumers, it was one of the first corporations to undertake such extensive means of market research and to seriously consider what women thought.

From market research available in the Maidenform Archive, I was able to see a pattern between the survey work completed by Maidenform and the corporate response to these surveys. While the market research in the Maidenform Archive is not a complete record of all survey work done by the corporation, it seems to be representative of the corporations attitude regarding customer satisfaction and product quality. A "Report on Lightweight Girdles" produced from informal interviews discusses the pros and cons of lightweight girdles, when and who wears lightweight girdles, a reaction to specific garments and recommendations for the improvement of lightweight girdles.[25] Perhaps the most significant finding in the report is the recognition that different women with different figure types have different needs. In other words, the report reflects an understanding that all women's bodies are not the same and may require different foundations and different levels of control, in order to match their bodies as closely as possible to the image of the ideal feminine form. The report also indicates that lightweight girdles were favored for informal occasions or by women who needed only light control. However, the report does seem to defend against women's criticisms concerning the lack of control inherent in lightweight girdles. "Lightweight girdles are seen to be lacking in control. This, of course, is more or less objectionable depending on a woman's build" (1). In this way, the report falls back on the notion of women's flawed bodies as it explains that it is a woman's build which is the problem not the lack of control of the foundation garment. The report also takes on the tone of a medical expert explaining what women need by way of a foundation garment. "Lightweight girdles are worn more for support than for control. This support is both physical and psychological — a psychological uplift as well as physical support to keep the woman straight and not tired. The lightweight girdle also provides neatness and solidity" (2). The language — keeping a woman *straight* and providing *solidity*—seems to convey a sense of prescriptive not unlike that which has been previously discussed.[26] At the same time, it seems clear that Maidenform feels a responsibility to its women customers to care for their physical and psychological well-being. The report even defines the terms support and control: "Support can be described as keeping the posture correct and keeping the woman from feeling tired. Control can be described as shaping the figure" (2). While clinging to their own position as experts in what women need with regard to support and control, the corporate attitude at Maidenform as evidenced by language choices in its inter-office communications and reports suggests that Maidenform respects the needs and preferences of its women consumers.[27]

Agency in Advertisements

The success of the twenty-two-year run[28] of the Maidenform "I dreamed" campaign may be largely attributable to this long-standing corporate attitude which sought to satisfy the demands of its women customers. Although initially the "I dreamed" campaign was met with adversity concerning the image of partially dressed women in public, the notion of women living out their dreams and desires in their Maidenform bras won out. James Stull explains this phenomenon in his article, "The Maidenform Campaigns: Reaffirming the Feminine Ideal." "Maidenform began offering cash prizes up to $10,000 for other original 'dream' situations, the public helped articulate, in effect, a collective fantasy which allegedly spoke to the repressed needs of middle-class American women" (1992, 1). The ads allowed women to envision themselves doing things and going places they could not have otherwise imagined. Stull acknowledges, "Women readers can participate in this fantasy by imagining that they, too, are confident and attractive enough—sexy enough—to appear in public exhibiting their own Maidenform bras" (1992, 2).

While the "I dreamed" ads provided women with new ideas of empowerment, independence and professionalism, they did little to disrupt the idealized image of woman. Stull maintains, "The campaign's supposed exhibi-

I dreamed I went shopping in my *maidenform bra*

Figure 5.1.   Maidenform Bra. Advertisement. "I dreamed I went shopping" 1950

tionist appeal just happened to coincide with the obsessive, even fetishistic appeal of breasts in the 1950s and the idealization of certain women (and body types)—Jane Russell and Marilyn Monroe, for example—whose ample bustlines and full figures represented the cultural ideal" (1992, 2). In this way the ad campaign demonstrates an element of limited agency that was available to women during the period. This agency and the iconic power of the ads was accessible to women viewers of the Maidenform "I dreamed" campaign. Figure 5.1 shows the first ad to run in the series, "I dreamed I went shopping in my Maidenform bra."[29] A woman sits or rather gracefully leans on a display table in a department store and stares admiringly at herself in a hand-mirror which she holds gently in her black-gloved hand. The formal attire of the woman including her chic hat and fitted waistline function as signifiers of upper class. The fact that she sits in this environment wearing a Maidenform bra can mean only one thing—that Maidenform bras must be worn by the finest women in the finest stores. Vicki Howard explains, "Maidenform's national 'I Dreamed' campaign linked the company with contemporary definitions of New Look glamour and femininity" (2001, 200). While this ad provides a fantasy of shopping without limits while wearing and being surrounded only by the most beautiful things, it actually heightens the readers understanding of ideal beauty and femininity.

The notion of being somehow trapped by feminine ideals is intensified in the "I dreamed I was sugar and spice in my Maidenform Bra 'n everything nice in my Maidenform Girdle"[30] ads (not pictured). The ad features three girls standing coquettishly in sealed glass jars. All three are blonde and petite. The first jar is labeled SUGAR and the girl in the jar stands primly in a curtsy with her arms flattened to her sides, her head cocked to one side with two tightly curled pigtails. She wears pantaloons with her Undertone bra. The second jar is labeled SPICE and contains a teenage girl wearing black-and white crop-pants with her Undertone bra. She leans against the side of the jar in a diminutive fashion while casting her gaze upward. The third jar is labeled 'N EVERYTHING NICE and the girl in this jar looks dead ahead in spite of the fact that she is holding open a book entitled *Little Women*. Her hair is pulled pack in a headband accentuating her sweet face and parted lip smile. Her feet are placed one in front of the other and she stands with the book almost covering her breasts and her CURTSY girdle exposed. All of the girls stand demurely, in feminine poses with their knees bent and heads slightly canted and they all wear Mary Jane shoes. They are meant to embody the ideal femininity of adolescent girlhood. Thus, the language of the ads is mirrored by the girls who are SUGAR and SPICE and EVERYTHING NICE. These ads, appearing in *Seventeen* magazine in February and June and in *American Girl* in

February and April 1960, marketed Maidenform bras and girdles in pairs to teens. The description of the Undertone bra reads:

> Mmmm—what a confection! My figure's perfection in UNDERTONE©, a honey of a bra that rounds my curves so sweetly, so neatly! And since variety is the you-know-what of life, Maidenform does Undertone in two delicious versions: Regular and Pre-shaped with a secret lining of light foam rubber, to add gentle new curves you'd swear were all you!

The play on words conveys the garments and the girls as delectable items of food to be consumed. The objectification and infantilization of the girls continues in the description of the girdle.

> Sweetness and light lacy elastic—that's what CURTSY© is made of! Add a portion (not a pinch) of curve-control, and you have the formula for a fabulous figure! Girdle or pantie, XS, S, M, L, Machine washable too!

Both descriptions drive home the point that these garments will enable young women to embody the appropriate femininity and will keep their bodies properly contained, limited and reduced. Additionally these ads reinforce the notion that girls are to embody the characteristics of sweetness and innocence while serving as beautiful objects to be looked at through glass jars. The jars themselves through which the girls can be seen but not heard magnifies their condition as captive objects—not unlike lightning bugs caught in children's jars (except here, there are no air holes). These young, silent, smiling and undeniably beautiful teens exemplify idealized teenage femininity and beauty. In this way, they are seen but not heard.

Such objectification is not unusual in Maidenform advertisements as demonstrated by the "I dreamed I was bookends in my Maidenform Bra" ad from 1959 (not pictured). This ad illustrates the extent to which women, particularly young women, are depicted as objects. Here the trope of two women, ostensibly twins, or one woman who is split, serve the menial task of holding up books. The titles of the books: *The Shape of Things to Come*, *Twice Over*, and *Sugar and Spice and Everything Nice* each signify the value and meaning of these young women's bodies in 1959. *The Shape of Things to Come* conveys the future of beauty standards embodied by the newer bras of the late 1950s, and *Twice Over* explains the repetitive nature of the image (suggesting we will see it again and again) and also plays with the meaning of two breasts and two bra cups. The final title, *Sugar and Spice and Everything Nice* reinforces the value and meaning of appropriately balanced girlish femininity as embodied by the women holding up these titles. In each case, the young women are reduced to the value of their bodies and in fact the enhanced value of their bodies in Maidenform bras. I reference the "sugar and spice and everything nice" and "the bookends" ads particularly because they are so confining and restrictive in their use of objectification. It is important to note the extent to which the "I dreamed" campaign mirrors the limited agency that women seem to experience as they choose and wear foundation garments.

Although the "I dreamed I was a lady editor in my Maidenform Bra" ad (not pictured) and "I dreamed I was Cinderella in my Maidenform Bra" ad (not pictured) appeared in 1951, the latter reinforces notions of ideal femininity while the former provides the reader with the promise of a professional work life and subverts traditional notions of the domestic sphere and ideal femininity for women consumers. The image of the lady editor provides a visual representation of a professional woman at work, an image that was rarely depicted before World War II. As Vicki Howard notes, "The occupation-oriented Maidenform ads reflected advertisers' recognition of changes in the make-up of the workforce. As more and more married women entered the workforce in this decade, a popular interest in working women and 'working couples' developed" (Howard 2001, 202).

Maidenform responded with several ads depicting women at work in their Maidenform Bras. Among them the "I dreamed I played in an all-girl orchestra in my Maidenform Bra," advertisement (not pictured) which conveys the idea that not only can a woman work, but she can be a professional musician (a profession not usually available to women in 1960). In fact, she will not be the only woman in the band, she can be part of an all-woman orchestra. However, as the copy reads, this is an *all-girl* orchestra. The use of the term girl rather than woman suggests that these musicians are not professionals, but just some girls "playing orchestra." To this extent, the professionalism articulated in the ad is somewhat undermined, but the image of an all-woman orchestra stays with the reader.

Not surprisingly Maidenform's "I dreamed" campaign drew many of its ideas about glamour, beauty and fashion from popular cultural icons. Vicki Howard points out, "Brassieres and girdles like those produced by Maidenform were necessary for the sweetheart silhouette popularized by such Hollywood actresses as Elizabeth Taylor" (2001, 200). Since Elizabeth Taylor so recently starred in *Cleopatra*, it isn't surprising that her figure influenced several Maidenform ads.[31] The "I dreamed I was an Egyptian dreamboat in my Maidenform Bra"[32] from 1955 (not pictured) takes on the glamorized image of the New Look.[33] Here a version of Cleopatra looks away from the camera into the distance and she is shown in silhouette thrust against the bow of a ship, leaning so far into the bow that she seems part of the boat. Her arms are outstretched behind her and she leads with her breasts covered only by her Maidenform Pre-lude © bra. The text of the ad reads:

> Look who's getting rave notices up and down the Nile! Me! Why, even the Sphinx thinks I'm a dreamboat in my Maidenform bra! What a lovely way to go sailing through life—high, light, and oh so secure! Cleopatra would be green with envy if she could see my form.[34]

Thus, the language of the ad acknowledges that this is an imitation of Cleopatra, but it also draws on the iconicity of Cleopatra, the Nile, the pyramids and the Sphinx while still conveying an amended 1950s version of the New Look. Stull comments, "The conical-shaped cups, the slim waist, the wrapped lower torso, as well as the repeated exhibitionist theme, reduce the Maidenform woman to a sexual stereotype, denying her an individual identity and presenting her as a passive, erotic spectacle constructed for the perusal of an admiring male (lover)" (1992, 3). While I recognize the vulnerability inherent in the image of the "Egyptian dreamboat," Stull's reading seems oversimplified and fails to take into account the complex power that may be attributable both to the iconic image of Cleopatra herself and to the Hollywood image of glamour, drama, grace and beauty embodied by Elizabeth Taylor.

Like the repetitive icon of Cleopatra, the iconic power of the Western leaps from the silver screen into Maidenform advertisements. In 1955 the "I dreamed I was queen of the Westerns in my Maidenform Bra," ad calls upon images of Annie Oakley and the Wild West (not pictured). The ad read, "From High Noon to Midnight, all the shootin's over me . . . the most-wanted figure in the wild'n woolly West! From Abilene to Santa Fe, the most fabulous curves in every round-up are mine, because I've got the best-known brand of the all . . . Maidenform." The woman in the ad stands beside a stagecoach with guns drawn sporting a cape and gunbelt. She wears skin-tight black pants and decorated black cowboy boots and hat with bags of money strewn at her feet. It seems clear she is robbing the stagecoach. While this representation may not be completely positive, it depicts a woman in action rather than in a passive stance such as the girls contained in the jars of the SUGAR AND SPICE AND EVERYTHING NICE advertisement.

This theme of the Western continues in 1960 where the wanted poster functions as an ad in the form of the "I dreamed I was WANTED in my Maidenform Bra" advertisement (not pictured). Interestingly the image of the WANTED poster appears most menacing and replicates the image of Jane Russell in Howard Hughes's popular film *The Outlaw,* released in 1945 and re-released in 1950. The double meaning of the word "wanted" as in desired and sought after for criminal activities is empowering both sexually and po-

UNDERTONE*makes the most of your young figure!

Each cup is edged with firm embroidery that holds the bra snug as it shapes and defines your curves. (The *best* definition of curves since algebra was invented!) The bottom edge of the bra can't possibly bind—it's scooped up in the middle to give you day-long comfort. Choose your Undertone 1.50 from a special range of sizes. One fits you perfectly! 28 to 36—AA, A, B cups.

Undertone also comes with a secret lining of thinnest foam that rounds out the smooth, shapely look you love. $2.00
*REG. U.S. PAT. OFF. ©1963 BY MAIDENFORM, INC., MAKERS OF BRAS, GIRDLES, SWIMSUITS

AMERICAN GIRL

Figure 5.2.   Maidenform Bra. Advertisement. "I dreamed I was wild in the west" 1963

litically. In 1963 the Western theme became more youthful than classic as shown in Figure 5.2, "I dreamed I was wild in the west in my Maidenform Bra."[35] James Stull argues that, "While the dramatization of female fantasies may initially seem liberating, the content of these ads is in fact quite conservative, even reactionary. They reflect and reinforce prevailing values, attitudes and beliefs by compressing social meaning into familiar and exaggerated—idealized roles" (1992, 3). While I agree that these Western theme ads do depict an aura of feminine passivity particularly through their use of the passive voice "I dreamed I was _____," the progression of the language connotes social change—from "the queen of Westerns" which suggests taking up an already feminized position as queen, to the double entendre evidenced in the WANTED poster, which indicates an acceptance of a more openly empowered feminine sexuality, to the acceptable use of the term "wild" being used in conjunction with the incarnation of a more modern teenage girl.

However, the sugar and spice model continues to play in Maidenform advertisements. The representation of the virgin-whore dichotomy—innocent but sexy, virginal but experienced— resurfaces in the early 1960s. In a Maidenform ad from 1963, a woman appears seated in the witness stand of a court room and looking away from the camera and wearing a strapless bra she swoons, "I dreamed I swayed the jury in my Maidenform Bra (not pictured)."[36] Certainly this ad blurs the line between passivity and sexual empowerment. The reader cannot be sure that the woman in the ad is innocent, but swaying a jury because of the size of one's breasts definitely crosses the line of social justice. That the woman appears doe-eyed and vulnerable perhaps suggests how difficult it is to know how to read the advertisement. It is in fact the complexity of the signifiers operating in this ad that prompts me to juxtapose the "I dreamed I swayed the jury" ad to Figure 5.3, "I dreamed I was a knockout in my Maidenform Bra."[37] In contrast to the "I dreamed I swayed the jury" ad, this advertisement articulates an empowered sexuality based on the double meaning of the term "knockout."

Clearly, the woman standing in the boxing ring is a blonde bombshell, a Marilyn Monroe look-a-like. She is a real "knockout," and she knows it. The reader also knows it. The model is not pulling any punches. She is a sexual powerhouse; she is putting it out there in the center ring for all to see. She does not appear doe-eyed and innocent. She is dangerous. Vicki Howard explains:

> The "I Dreamed" campaign reveals the complexity of gender ideology in the 1950s. The campaign was built around the idea of women taking on the new, "feminine" identities in their Maidenform bras. These identities did not reflect the popular stereotype of the 1950s white woman as a suburban, middle-class mother and housewife. Rather they seemed more akin to other popular images of women at that time, like the pinup or the Hollywood sex goddess. Ads sought to be risqué in their representation of sexuality through the half-clothed female body. These identities challenged notions of middle-class decorum and restraint. (2001, 201)

I dreamed I was a knockout
in my *maidenform* bra

Arabesque*...*new Maidenform bra*...has bias-cut center-of-attraction for *superb*
 separation...insert of elastic for *comfort*...floral circular stitching for the most *beautiful* contou
White in A, B, C cups, just 2.50. Also pre-shaped (light foam lining) 3.50.

PAT. OFF. BY MAIDENFORM, INC.—MAKER OF BRAS, GIRDLES AND SWIMSUITS. ©1961

Figure 5.3.   Maidenform Bra. Advertisement. "I dreamed I was a knockout" 1961

I dreamed I walked a tightrope
in my *maidenform bra*

Sweet Music*...new Maidenform bra...has fitted elastic band under the cups for easy breathing; and reinforced undercups to keep you at your peak of prettiness! White in A, B, C cups, 2.50

PAT. OFF BY MAIDENFORM, INC.—MAKER OF BRAS, GIRDLES AND SWIMSUITS ©1961

Figure 5.4   Maidenform Bra. Advertisement. "I dreamed I walked a tightrope" 1961

While her beauty is certainly a product of the cheesecake pin-up girl, her representation of empowered sexuality and the image of her standing proudly in a boxing ring, a man's arena for testing strength, flies in the face of passive femininity.

While many of the ads do rely on the passive voice as previously noted in reference to the Western-themed ads, several of the Maidenform advertisements use active verbs to convey the physical strength and capacity of women's bodies. Figure 5.4 from 1961, "I dreamed I walked a tightrope in my Maidenform Bra"[38] accentuates how a woman's poise, grace, balance and strength may be used not only as a means of locomotion, but as a means of escape. The woman in the ad appears liberated, walking high above the city with arms outstretched and her bustle billowing (almost as if it were a cape worn by a super hero). There is perhaps even a sense of rescue here. Of course, it should be noted the extent to which walking a tightrope is the well-used metaphor of femininity wherein women must balance work and family, commitments to husband and children, and still have dinner ready at six o'clock. While the social and cultural demands of women's lives have changed historically, the metaphor continues to accurately describe what many women experience in their daily life today. However, this woman wears a look of elation and pleasure and does not appear to be hampered by the struggle to balance the demands of her life. In essence, she has the world at her feet. She is literally on top of the world. The sky is the limit. However, the tightrope walk almost always signifies the need to control and limits which direction she can move, and we must be mindful of the fact that one wrong move can mean her death. Thus, the paradox of limited agency still continues even when the passive voice is absent from the advertisement and the woman seems in control of her destiny.

Similarly an ad from 1961 illustrates a sense of release, of play, of pleasure as the woman appears to effortlessly sail through the air. The copy reads, "I dreamed I flipped in my Maidenform Bra (not pictured)."[39] The physical competence and freedom evident in the ad may indeed be linked to the target audience of the ad, an active teen or young woman who may be free in ways not previously available to her older and/or married counterparts. Similarly, an ad from 1969 proclaims "I dreamed I stretched from here to there in my Maidenform Bra (not pictured)."[40] These ads suggest a physically freeing and empowering experience. The young woman in the ad literally stretches her body thereby demonstrating its flexibility, its capacity to move freely and to be enjoyed by the woman. There does seem to again be a question of how far a woman is willing to stretch to satisfy societies demands of her looks, her work performance, and her commitment to family, but again this question is not articulated only suggested. Finally, in Figure 5.5, the title reads, "I

Figure 5.5. Maidenform Girdle. Advertisement. "I dreamed I felt free" 1969

dreamed I felt free. . . really free in my Maidenform Concertina." Here the women are literally racing through life in their girdles. It seems that this ad represents a last attempt by Maidenform to hold onto a youth market in girdling by proffering the freedom of wearing foundationwear. The ad copy harkens back to the prescriptives of what not to wear from the Corset Contortionist[41] as it reads:

> You'll never yank at a girdle again. At least not Maidenform's Concertina©. The girdle with the "action insert." Bend, it opens. Stand, it closes. The only time you pull this girdle up is when you put it on. Made with Lycra© with panels to smooth you front and back. Pastels, black, white. With matching bras and lingerie.

The fact that Maidenform names the girdle/bra set Concertina© is disconcerting as the wire is suggestive of prisons and other internment camps; however, the language and indeed the tone of the ad imply that the Maidenform "I dreamed" campaign is coming to a close as women have become many of the things they once dreamed of becoming through the Maidenform ads. Ultimately, these later ads move away from the pin-up, sex goddess described by Howard and move toward a physical empowerment that indicates the unlimited capacity of women's bodies even if their places in society are still in question.

Although Howard and Stull clearly disagree in their critical readings of the Maidenform "I dreamed" campaign ads with regard to the degree of social, political and physical freedom proffered in the advertisements, both provide valuable insight into the historical constructedness of the advertising campaign. Their seemingly oppositional critiques actually reinforce the notion that there is a palpable agency, albeit a limited agency, available to women who read these ads. While Stull seems to fall into a cultural dupe analysis of the ads, Howard accepts a more celebratory consumerist model of analysis. Still, I find that although these theories may work with semiotic analyses of the Maidenform ads and consequent discussions of agency proffered to readers, they do not make space for a discussion of the ways in which women experience their lives and their bodies during the ongoing struggle of contestation and consent within fashion and beauty cultures. While it is important to understand how fashion change takes place, it is also important to recognize how women live and experience their bodies as they negotiate between the individual and social body. While cultural hegemony theory provides an ample description of how consent and resistance occurs within the political, economic and even the cultural and social spheres, it does not satisfactorily address or explain the experiences of the lived feminine body. Cultural hegemony may explain the shared adoption of particular signifiers, but it does not explain the shared experience of wearing foundation garments and the restrictions and possibilities that their materiality entails.

NOTES

1. For a discussion of telephone survey methods and survey questionnaire, see introduction. See also variable frequencies in appendix A.
2. See variable v36 in appendix A.
3. See variable v41 in appendix A.
4. See variable v27 in appendix A.
5. See variable v24 in appendix A.
6. See variable v31 in appendix A.
7. See variable v26 in appendix A.
8. See variable v37 in appendix A.

9. See variable v31 in appendix A.

10. See variable v34 in appendix A.

11. See variable v44 in appendix A.

12. See variable v40 in appendix A.

13. See variable v43 in appendix A.

14. See variable v42 in appendix A.

15. See Juffer 1996 and 1998 for a detailed discussion of ways in which women subvert the intended use of Victoria's Secret lingerie catalogs.

16. Several such accounts are profiled in chapter 2.

17. For a detailed description of hegemony, see Gramsci 1971.

18. See Peiss 1998, and Scranton 2001.

19. See Box 23, Series 5, Subseries A: Market Research 1947–1966, Maidenform Collection, Archives Center, Smithsonian Museum of American History.

20. See Folder 3, Box 23, Series 5, Subseries A: Market Research 1947–1966, MC.

21. The report references difficulties in new product introduction with regard to girdles.

22. See Folder 26, Box 23, Series 5, Subseries A: Market Research 1947–1966, MC

23. See appendix b Maidenform market survey questionnaire.

24. See Folder 5, Box 23, Series 5, Subseries A: Market Research 1947–1966, MC.

25. See Folder 8, Box 23, Series 5, Subseries A: Market Research 1947–1966, MC.

26. See Chapter 2 for a discussion of prescriptives for femininity.

27. The language used in Maidenform marketing reports suggests a more respectful attitude toward its consumers than later Victoria's Secret marketing information.

28. A total of 163 "I dreamed" ads ran in 70 countries from 1949 to 1971 making it one of the longest running ad campaigns in history (Stull 1992). For a detailed list of Maidenform Advertisements I reviewed, see appendix C.

29. See Folder 6, Box 73, Series 6, Subseries A: Advertisements 1929–1996, MC.

30. Ibid

31. See also "I dreamed I barged down the Nile in my Maidenform Bra" from chapter 4, page 84 and 91, Cleopatra references in the index.

32. See Folder 6, Box 73, Series 6, Subseries A: Advertisements 1929–1996, MC.

33. For a more detailed discussion of The New Look, see Ann Beth Presley 1998.

34. This ad ran in *Life* magazine, *Glamour*, *Woman's Home Companion*, *Woman's Day* and was included as a Sunday supplement in the *New York News*, *Chicago Tribune* and the *Philadelphia Inquirer*.

35. See Folder 6, Box 73, Series 6, Subseries A: Advertisements 1929–1996, MC.

36. Ibid.

37. Ibid.

38. Ibid.

39. Ibid.

40. Ibid.

41. See Figure 1.1 in chapter 1.

Chapter Six

Minding Our Bodies: Displacing the Foundations of Femininity

It is the gaze, the projects of men that are culturally definitive. Hence women are not full cosubjectivities, free to experience from a tacit body. They must maintain a constant awareness of how they appear to men in terms of physical attractiveness and other forms of acceptability. Women are thus expected to pay meticulous attention to their surface appearance, including hairstyle, make-up, dress, weight, figure and skin tone.

Drew Leder, *The Absent Body*

Women's struggles to negotiate between the meanings of the individual body and the social body through the process of shaping their bodies with foundationwear represent the potential for a collective and personal move toward reconfiguring traditional feminine embodiments. I offer here an analysis of contemporary foundation garments—bras, slimmers, shapers, smoothers—and gendered performativity while exploring the ways in which these garments encourage, train, and police women's performances of normative feminine motility, spatiality, and comportment. Along with several feminist theorists,[1] such as Leslie Heywood (1998a, 1998b), Iris Young (1989), and Susan Bordo (1993), I maintain that this type of normative feminine embodiment deters many women from experiencing their bodies as capacities while encouraging women to treat their bodies as objects to be controlled, maintained and prodded along. In response to this problem, I advocate that women actively engage their bodies as capacities in order to disrupt and offset normative modes of feminine comportment, spatiality, and motility that have been reinforced by the habituated practices of wearing foundation garments.

As I examine the performatives of contemporary normative, ideal femininity and their connection to inhibited intentionality, ambiguous transcendence, and discontinuous unity, I look to the possibility of subversive performatives vis-á-vis the strengths of women to proliferate categories of gender and to potentially displace current notions of what it means to become woman. Coming at the problem of becoming gendered through Monique Wittig's 1992 revolutionary turn on Simone de Beauvoir's work,[2] Judith Butler describes in *Gender Trouble* how the repetition of gendered performatives leaves space for gender transformation, as "the arbitrary relation between such acts, in the possibility of a failure to reappear, a de-formity, or a parodic repetition exposes the phantasmatic effect of abiding identity as a politically tenuous construction" (1999, 179). Recognizing Butler's early work in *Gender Trouble*, I look to other critiques from theorists and practitioners: bell hooks (1992), Leslie Heywood (1998a, 1998b), Judith Lorber (1998), Janice Yoder (1989) and the *Body Outlaws* (2000)[3] who offer subversive and resistant alternatives to normative, ideal femininity and who suggest multiple modes of becoming woman.

In my own case, becoming woman meant losing my ability to connect with the capacities and strengths of my body. It was not until I began waiting tables that I experienced again, the real pleasure of engaging my intentionality in the fluid movements of my body as I passed easily through a crowded kitchen and dining room to serve margaritas in top-heavy glasses and steaming fajitas on searing cast-iron skillets. The thrill of enacting my intentions in displays requiring strength (fajita pans aren't light), grace (it's not easy to serve a tray of margaritas without spilling on your customers), and endurance (working sixteen-hour double shifts on Saturdays) drew me into restaurant work. I found physical empowerment in this labor and have returned to waiting tables on and off for seventeen years (for the duration of high school and through graduate school). While I locate this labor as a turning point in my perception, moving from experiencing my body as a thing to be seen to experiencing my body as a capacity to be enacted, I have come to recognize the value of physical empowerment in a range of labor and sport. Engaging this intentionality in everyday life continues to be a struggle.

What I seek to uncover in this chapter is an understanding of how spatiality, comportment, and motility are gendered particularly in the feminine, how these performatives are habituated, and how women are "marked as woman" as they operate their bodies in modes of femininity. As gender theorist and transperson Riki Wilchins explains, the cultural requirements of gender displays are universally understood in the context of U.S. culture: masculine displays indicate power and dominance, while feminine displays indicate submission and vulnerability (1997, 132). While I concede that even normative, ideal femininity can be pleasurable and enlivening, I agree with Wilchins that there is a quality of vulnerability and submission in most feminine gender displays.

When I compare my own version of gendered initiation to that experience detailed by Wilchins who remembers the experience of becoming boy/man, I must consider the overwhelming circumstances of habituated gender performatives wherein girls become women and boys become men. Wilchins explains:

> My first and best lesson in emotional camouflage came from boys' locker-rooms. It was normal to engage in pecking-order displays, like put-down fights in which we insulted each other's mothers and sisters with the lewdest possible lines. If I went numb and cold, if I concentrated on envisioning myself as muscular, angry, and aggressive, I could get by. Guys would leave me alone. The harassment stopped. It was replaced by respect, or at least distance, which was all I wanted from them. Actually it was what I preferred. I had learned to be a "boy." (1997, 153)

When I examine Wilchins' description of denying the emotional desire to be other than muscular, angry, and aggressive, I am reminded of the emotional desire of "the girl" described by Simone de Beauvoir to be other than pretty, kind, and timid (1989, 357–58). In either case, however, the performance of gender, the displays of masculinity and femininity, are those which define and separate the girl child from the boy child, and frame the initiation of the girl into womanhood and the boy into manhood.

These displays—the gestures, the postures, the movements—form the basis for my interrogation of the issues of spatiality, comportment, and motility of the feminine body. As Wilchins reflects on that locker-room experience, she also points out that those tools of posturing, learned as a boy, are ones she can take up to defend herself at anytime. She notes, "I kept those images in my head for years, that particular sense of myself. I still use it today when I'm out alone late at night and have to walk in a dangerous neighborhood, or I see someone sizing me up from across a darkened street. That self-image re-emerges forcefully in my stride, in the way I hold myself, clench my fists, and scowl" (Wilchins 1997, 153). In this way, Wilchins explores what it is like to put on a gendered identity at least externally. In fact, this is one of the key arguments of her work—to explain what it is like to operate externally along the narrow lines of acceptable genders as defined by American culture and society. What she describes is a process in which she actually recalls the habituated spatiality, comportment, and motility of her boyhood and is able to activate them as a defense. She is in the moment of defense becoming masculine and hearkening back to those external body signifiers of boyhood masculinity.

Wilchins relays her own frustration in failing to convey these qualities in her own gendered performance. A butch woman in a transperson support group critiques Wilchins' gendered performance. She declares:

> You sometimes—I don't want to hurt your feelings—but you sit cross-legged in meetings and sometimes it takes up some of the space of the woman next to you. As a woman, I just wouldn't do that. It's your male training like the men on the subway who have to spread their legs to take up two seats. You don't understand how intimidating to women male behavior can be. (qtd in Wilchins 1997, 42)

In this way Wilchins' habituated masculinity gives her away and exposes her as a transperson who was originally trained to perform masculinity.

Sociologist Pierre Bourdieu describes how these performatives become habituated through imitations of adult gestures, movements, and postures (1977, 87). Bourdieu observes, "the awakening of consciousness of sexual identity and the incorporation of the dispositions associated with a determinate social definition of the social functions incumbent on men and women come hand in hand with the adoption of a socially defined vision of the sexual division of labour" (1977, 93). He articulates that it is precisely by this process of gendering (which Wilchins contests) according to social definitions that women and men are determined, so that they come to understand their separate roles in society. He asserts that it is through "the seemingly most insignificant details of dress, bearing, physical and verbal manners" that the content of the culture is maintained (Bourdieu 1977, 94). Thus, what Bourdieu concludes is that bodily hexis—"treating the body as memory"—operates within the system of the habitus to produce and reproduce culture. The habitus perpetuates and sustains culture "through injunctions as insignificant as 'stand up straight' or 'don't hold your knife in your left hand'" (Bourdieu 1977, 94). What this means in terms of drawing up the lines for performatives of gender is that these seemingly insignificant details are involuntarily learned by boys and girls from their parents and other adults, and that they are determined and defined by socio-historico-cultural definitions of gender in part to perpetuate the gendered division of labor. In this way, Bourdieu confirms and supports both Wilchins' descriptions of learned masculine performatives, whereby boys become men, and Beauvoir's descriptions of trained feminine performatives, whereby girls become women.

However, as I consider these trained gender performatives, I must note how the postures, gestures, and movements of gender come to be constituted as habit through the everyday experience of the lived body. The issues of spatiality and motility are key concepts in making such determinations. If I consider the relationship of the body to motion or space, I must recognize that it is the lived body that is at work here. Embodiment theorist Maurice Merleau-

Ponty points out that "Consciousness is being towards the thing through the intermediary of the body" (1962, 138-39); however, "We must avoid saying that our body is in space, or in time. It inhabits space and time" (1962, 139). Thus, it is at the level of the lived body, at the level of performativity where an aim or intentionality becomes enacted, that the lived body becomes at home in the world. The lived body inhabits time and space and becomes at home in the world; in the moment that an intentionality is achieved. This explains how it is that Wilchins can sit cross-legged taking up the space of the woman next to her and not be aware that this exercise in spatiality is a masculine performative. She is unconscious of what space her lived body inhabits. Because this inhabiting occurs at the level of the lived body and its performativity, it occurs before, beyond, and besides her consciousness. Her lived body inhabits the space on the floor by achieving an intentionality to sit. The performativity that results in the achievement of the aim to sit does not occur to her. Her lived body simply aims to sit and does so.

In considering the intentionality of the feminine body in terms of comportment, spatiality, and motility, I must recognize that it is able to operate only within its habituated understanding of intentionality and what it is given. The habituation that makes women feel comfortable is gendered as it is raced and classed, but the way it is gendered for women can be particularly alienating and antithetical to their capacity to act. Beauvoir articulates this rift as she describes how the girl becoming a woman experiences her body as foreign from her during this process of becoming (1989, 308). She explains how a girl experiences her body as a thing that limits her and seems distant from her (Beauvoir 1989, 308). This description illuminates the process wherein the girl experiences her body not as a part of her, but as a separate entity which draws attention to her, exposes her, brings her out into the open, the public, the world of men. The intentionality of the girl walking like a woman in a woman's flesh in public is an imitated and trained performance of the body since the girl is "treated like a live doll and is refused liberty. She is taught that to please she must try to please, she must make herself an object; she should therefore renounce her autonomy" (Beauvoir 1989, 280). Her intentionality is to become a woman, to make herself an object. These intentions are all taken up and put into practice by the body. Her body becomes the site of alienation as the integrity of perceptual giveness of the lived body is compromised in order to become an object for the male gaze.

This conflict is also taken up by Wilchins, who comments, "What I am interested in is the original cultural gesture to regulate and contain what your body and mine can mean, or say, or do" (1997, 87). What is at stake here then, at least initially for the feminine body, is the right to be read as a body having the capacity to act, and having that capacity take precedence over the recognition of the feminine body as object. Iris Young explains in "Throwing Like a Girl" that as a result of this conflict, the feminine body is overlaid with immanence and experiences ambiguous transcendence, and "woman often lives her body as a burden which must be dragged and prodded along, and at the same time protected" (1989, 59). Such a disruption is caused by, as Young suggests, an inhibited intentionality in which the "feminine body underuses its real capacity, both as the potentiality of its physical size and strength and as the real skills and coordination which are available to it" (1989, 59). The feminine body operates in a state of inhibited intentionality which does not allow the full commitment of the body to a given task—hence the title, "Throwing Like a Girl"; a girl does not use her entire body to put the ball into motion, she only uses those parts of her body that are entirely necessary.[4] Inhibited intentionality represents the first kind of alienation that woman experiences. I have described it previously in discussions with friends as a perceived inefficiency or incompetence. Young describes it in terms of a woman's distrust of her own bodily capacity. She notes, "A woman frequently does not trust the capacity of her body to engage itself in physical relation to things" (Young 1990, 59). Young points out that this inefficiency in performance yields not only an alienation in terms of inhibited intentionality, but as women are trained to perform inefficiently as feminine bodies, this training produces a second kind of alienation as it violates their experience of themselves as transcendent subjects (1989, 56).

Young also argues that this inefficiency is experienced by woman in regard to a division in her "attention between the task to be performed and the body which must be coaxed and manipulated into performing it" (1989, 61). What this means is that woman's intentionality is inhibited by this division, and also that this division is emphasized by woman's awareness of how her body looks as she performs the task. Young states, "Finally, feminine bodily existence is self-referred to the extent that the feminine subject posits her motion as the motion that is looked at" (1989, 61). This becomes significant when I consider woman's awareness of her own appearance in performing tasks that are physically demanding. This is the tension between experiencing the body as subject, an intentionality that reaches out into the world, and experiencing the body as object, a mere thing to be gazed upon. Young confirms that the bodies of men and women carry this double meaning, but with women this experience of the body as both subject and object is simultaneous and therefore debilitating and disruptive of the harmony of the transcendent subject at home in the world.

Thus, I can consider Wilchins' text in yet another light. While she sets up her book in terms of a gender conflict between being read as masculine or as feminine, in many cases it seems that the conflict she describes concerns being read as an object, while seeing herself as a subject. As a man, she most likely did not experience herself simultaneously as subject and object and did not receive the kinds of objectifying attention that she describes experiencing as a transperson. She confides, "What causes me pain is having my body read against me," (1997, 147) but later she describes what being read as a woman meant to her. Wilchins comments, "When people started reading me as a woman, I had to very consciously learn how they saw me in order to use the restroom. I had to learn to recognize my voice, my posture, the way I appeared in clothing" (1997, 151). She explains here that she must learn to perform femininity satisfactorily, to have her body read as feminine in order to survive in society.

Embodiment theorist Sandra Bartky provides a framework for understanding Wilchins' dilemma in terms of learning the difference between masculine and feminine motility, spatiality, and comportment because "women are far more restricted than men in their manner of movement and spatiality" (1988, 66). She articulates these restrictions in terms of their limits on woman's spatiality. Bartky notes, "The woman holds her arms closer to her body, palms against her sides; her walk is circumspect. If she has subjected herself to the additional constraint of high-heeled shoes, her body is thrown forward and off balance: The struggle to walk under these conditions shortens her stride more" (1988, 67). Thus, as Bartky and Young suggest, woman operates within an enclosed space in which she hopes to be protected, but she is simultaneously limited in that space. Bartky describes the contemporary frame for feminine comportment as "a whole new training: a woman must stand with stomach pulled in, shoulders thrown slightly back and chest out, this to display her bosom to maximum advantage. While she must walk in the confined fashion appropriate to women, her movements must at the same time, be combined with a subtle but provocative hip-roll" (1988, 68). Thus Bartky articulates the requirements of contemporary, normative, ideal feminine comportment.

However, bell hooks (1992) hones these feminist critiques of normative femininity described by Beauvoir, Young, Bartky, and Wilchins as she enumerates the specific oppressions circulating in the myth of woman, the myth of femininity. In her essay, "Is Paris Burning?," hooks critiques the subversion involved in gay black men performing "white, heterosexual, ruling-class femininity" (1992a, 148). She suggests that in such parody, these performers pay homage to an ideal femininity in which whiteness plays the largest role. Her critique moves against Butler's theoretical model as she argues that while gender bending may offset power relations of the phallocratic economy, the balance of white supremacy is not offset (1992, 147). She concludes that the political implications of a dominant, normative femininity—white, heterosexual and ruling-class—operating hegemonically in the capitalist North serves only to divide and limit the potential for resistant and subversive modes of femininity. hooks points out the reality of the struggle to resist racism, heterosexism, and classism that many women confront daily in their workplaces, communities, families and relationships.

In Ophira Edut's anthology, *Body Outlaws*, several young women argue that resistance and the potential for subversive actions rests with ourselves as we recognize our own femininities as empowered and proud while breaking the hold that dominant ideal femininity has on us. Erin J. Aubry's essay, "The Butt," details the kind of resistance she engages in every day. Aubry comments, "It was tricky, but I absorbed the better aspects of the butt stereotypes, especially the Tootsie-Roll walk—the wave, the undulation in spite of itself, the leisurely antithesis of the spring in the step" (2000, 28). Aubry articulates her experience of resisting the ideal feminine comportment that Bartky describes on behalf of a comportment that suits her body, her butt, her situatedness. She explains, "I liked the walk and how it defied that silly runway gait, with the hips thrust too far forward and the arms dangling back in empty air. That is a pure apology for butts, a literal bending over backward to admonish the body for any bit of unruliness" (Aubry 2000, 28).

However, Aubry acknowledges that this process of embracing the stereotypical unruliness of her butt as a resistance to the myths of ideal femininity is not easy. Aubry states, "If we [black women] are always put on the butt defensive, as it were, we'll never have the psychic space to assess how we *really* feel about wearing Lycra—and a woman with a sizable butt *must* have an opinion about it" (2000, 25). Thus, subverting the performatives of normative femininity requires vigilant dedication and a willingness to confront the products of the dominant culture—ideal bodies in Lycra power-slips, push-up bras, and microfiber underwear, performing white, ruling-class, heterosexual femininity. Aubry closes her essay by arguing that the potential for subversion rests with a willingness to deal with our bodies, to confront the images of ideal femininity in popular culture.[5]

However, as Aubry and hooks point out, this is difficult work because ideal femininity may be evidenced everywhere in popular culture—billboards, fashion magazines, television, and even in catalogs sent directly to our homes. Women are constantly reminded of fashion's ideal body and what performing ideal femininity means for this body. This is perhaps no better demonstrated than in the role that contemporary foundation garments play in the lives of American women. These bras, bustiers, slimmers, shapers, microfiber shaping underwear, thongs, power-slips, and push-up bras *work on* the feminine body not only to shape, mould, sculpt, and decorate, thus facilitating the feminine body as object, but these garments also *work for* the feminine body, keeping it separated and enclosed, confined and protected, thus facilitating the feminine body as autonomous. Thus, the foundation garment precariously frames the feminine subject/object contradiction and as such performs itself as a signifier of the oppression of woman—who has been habituated into the performatives of feminine gestures, movements, and motilities all while remaining confined within the moving frame of fashion's ideal body.

A contemporary framing is depicted here in Figure 6.1 from Victoria's Secret Catalog.[6] The model wears what is called "The Sensual Shapers" slip which "has tummy control insets to cinch the waist . . . [and] lace trim with hidden elastic for a stay put fit." This image illustrates precisely the stance that Bartky outlines, but what is perhaps more noteworthy is that as the image in the advertisement suggests, it is the foundation garment, "The Sensual Shapers" slip, that manipulates the body into its correct feminine posture.

This controlled, contained, and restricted feminine posture serves to enclose the feminine body in a protective move, to shield it from the gaze, or as Bartky points out, to prevent an assault on female genitalia. Bartky argues, "The fact that women tend to sit and stand with legs, feet, and knees close or touching may well be a coded declaration of sexual circumspection in a society that still maintains a double standard, or an effort, albeit unconscious, to guard the genital area" (Bartky 1988, 74). This posture is demonstrated in Figure 6.2 where the sitting posture of a woman in a satin corset reflects the posture that Bartky details. The model appears with shoulders back, stomach pulled in, and chest out—in a move that suggests an invitation for objectification—while her legs, and knees are positioned close together, almost touching—in a move that suggests as Bartky does, the need to guard the female genitals. However, the model's feet are far apart, which might be taken as a suggestion of an acceptable degree of provocative femininity.

What I wish to point out in incorporating these contemporary foundationwear advertisements into this analysis is an understanding of how these garments support and facilitate notions of restricted feminine comportment; however, I do not simply argue that these garments serve to limit woman's performativity. I argue that they work to maintain a social control of feminine comportment that operates whether women wear these garments or not (not unlike the previously mentioned concept of internalizing girdles)—and, perhaps more complexly, that part of the rationales for women wearing such garments stems from an unconscious idea that the female body in general, and the female genitals in particular, must be protected. If I add to this analysis a recognition that there has in recent years been a resurgence and indeed a proliferation of foundation garments in fashion—in the form of contemporary shapewear—the suggestion that women are coming back to these garments in

Figure 6.1.   Sensual Shaper's Slip. *Victoria's Secret Catalog.* **Fall 1999**

Figure 6.2.   The Satin Corset. *Victoria's Secret Catalog.* Fall 1999

response to a conservative social backlash[7] underscores the significant role of foundationwear not only in terms of restricting the feminine body but also in terms of protecting it.

However, in recognizing woman's desire to protect the feminine body by enclosing and restricting it, whether in terms of foundation garments or the comportment they serve to reinforce, I must also be concerned with the consequences of limiting the feminine body in this way. Susan Bordo (1993) comments on the significance of foundation garments in their reinforcement of the cultural contrast between the male and female forms in the nineteenth century:

"Consider this particularly clear and appropriate example; the nineteenth-century hourglass figure, emphasizing breasts and hips against a wasp waist, was an intelligible, symbolic form, representing a domestic, sexualized ideal of femininity. The sharp cultural contrast between the female and male form, made possible by the use of corsets and bustles, reflected in symbolic terms, the dualistic division of social and economic life into clearly defined male and female spheres. At the same time, to achieve a specified look, a particular feminine praxis was required—straightlacing, minimal eating, reduced mobility—rendering the female body unfit to perform activities outside its designated sphere" (1993, 181).

As Bordo points out, it is the performativity that must be altered to coincide with the body ideal which renders the feminine body inefficient outside its own sphere of operation. To my mind this phenomenon as described by Bordo continues to threaten women because contemporary notions of ideal bodies have and continue to determine normative femininity in spite of the fact that dimensions of shape and size demanded of the feminine form have varied historically.[8]

In her book, *Fifty Years of Fashion*, fashion historian Valerie Steele states, "From stiletto heels and waspie girdles to white gloves and aprons, women's fashion promoted restrictive images of femininity" (1997, 29). Steele also cites Anne Fogarty's book from 1959, *Wife Dressing*, wherein Fogarty compares girdle wearing to Chinese foot binding, and confirms that in the 1950s she favored wearing "cocktail dresses so tight that sitting was impossible" (Fogarty 1959). "You're not meant to suffer," she reassured her readers, but the feeling "should be one of *constraint* rather than comfort" (Fogarty 1959). However, if in recognizing that women are no longer bound by the social, cultural or physical constraints of the 1950s—no longer obligated to wear cocktail dresses so tight they cannot sit down—I argue that women have been released from these body ideals, then I am forgetting that now as ever women chase after fashion's ideal body. Many women continue to devalue their bodily capacities while striving to meet conventional beauty standards.[9]

As feminist theorist Leslie Heywood suggests in her book, *Bodymakers,* patriarchal notions of ideal femininity and its rigid body ideals continue to limit what women can do. Heywood notes, "Seeking beauty, denying strength women line up at the Stair Masters in the gym in pursuit of the hot fitness body; the corset and the Wonderbra have come back, implants and plastic surgery are presented as avenues to individual power, [and] advertisements are fond of corpses" (1998, 55). Heywood conveys the extent to which women's bodies have become so thin that they appear like corpses. She explains how the fitness movement has eclipsed female body building in a move that eliminates the option of a visibly muscular body ideal for women in favor of a lean-looking one. Heywood expresses this exchange in the terms "seeking beauty and denying strength."

In her essay, "Part Animal, Part Machine," feminist theorist Leigh Shoemaker agrees with Heywood's assessment that while body ideals change historically, one form of bodily constraint is exchanged for another. Shoemaker adds that advertising typically proffers freedom while substituting one kind of social constraint for another. She concludes:

> Thanks to the second wave feminist analysis of beauty culture, we can see that fashion gives us corsets, hose, high heels, underwire bras; the "health and beauty" industry gives us paints, powders, dyes, silicon, liposuction; "nutrition" centers offer diets and other ways to become smaller and less present while remaining in continual states of paralyzing obsession; the mental health industry offers Xanax, Valium, and Ativan; and advertising tells us, "You've come a long way, baby," pretending to offer freedom by actually turning the key on a new form of imprisonment. Femininity now, as in the second wave and before, is about constriction. (1997, 112)

Shoemaker articulates the reality of contemporary American society in which women are bombarded with images of what they are supposed to have come a long way to be. These images serve only to reify the feminine body as a manageable and alterable site, one that is kept under control through a myriad of bodily disciplines that subjugate the feminine body, keeping it captive in its own habitual practices. As Bartky notes, "The influence of media is pervasive, too, constructing as it does an image of the female body as spectacle, nor can we ignore the role played by 'beauty experts'" (1988, 74). The proliferation of beauty experts in television programs like "Fashion Emergency" suggests the extent to which women are subjected to a constant barrage of fashion dos and don'ts, but much of the advice of "fashion and beauty experts" goes beyond the surface of the body. This advice operates on the body itself. It attempts to reconstruct the ideal body while coping immediately and directly with design flaws in the lived body.

This fixation with reshaping the female body is exemplified in a "Fashion 101 Lesson" from *In Style* Magazine, February 2000 (not pictured), and is entitled "Problem Solvers." This article/advice column gives advice to women regarding what they can do in order to solve "bra problems." The language reads, "bra problems," but the majority of advice blocks focus on "breast problems"—"two different sizes, small breasts, large breasts, breasts too far apart." These bras are specially made to work on the breasts that do not fit the requirements of fashion's ideal body. In this way, the "experts" tell women what form of discipline is appropriate for their particular flawed body. This is further demonstrated in a "Fashion 101 Lesson" two years later from *In Style,* February 2002 (not pictured), in which thongs are articulated as "problem solvers [which] do more than eliminate panty lines." The thongs are touted as "all-reason thongs" and are made to fix every type of problem from pregnancy to general tummy control. New microfiber materials make these thongs and the majority of "light to heavy control" seamless underwear "invisible under clothes." Women are encouraged to wear thongs because they are sexy, they eliminate panty lines and they can help to solve body problems.

Thus, the concern with fixing the problem body continues to be at the center of woman's responsibility in American culture. I have cited previously Susan Bordo's critique of this fixation on self-modification in terms of the pursuit of the elusive ideals of femininity and fashion's ideal body resulting in docile bodies (1993, 166). This drive to make our bodies better, to self-regulate and self-police our problem bodies is a growing concern for women in American culture. In her acclaimed educational film *Killing Us Softly Three*, Jean Kilbourne interrogates the representations of women circulating in American advertising culture, what she deems a "toxic culture" (2000). Thus, women engage in the habituated practices and performatives of regulating their bodies, of making them satisfactory for cultural consumption. Sandra Bartky confirms this notion of self-regulation as she maintains, "The disciplinary techniques through which the 'docile bodies' of women are constructed aim at a regulation that is perpetual and exhaustive—a regulation of the body's size and contours, its appetite, posture, gestures and general comportment in space and the appearance of each of its visible parts" (1988, 80). What Bordo, Kilbourne and Bartky conclude is that such extreme regulation of the feminine body keeps woman occupied with achieving an ideal femininity that is always kept just beyond her reach.

Thus, as Beauvoir and Young have suggested, woman is encouraged to take up the body as an object in order to achieve or attain her desire. An example of this can be seen in another "Fashion 101 Lesson" from *In Style*, February 2000, entitled "Sexy Looks." The article advises, "A bra is one of your most functional garments, but never forget that it can also be your most enticing. Besides the obvious sex appeal of a push-up, details like embroidery, lace, feminine colors and appliqués can make your bra a tool of seduction that won't be denied." The article encourages women to take up the performativity of bra wearing, in a move that exhibits the body as sex object. The body becomes sexually enticing as it is prepared as an object for consumption. The breasts are pushed-up and decorated with "embroidery, lace, feminine colors and appliqués." These bras are tools of seduction that, when applied to the feminine body, render it as object.

That women's bodies have been exploited as commodities for centuries is a well-known fact. That images of women have circulated in the media as "sex symbols" is similarly understood; however, the fact that more and more women "are spending more time on the management and discipline of our bodies than we have in a long, long time" is perhaps a lesser known fact (Bordo 1993, 166). "New too is the spread of this discipline to all classes of women and its deployment throughout the life cycle. What was formerly the specialty of the aristocrat or courtesan is now the routine obligation of every woman, be she a grandmother or a barely pubescent girl" (Bartky 1988, 81). The proliferation of the demographic groups of women engaged in disciplining the feminine body, coupled with the proliferation in the amount of time spent engaged in such disciplining, constitute the present crisis of/for the feminine "docile body."

As Bartky notes, "The disciplinary power that is increasingly charged with the production of a properly embodied femininity is dispersed and anonymous; there are no individuals formally empowered to wield it; it is as we have seen, invested in everyone and in no one in particular" (1988, 80). Bordo concurs and notes, "We must abandon the idea of power as something possessed by one group and leveled against another; we must instead think of the network of practices, institutions, and technologies that sustain positions of dominance and subordination in a particular domain" (1993, 167). Thus, as women continue to sit in the precarious and dangerous position of simultaneous subject/object, they must choose the correct performative in a given moment to ensure survival.

But women should be doing more than surviving in society. They should not be reduced or limited by conditions in which the habituated practices and performances of everyday life subsume them. They should recognize that their repeated gendered performatives have the capacity to proliferate subjectivities. As Butler argues in *Gender Trouble*, "The task is not whether to repeat, but how to repeat or, indeed, to repeat and, through a radical proliferation of gender, to displace the very gender norms that enable the repetition itself" (1999, 189). What I suggest with regard to Butler's call to action is an enactment of our bodily capacities. We should open up and inhabit spaces in which we can experience ourselves in terms of our intentionalities and aims. I suggest a return to the 1968 feminist protest of the Miss America Pageant in

which women removed their bras in an effort to confront the physical oppression of restrictive gendered clothing. We should wear sports bras or go
bra-less[10] instead of wearing push-up bras while engaging in the repetitions
of lifting, carrying, stretching, walking, running, and overall strength training.
This does not come in response to notions that women should attempt to be
muscular like men, but that women should aspire to be strong like women by
engaging their bodies to their fullest capacities and using feminine
strengths—lower body strength, flexibility and endurance—to achieve aims
and accomplish objectives.[11]

Judith Lorber details such an example of subversive performativity in her
article "Believing is Seeing: Body as Ideology." Lorber explains, "When
women were accepted as West Point cadets, it became clear that the tests of
physical competence, such as rapidly scaling an eight-foot wall, had been
constructed for male physiques—pulling oneself up and over and using up-
per-body strength" (1998, 19). The women's answer to this challenge was,
however, not to go over the wall like the men, but to figure out a way to use
their own strengths to get over. Yoder comments, "I was observing this obstacle one day, when a woman approached the wall in the old prescribed way,
got her fingertips grip, and did an unusual thing: she walked her dangling legs
up the wall until she was in a position where both her hands and feet were
atop the wall. She then simply pulled up her sagging bottom and went over.
She solved the problem by capitalizing on one of women's physical assets:
lower-body strength" (1989, 530). Women's lower body strength facilitated
completion of the same obstacle that men used upper body strength to overcome. This example serves to explain how women can use their bodies to
achieve aims in ways that are different from men. Women do not have to become like men to be physically efficient, capable, or confident. They must
simply find their own ways to achieve their own goals.

My recommendations for women to actively strengthen their bodies, to engage in the subversion of women's docile bodies—bodies that are only considered fit in terms of appearance—stems from the work of Lorber, Yoder and
Heywood. Heywood adds to the work of Lorber and Yoder in which they recognize the subversive capacity of the feminine body to achieve physical goals
vis-á-vis a deployment of innovative feminine performatives. Heywood argues that through strength training, women can engage in subversion of feminine body ideals such as "the hot fitness body"—the feminine body as lean,
but weak. She also argues, perhaps most significantly, that women who
strengthen their bodies also raise their capacities to do and to be: "I have seen
them go out of the gym with their shoulders back and their heads held high,
a little bit more confident about their positions in the world, a little less
bounded by limits that they've internalized from years of absorbing cultural

mythologies that impose drastic limits on women's strength and potentials" (Heywood 1998a, 59–60). In merging the work of Lorber, Yoder, and Heywood, I can recognize my own response to the physical empowerment I experienced waiting tables. I can understand how focusing on the physical strengths of women—lower body strength, endurance, and flexibility—have the potential to displace feminine gender norms and constitute a very different kind of subjectivity. Being at home in our bodies and enacting our intentionalities should be the goal whether we are tootsie-rolling walkers, baby-carrying moms, tray-toting servers, wall-climbing cadets, or weight-lifting scholars. Engaging in these performatives may not seem subversive at all; however, if women can experience their bodies as capacities, they can inhabit a space of healthy subjective empowerment. As Heywood points out, "[weight] Lifting can make a woman who has been culturally devalued in any of the usual ways—'You throw (or talk or act) like a girl'—feel stronger, more certain of herself and her place in the world, the right she has to take up space" (1998a, 187).

Women who can take up space, live in harmony with their bodies, be at home in the world, operate their bodies to their fullest capacities—these are not the representations of most women we see on television or in magazines. Most of the images we see are of women who: constrain their bodies—through dieting, wearing foundation garments and even undergoing surgery—to present themselves in feminine postures and gestures that render them objects, enclose their bodies within the same garments to maintain any small measure of subjectivity, control and manage their docile bodies in a race toward an elusive femininity that is perpetual and exhaustive. We have been taught to desire to be the women we see most in the media, but we want to be constituted as women of the first set, the ones we do not see as often. We want to be able to engage in repeated subversive performatives that displace notions of normative femininity and proliferate gender norms so that it becomes possible for us to be who we are, ourselves. We do not want to exchange one ideal body for another, which is the trap that seems to be laid for us in so many gym and fitness advertisements. We do not desire a body that is like the one on television or in the magazines. We want our bodies to be reflections of ourselves, empowered by our intentionalities and imaginations. In wanting this, in moving toward this, we must be critical of the demands of normative, ideal femininity and choose to parody those performatives that have disciplined us. In her book, *Pretty Good for a Girl*, Heywood finds subversion in her weight-lifting repetitions. She declares:

Each rep. Yes. Here I go. Here's one for all the times someone told me a girl should be feminine and petite, that I'd better watch out or I'd get too big. Here's another for each time I spoke or screamed and my voice spun through the air like dust. And here's my last tortured rep for those who said they could love me if only I could be just a little bit nicer and quieter, please, not quite so intense. Here we go, 205 to the sky: feel much better already baby. (Heywood 1998b, 194)

While I maintain that a deployment of physical empowerment via a focus on the strengths of women—lower body strength, flexibility, and endurance—and a removal of confining contemporary foundation garments are moves to displace gender norms, what I really am calling for here is a raising of consciousness, a critical eye toward feminine performatives, and a recognition that the feminine body cannot continue to bear the weight of culture upon its embattled frame. Foundation garments may cover the wounds and seem to protect the body, but underneath it all, the feminine subject is struggling to reconstitute itself. We cannot continue to allow ourselves to be habituated as weak, diminutive, docile. By removing the strictures of normative feminine performatives and ideal bodies, we make the move of freeing ourselves from structures that limit our intentionalities, reduce our capacities, and stymie our imaginations. Ultimately, we free our embodied subjectivities by displacing the foundations of femininity.

NOTES

1. I would like to personally thank Debra Bergoffen for her diligence and persistence in pushing me to revise this piece as well as my own perceptions of feminine embodied experience. I am also grateful for advice and comments given to me by Gail Weiss, Iris Young, Susan Bordo, Riki Wilchins, and Leslie Heywood. It seems important to note that I see a strong connection between feminist theories of the body and women and sport, and I am equally indebted to those who publish in each field.

2. See Beauvoir 1989, 267 and Butler 1987.

3. See for example Aubry 2000.

4. This is not to say that women cannot overcome this condition, nor is this to say that there are women who do not experience their bodies in this way. I agree with Young that women frequently underuse the capacities of their bodies; however, many women—athletes and those who labor with their bodies—may not experience immanence and/or inhibited intentionality in the moment of performance of a specified or repeated task. Yet, athletes are particularly susceptible to other kinds of alienation. For more on women athletes, "feminine apologetic" and "muscle gap," see Theberge 2000 and Cahn 1998.

5. For a discussion of representations of raced bodies in high fashion magazines and catalogs, see hooks 1992.

6. For a comparison of class in the catalogs of Victoria's Secret and Frederick's of Hollywood, see Valdivia 1997.

7. For a discussion of a return to Victoriana, see Workman 1996.

8. See also Melinkoff 1984 and Presley 1998.

9. For a discussion of the use of plastic surgery to achieve dominant ideal beauty, "which is male-supremacist, racist, ageist, heterosexist, anti-Semitic, ableist and class-biased," see Morgan 1998, 156.

10. I agree that women can and should, of course, choose not to wear bras if they feel comfortable doing this. A good friend of mine offered that if we lived in a culture where elongated breasts were valued, she would not wear a bra at all.

11. See Gloria Steinem's "The Politics of Muscle" (1994) for a discussion of the importance of physical empowerment and the women's movement.

Chapter Seven

Conclusions and Some Afterthoughts

Women are encouraged to aspire to the idealized body and the clothed image wrapped around it. In this sense, women become not only the consumers of clothes, but the consumers of the meaning and promise of idealized womanhood.

Ali Guy, Eileen Green and Maura Banim, *Through the Wardrobe*

By now, it should be clear that fashion's ideal body, ideal femininity and idealized womanhood are inextricably linked. This entanglement is of course not a natural one, but rather one that is culturally produced. It is important to note that the category of woman and all its cultural meanings are almost always reduced to the image of fashion's ideal body. That feminists have fought the ever strengthening vines of this intertwined concept of woman/body suggests the depth of the roots of the myth: woman = body. Although women can most certainly not live without their bodies, women cannot and should not be alienated from their capacities, their strengths, their beauties or their bodies' transformative powers.

Simone de Beauvoir heightens awareness of this myth of woman as body in her introduction to *The Second Sex*, as she describes the process in which women are reduced to this myth and explains how this myth stigmatizes and devalues womanhood and femininity (1989). In addition, Beauvoir connects the myth of woman and the stigma of the female body to woman's complicity with man noting the unique bond that woman shares with her oppressor. Beauvoir states, "When man makes of woman the *Other*, he may, then expect her to manifest deep-seated tendencies toward complicity. Thus, woman may fail to lay claim to the status of subject because she lacks definite resources, because she feels the necessary bond that ties her to man regardless of reciprocity, and

141

because she is often very well pleased with her role as the [inessential] *Other*"
(1989, xxvii). In this way, Beauvoir provides the theoretical groundwork for
an argument concerning not only the oppression of woman, but also the complicit role of woman in this oppression. By the conclusion of her argument,
Beauvoir submits that the relationship of woman to man is complicated by the
gendered division of labor and economic concerns. Beauvoir points out, "We
must not believe, certainly, that a change in woman's economic condition
alone is enough to transform her, though this factor has been and remains the
basic factor in her evolution; but until it has brought about the moral, social,
cultural and other consequences that it promises and requires, the new woman
cannot appear (1989, 725). In this way, Beauvoir demonstrates the nuance of
her argument concerning the oppression of woman to include recognition of
the double-bind of patriarchy and capitalism. It is important to note that she
does not address racism, although many theories of race invoke it as a product of classifying under the terms of economic systems including feudalism,
mercantilism, colonialism and now globalism. Neither does she discuss the
extent of the double-bind of patriarchy and capitalism in terms of the strength
of these power structures, but she alludes to their effects on the situation of
woman who lives under the material and historical conditions produced by
patriarchal capitalism, what bell hooks would call white supremacist capitalist
patriarchy (1992).

In her discussion of the situation of woman Beauvoir continuously returns
to the lived experience of woman and to the lived body. This continuous return to the grounded experience of woman conveyed through a phenomeno-
logical discourse allows Beauvoir to examine complex power relations
through the lens of the lived body. Thus, Beauvoir concludes, "She [the
woman of today] appears most often as 'true woman' disguised as a man, and
she feels herself as ill at ease in her masculine garb. She must shed her old
skin and cut her own new clothes. This she could do only through a social
evolution" (1989, 725). Even Beauvoir's use of language—garb, skin and
clothes—alludes to the significance of women's bodies and clothing in the
revolutionary change concerning the situation of woman. She explains the
difficulty in interrupting the complicity of woman in relation to man via a
new production of woman; however, she maintains the importance of engaging in this change for the benefit of humanity. She asserts, "Every subject
plays his part as such specifically through exploits or projects that serve as a
mode of transcendence; he achieves liberty only through a continual reaching
out toward other liberties" (Beauvoir 1989, xxxiv).

This complicit relationship is particularly appropriate to the discussion of
women's perpetuation of their own oppression through fashion and beauty
cultures,[1] and Beauvoir lends to this project an understanding of such com-

plicity on the part of women, both interviewed and surveyed, who maintain that they are happy with their choice of foundation garments even if they are not happy with their bodies. In response to this conflict, Beauvoir seeks to clarify the difference between happiness and liberty. She argues:

> But we do not confuse the idea of private interest with that of happiness, although that is a common point of view. Are not women of the harem more happy than women voters? Is not the housekeeper happier than the working woman? It is not too clear just what the word happy really means and still less what true values it may mask. There is no possibility of measuring the happiness of others, and it is always easy to describe as happy the situation in which one wishes to place them. In particular those who are condemned to stagnation are often pronounced happy on the pretext that happiness consists in being at rest. (1989, xxxiv)

Beauvoir's distinction between happiness and liberty underscores the predicament of women under late capitalism who find themselves identified as subjects primarily through consumption. Materialist feminist Rosemary Hennessy describes the historical production of this type of consumer subjectivity, which occurs in the aftermath of World War II. Hennessy notes:

> A new growing mass media, including the advertising industry, displaced unmet needs into new desires and offered the promise of compensatory pleasures, or at least the promise of pleasure in the form of commodity consumption. The inducement of social demand and consumer desire was one of the key components of the new consumer culture and a crucial mechanism through which capitalist overproduction was managed ideologically. This process took place on multiple fronts and involved the formation of newly desiring subjects, forms of agency, intensities of sensation, and economies of pleasure that were consistent with the requirements of a more mobile workforce and a growing consumer culture. Most significantly, the position of desiring subject was gradually being opened up to women who would eventually be recruited as ideal and consummate consumers. (2000, 99)

Hennessy provides an understanding of the situation of woman as it is at once bettered, worsened and complicated by the capitalist identities ascribed to women: consummate consumers and desiring subjects.

Beauvoir and Hennessy each explore the social, cultural, political and economic forces which produce the situation of woman. The interview and survey data from this project provide an example of the impact of these force relations on the individual lives of women as they struggle with their bodies, their identities and their subjectivities. Certainly, Hennessy and Beauvoir raise the stakes for women's consumption of fashion's ideal body as they articulate the problematic status of woman under the systems of patriarchy and capitalism; however, bell hooks reminds us that racist oppression intersects the class and gender oppressions rooted in capitalism and patriarchy.[2] hooks's articulation of the interlocking systems of oppression, "white supremacist capitalist patriarchy," provides a triangulated perspective for examining fashion and beauty cultures (1992a). White supremacist capitalist patriarchy allows for multiple analyses of the power dynamics involved in the consumption and production of fashion's ideal body. Marxist notions of commodity fetishism and even the Althusserian model of repressive state apparatuses and ideological state apparatuses are incorporated into analyses of consumption, production and cultural practice (Althusser 1970). Adorno and Horkheimer's critique of the culture industry is likewise incorporated into this polyvalent analysis (1987). This is to say that none of these models of power are absolute or monolithic. Hence, as cultural historian Jill Fields[3] has pointed out, a cultural hegemony model becomes particularly useful as it allows for analysis of interconnected systems of economic, political, social and cultural power (1997, 72). Women's bodies have meaning and significance in all of these domains, and as such traffic as cultural capital or stigma. Fashion and beauty cultures have cashed in on this reality for women, who are desiring subjects and consummate consumers. Thus, shapewear, as an innovative contemporary commodity, both facilitates American women's desires for fashion's ideal body and codifies economic, political, social and cultural boundaries for women's bodies.

The significance of these interlocking systems of oppression still leaves room for negotiating cultural meanings and practices, and Foucauldian theories of power can also help to explain the shifts in value for specific fetishized objects and practices. Certainly, women may be read as docile bodies that are subject to the mass media, advertising and the dominant culture's articulation of fashion's ideal body, and recognizing that this ideal is elusive is the key to understanding its cultural power. However, women still negotiate the meaning of their bodies within the shifting social body which includes subcultural values. While the system of global capitalism moves toward a global hegemonic culture and the proliferation of dominant cultural ideals including fashion's ideal body, there is still the possibility of resistance within the flux of these articulations. Indeed the very speed at which these ideals ebb and flow creates circuits of meaning that are polyvalent. The example of internalized girdling as expressed by Susan Bordo provides us with a glimpse of how a fashion requirement like foundationwear can be internalized by the social body. Hence, a resurgence of contemporary shapewear may not change the external appearance of fashion's ideal body. The ideal slender body may prevail either with or without shaping garments.

Figure 7.1. Lord and Taylor. Advertisement. "Buy 2 Get 1 Free" March 2003

Figure 7.1 demonstrates that contemporary shapewear continues to be marketed into the new millennium and is not a passing fetish of the late 1990s. This advertisement for contemporary shapewear came unsolicited to my mailbox in the spring of 2003. It heralds the longevity of girdle resurgence in the form of contemporary shapewear and indicates that foundationwear corporations continue to shape fashion's ideal body. It is significant that Warner's who produced the Lastex net slipover profiled in chapter 1 is still going strong with many lines of contemporary shapewear. Other brand names such as Vanity Fair and Flexees have been equally long-standing. It is likewise important to note that while many of the brands have been bought by multinational corporations, consumers recognize and are loyal to brand names.[4] Table 7.1 represents the Big Four Foundationwear conglomerates and their brands.

Fashion's slender ideal body continues to take center stage in the commodity fetishism of foundationwear. A good example of this comes from a Fashion 101 article from *In Style* Magazine, October 2004 and is titled "Selecting the Right Body Shaper." The introduction to the article reads:

> No garment can whittle a body down two sizes, but today's shapewear *will* help you look better in your clothes. Firm-control tummy toners can flatten the abdomen, giving you a sleek, fit look, while full-body shapewear can smooth out bulges or provide an antijiggle foundation for formfitting clothing. Recent improvements include strong but lightweight fabrics that breathe (no more sweating in girdlelike garments), seamless construction (bye-bye, telltale lines), and new silhouettes like bike-pants thigh slimmers and spaghetti-strap control slips. (*In Style*, October 2004, 256)

The fetishized object is fashion's ideal body, and these contemporary shapers promise to resolve the problem body—"to smooth out bulges or provide an antijiggle foundation." This Fashion 101 example underscores not only the desire for fashion's ideal body, but the desire to solve the problem body, the flawed American woman's body. It also illustrates the longevity of the cult of thinness and the consequent girdle resurgence in the form of contemporary shapewear (even if there is a distancing from the g-word through the use of technological advances such as improved microfiber fabrics).

Table 7.1.   Big Four Foundationwear Corporations and Brands

BIG FOUR FOUNDATIONWEAR CORPORATIONS & BRANDS			
Warnaco	*Sara Lee*	*VF Corporation*	*Maidenform Worldwide*
Warner's	Bali	Vanity Fair	Maidenform
Calvin Klein	Playtex	Vassarette	Flexees
LeJaby	Wonderbra	Bestform	Lilyette
Olga	Barely There	Lily of France	Sweet Nothings
Olga's Christina	Hanes	Curvation	Self Expressions
BodySlimmers	Lovable	Tommy Hilfiger	Rendezvous
Axcelerate	Gossard		Bodymates
	Un-d's		Subtract

When I began this project in the spring of 1999, I could not have predicted the evolution of shapewear into the new millennium. Nonetheless, the trend has continued.[5] Another example of the proliferation of shapewear in mainstream culture comes from the "Style File" from *In Style* Magazine, November 2006 and is titled "Fashion Prop Kit: Shape Up (Instantly!)." The introduction to the product line reads, "These secret weapons lift, tighten and give you all the right curves" (*In Style* November 2006, 186). The Style File profiles a Hip Slip described as "A deft mixture of spandex and nylon [that] makes this possibly the finest chemise of all time" thus high-lighting the effects of new technology on producing a better fitting, better working, shaping garment (2006, 186). This technological advancement is part of the culture of improvement and yet another dimension of commodity fetishism.[6] The "Style File" also recommends the Thigh Toner. The text reads, "These mid-thigh shapers provide extra toning as well as a smooth line under the skimpiest of pieces" (2006, 186). Once again the focus is on improving the body, using the newest technology, the latest in shapewear. The fetishistic desire for a flabless gym-honed body is exploited by foundationwear manufacturers who employ the discourses of improved technology, colorful fabrics and fashion's ideal body to sell new shapewear lines.

In this way contemporary foundation garments shape not only the bodies of American women, but shape the subjectivities of American women particularly within fashion and beauty cultures. While the practices of girdling were certainly more monolithic and intrusive than the recommendations for shapewear found in contemporary magazines, there has been a proliferation of the "Fashion 101" and "Fashion Emergency" discourses in popular media in the last decade with entire television programs dedicated to fashion and beauty makeovers. In fact, even the negative prescriptives found in early discourses of girdling have cropped up in television programs such as TLC's *What Not to Wear* and Entertainment Television's *Fashion Emergency*. The discourses of these programs and fashion magazines confirm the use of women's bodies as a locus of social control. Prescriptives for shaping and smoothing the body with the right foundationwear and articulations of fashion don'ts with regard to women's bodies perpetuate the identities of American women as consummate consumers, as desiring subjects in pursuit of fashion's ideal body.

Survey and Interview Findings

Although many American women may pursue fashion's ideal body, they negotiate what they are willing to do to achieve this goal. In this way, pursuing shapewear as an option for body augmentation is arguably preferable to plastic surgery options such as liposuction, breast implants, or tummy tucks. Women who participated in surveys and interviews for this project recognized that women's value in society is often equated with their bodies; however, these same women overwhelmingly identified the standards for ideal beauty and fashion's ideal body as Eurocentric, racist, classicist and ageist and ableist.[7] While many women acknowledge that they are not happy with their bodies, and that foundation garments help them to be happier with their bodies, few women describe themselves as being caught in a cycle of the beauty myth. Most women measure their bodies against the standard of the ideal body and can explain how their bodies fail to meet the standard. Still, they do not describe themselves as caught or trapped in the pursuit of idealized womanhood. However, almost every woman interviewed became uncomfortable when asked about their bodies' physical capacities. They did not seem to want to discuss the object/subject dilemma that continues to circulate in feminist discourse. Discussions of bodily appearance versus physical capacities fell flat, in spite of the fact that many women openly disagreed with objectified images of women in popular media. However, it is important to note that when surveyed, 76 percent of women strongly agreed and 15 percent of women somewhat agreed with the statement that: The fashion industry places unrealistic demands on women's bodies.[8] It is also important to note the extent to which fashion has become one of the most contested cultural terrains. The fashion industry is at the center of this contestation with regard to fashion's ideal body, but the industry is supported not only through commodity fetishism fueled by the mass media, but also through social institutions such as the church and the family, through traditional patriarchal ideals of femininity and the gendered division of labor, through white supremacist notions of ideal beauty, and through cultural practices and values that reinforce these power structures. The complex intersection of social, cultural, political and economic factors all shape the bodies of American women.

Ideal womanhood, ideal femininity, dress codes, and even religious rituals affect American women's subjectivities, but even amidst these force relations, women seek individualized identities and their own subjectivities. In this way cultural dupe and celebratory models[9] of commodification are inadequate to express women's experience at the level of the lived body. Thus, it is imperative that women's lived accounts and embodied experiences become central to this type of exploration. It is the work of this project to confront the complex conditions of women's lived experience, raise awareness of these conditions and to articulate ways in which women may benefit from the individual and collective struggles of other women as they reach out toward other bodily liberties. As Guy, Green and Banim argue, "women become not only the consumers of clothes, but the consumers of the meaning and promise of idealized womanhood" (2001, 6). This has been the point of this project, to interrogate the meaning and promise of idealized womanhood as they are articulated in the production and consumption of foundation garments. Listening to the voices of women as they experienced their bodies within and without foundationwear clarified and altered theories of female embodiment.

Recognizing the rituals and practices of wearing foundation garments enables us to identify the intricate connections between cultural requirements of femininity and these effects on women's lives. Delving into areas of the individual and social body, we can become more aware of the struggle women engage in as they strive to fit their own bodies into frames of idealized womanhood. I am mindful, however, not to suggest that women are merely victims of fashion or that they do not contribute to the production of their roles as consumers of idealized womanhood, but as Beauvoir, Hennessy, hooks and so many others suggest, women's roles as consumers carry with them a certain responsibility. It is in this space where my research lands up at the point where we must take charge of our limited and albeit conflicted agency in our consumption of the meanings and promises of foundationwear that proffer the perfect union of the ideal body and idealized womanhood. It is up to us to use the transformative and productive capacities of our bodies to reach out toward other liberties, to shed our old skins, to cut out new clothes and to destroy the myth of woman = body.

My conclusions coincide with much feminist work, which claims that women must see through the ideology of dominant ideal beauty, but I also suggest that women must remember to value themselves in terms of their bodily capacities. Casting off the trappings of femininity is not enough. It may be a first step. Some women who wear foundations may in fact value their bodily capacities more than others may. My prescriptive is for women to actively engage and revel in the capacities of their bodies. Raising consciousness regarding the consumption of the promises and meanings of idealized womanhood remains a constant in almost all feminist work. It should be followed with more women-centered research. Feminist researchers have an obligation to let women speak, and in this way to catapult women's voices to the fore of their research and their findings. I maintain that raising consciousness through communication and shared experience of the lived body is the clearest path to social change.

NOTES

1. For more on oppression and resistance in fashion and beauty cultures, see Peiss 1998; Warwick and Cavallaro 1998; Poulton 1997; Melinkoff 1984; Weitz 1998; Scranton 2001; Benstock and Ferris 1994.

2. See chapter 6 and hooks 1992a, 148.

3. See also Fields *An Intimate Affair: Women, Lingerie and Sexuality* 2007.

4. BodySlimmers was purchased by Warnaco, one of the Big Four shapewear giants.

5. For projections of foundation garment sales, see chapter 1, table 1.1.

6. See chapter 1, page 1: quotation from Fields 1997.

7. See Morgan 1998 for a discussion of how plastic surgery is male-supremacist, racist, ageist, heterosexist, anti-Semitic, ableist and class-biased.

8. See appendix A, variable v42.

9. See chapter 5; McRobbie 1999; and Adorno and Horkheimer 1987.

Appendix A: Telephone Survey Variables and Frequencies

tab v4

Who helped you pick first	Freq.	Percent	Cum.
Mother	174	65.17	65.17
Father	2	0.75	65.92
Sister	8	3.00	68.91
Girlfriend	5	1.87	70.79
Other	74	27.72	98.50
DK	3	1.12	99.63
Ref	1	0.37	100.00
Total	267	100.00	

. tab v5

Slimmers,shapers or smoothers	Freq.	Percent	Cum.
Yes	46	17.23	17.23
No	219	82.02	99.25
98	2	0.75	100.00
Total	267	100.00	

. tab v6

Push-up bras	Freq.	Percent	Cum.
Yes	78	29.21	29.21
No	189	70.79	100.00
Total	267	100.00	

(continued)

151

. tab v7

Non-underwire bras	Freq.	Percent	Cum.
Yes	158	59.18	59.18
No	109	40.82	100.00
Total	267	100.00	

. tab v8

Control-top pantyhose	Freq.	Percent	Cum.
Yes	156	58.43	58.43
No	110	41.20	99.63
98	1	0.37	100.00
Total	267	100.00	

. tab v9

Shaping panties	Freq.	Percent	Cum.
Yes	50	18.73	18.73
No	215	80.52	99.25
98	2	0.75	100.00
Total	267	100.00	

. tab v10

Type unmentioned	Freq.	Percent	Cum.
Yes	49	18.35	18.35
No	218	81.65	100.00
Total	267	100.00	

. tab v11

Wearing frequency	Freq.	Percent	Cum.
Special	78	29.21	29.21
Monthly	4	1.50	30.71
Weekly	36	13.48	44.19
Everyday	136	50.94	95.13
Other	9	3.37	98.50
DK	3	1.12	99.63
Ref	1	0.37	100.00
Total	267	100.00	

. tab v12

Earlier period	Freq.	Percent	Cum.
Yes	109	40.82	40.82
No	157	58.80	99.63
98	1	0.37	100.00
Total	267	100.00	

. tab v13

Corset	Freq.	Percent	Cum.
Yes	11	9.73	9.73
No	102	90.27	100.00
Total	113	100.00	

. tab v14

Corselette	Freq.	Percent	Cum.
Yes	5	4.42	4.42
No	108	95.58	100.00
Total	113	100.00	

. tab v15

Long-line bras	Freq.	Percent	Cum.
Yes	23	20.54	20.54
No	89	79.46	100.00
Total	112	100.00	

. tab v16

Girdle	Freq.	Percent	Cum.
Yes	76	67.86	67.86
No	36	32.14	100.00
Total	112	100.00	

. tab v17

Open-bottom girdle	Freq.	Percent	Cum.
Yes	29	37.18	37.18
No	48	61.54	98.72
98	1	1.28	100.00
Total	78	100.00	

. tab v18

Panty girdle	Freq.	Percent	Cum.
Yes	64	82.05	82.05
No	12	15.38	97.44
98	2	2.56	100.00
Total	78	100.00	

. tab v19

Boy-leg girdle	Freq.	Percent	Cum.
Yes	26	33.33	33.33
No	49	62.82	96.15
98	3	3.85	100.00
Total	78	100.00	

(*continued*)

. tab v22

Feel feminine with	Freq.	Percent	Cum.
Stg Agr	52	19.48	19.48
Some Agr	115	43.07	62.55
Some Dis	52	19.48	82.02
Stg Dis	45	16.85	98.88
DK	2	0.75	99.63
Ref	1	0.37	100.00
Total	267	100.00	

. tab v23

Feel exposed without	Freq.	Percent	Cum.
Stg Agr	45	16.85	16.85
Some Agr	55	20.60	37.45
Some Dis	59	22.10	59.55
Stg Dis	107	40.07	99.63
Ref	1	0.37	100.00
Total	267	100.00	

. tab v24

Others find me more attractive with	Freq.	Percent	Cum.
Stg Agr	47	17.60	17.60
Some Agr	73	27.34	44.94
Some Dis	49	18.35	63.30
Stg Dis	66	24.72	88.01
DK	31	11.61	99.63
Ref	1	0.37	100.00
Total	267	100.00	

. tab v25

Enjoy wearing	Freq.	Percent	Cum.
Stg Agr	59	22.10	22.10
Some Agr	79	29.59	51.69
Some Dis	45	16.85	68.54
Stg Dis	79	29.59	98.13
DK	3	1.12	99.25
Ref	2	0.75	100.00
Total	267	100.00	

. tab v26

Feel Sexy with	Freq.	Percent	Cum.
Stg Agr	49	18.35	18.35
Some Agr	95	35.58	53.93
Some Dis	49	18.35	72.28
Stg Dis	66	24.72	97.00
DK	7	2.62	99.63
Ref	1	0.37	100.00
Total	267	100.00	

. tab v27

Clothes look better with	Freq.	Percent	Cum.
Stg Agr	127	47.39	47.39
Some Agr	95	35.45	82.84
Some Dis	22	8.21	91.04
Stg Dis	21	7.84	98.88
DK	2	0.75	99.63
Ref	1	0.37	100.00
Total	268	100.00	

. tab v28

Am comfortable with	Freq.	Percent	Cum.
Stg Agr	132	49.25	49.25
Some Agr	85	31.72	80.97
Some Dis	27	10.07	91.04
Stg Dis	23	8.58	99.63
Ref	1	0.37	100.00
Total	268	100.00	

. tab v29

Move freely with	Freq.	Percent	Cum.
Stg Agr	125	46.64	46.64
Some Agr	97	36.19	82.84
Some Dis	25	9.33	92.16
Stg Dis	18	6.72	98.88
DK	2	0.75	99.63
Ref	1	0.37	100.00
Total	268	100.00	

(continued)

. tab v30

Most women wear shaping garments	Freq.	Percent	Cum.
Stg Agr	156	56.12	56.12
Some Agr	79	28.42	84.53
Some Dis	22	7.91	92.45
Stg Dis	9	3.24	95.68
DK	12	4.32	100.00
Total	278	100.00	

. tab v31

All women look better with	Freq.	Percent	Cum.
Stg Agr	58	20.86	20.86
Some Agr	70	25.18	46.04
Some Dis	83	29.86	75.90
Stg Dis	60	21.58	97.48
DK	7	2.52	100.00
Total	278	100.00	

. tab v32

Without women jiggle	Freq.	Percent	Cum.
Stg Agr	81	29.14	29.14
Some Agr	88	31.65	60.79
Some Dis	62	22.30	83.09
Stg Dis	34	12.23	95.32
DK	13	4.68	100.00
Total	278	100.00	

. tab v33

Today's garments don't limit movement	Freq.	Percent	Cum.
Stg Agr	69	24.82	24.82
Some Agr	112	40.29	65.11
Some Dis	44	15.83	80.94
Stg Dis	33	11.87	92.81
DK	18	6.47	99.28
Ref	2	0.72	100.00
Total	278	100.00	

. tab v34

All women need to wear	Freq.	Percent	Cum.
Stg Agr	38	13.67	13.67
Some Agr	48	17.27	30.94
Some Dis	73	26.26	57.19
Stg Dis	116	41.73	98.92
DK	2	0.72	99.64
Ref	1	0.36	100.00
Total	278	100.00	

. tab v35

Women give up freedom for looks	Freq.	Percent	Cum.
Stg Agr	30	10.79	10.79
Some Agr	82	29.50	40.29
Some Dis	93	33.45	73.74
Stg Dis	59	21.22	94.96
DK	12	4.32	99.28
Ref	2	0.72	100.00
Total	278	100.00	

. tab v36

Women wear to mask flaws	Freq.	Percent	Cum.
Stg Agr	123	44.24	44.24
Some Agr	111	39.93	84.17
Some Dis	32	11.51	95.68
Stg Dis	8	2.88	98.56
DK	3	1.08	99.64
Ref	1	0.36	100.00
Total	278	100.00	

. tab v37

Make women sexier	Freq.	Percent	Cum.
Stg Agr	35	12.59	12.59
Some Agr	109	39.21	51.80
Some Dis	61	21.94	73.74
Stg Dis	56	20.14	93.88
DK	15	5.40	99.28
Ref	2	0.72	100.00
Total	278	100.00	

(continued)

. tab v38

Most women should wear	Freq.	Percent	Cum.
Stg Agr	51	18.35	18.35
Some Agr	71	25.54	43.88
Some Dis	70	25.18	69.06
Stg Dis	80	28.78	97.84
DK	5	1.80	99.64
Ref	1	0.36	100.00
Total	278	100.00	

. tab v42

Fashion industry demands	Freq.	Percent	Cum.
Stg Agr	211	75.90	75.90
Some Agr	42	15.11	91.01
Some Dis	10	3.60	94.60
Stg Dis	9	3.24	97.84
DK	5	1.80	99.64
Ref	1	0.36	100.00
Total	278	100.00	

. tab v43

Help women keep up with demands	Freq.	Percent	Cum.
Stg Agr	62	22.30	22.30
Some Agr	153	55.04	77.34
Some Dis	33	11.87	89.21
Stg Dis	23	8.27	97.48
DK	6	2.16	99.64
Ref	1	0.36	100.00
Total	278	100.00	

. tab v44

Marital status	Freq.	Percent	Cum.
Mar	136	48.92	48.92
Div	22	7.91	56.83
Sep	2	0.72	57.55
Wid	17	6.12	63.67
Never	86	30.94	94.60
Other	14	5.04	99.64
Ref	1	0.36	100.00
Total	278	100.00	

. tab v39

Protect women's bodies	Freq.	Percent	Cum.
Stg Agr	21	7.55	7.55
Some Agr	76	27.34	34.89
Some Dis	80	28.78	63.67
Stg Dis	89	32.01	95.68
DK	11	3.96	99.64
Ref	1	0.36	100.00
Total	278	100.00	

. tab v40

Fashion requirement	Freq.	Percent	Cum.
Stg Agr	48	17.27	17.27
Some Agr	120	43.17	60.43
Some Dis	56	20.14	80.58
Stg Dis	50	17.99	98.56
DK	3	1.08	99.64
Ref	1	0.36	100.00
Total	278	100.00	

. tab v41

Achieve what nature didn't give	Freq.	Percent	Cum.
Stg Agr	48	17.27	17.27
Some Agr	128	46.04	63.31
Some Dis	49	17.63	80.94
Stg Dis	46	16.55	97.48
DK	3	1.08	98.56
Ref	4	1.44	100.00
Total	278	100.00	

. tab v45

Race	Freq.	Percent	Cum.
Nat Am	6	2.16	2.16
Black	12	4.32	6.47
Asian	5	1.80	8.27
Hispanic	9	3.24	11.51
White	236	84.89	96.40
> 1	2	0.72	97.12
Other	6	2.16	99.28
Ref	2	0.72	100.00
Total	278	100.00	

(*continued*)

. tab v48

Income	Freq.	Percent	Cum.
-20k	32	11.51	11.51
20-40k	50	17.99	29.50
40-60k	38	13.67	43.17
60-80k	43	15.47	58.63
80-100k	33	11.87	70.50
100+k	15	5.40	75.90
DK	8	2.88	78.78
Ref	59	21.22	100.00
Total	278	100.00	

. tab v49

Class	Freq.	Percent	Cum.
Upper	18	6.47	6.47
Middle	185	66.55	73.02
Working	66	23.74	96.76
Lower	3	1.08	97.84
DK	1	0.36	98.20
Ref	5	1.80	100.00
Total	278	100.00	

Appendix B:
Maidenform Survey 1959

Appendix B Maidenform Survey 1959

1. Which one type of brassiere do you most regularly wear at the present time?

   Padded ☐   Unpadded ☐

2. The last time you purchased a brassiere, did it come in an individual package or was it unpackaged?

   Packaged ☐   Unpackaged ☐

3. What was the brand of the last brassiere you purchased?   Brand_____

   (write in)

4. Following are four statements which deal with the type of brassiere you could prefer for everyday wear and/or dress up wear.....check the one (1) statement which best describes the brassiere you prefer for everyday wear and for dress up wear.

	Everyday Brassiere (check 1)	Dress Up Brassiere (check 1)
1. Brassiere which has no embroidery, practically no stitching on cup	☐	☐
2. Brassiere which is partly embroidered, practically no stitching on cup	☐	☐
3. Brassiere which is entirely embroidered, practically no stitching on cup	☐	☐
4. Brassiere with a stitched cup, no embroidery	☐	☐

4a. The following table shows a list of fabrics brassiere cups come in.....
Write in your 1st and 2nd choice of fabric for the brassiere you checked for everyday wear and dress up wear in the question above.

Fabric	Everyday Wear (1st and 2nd choice only)	Dress Up Wear (1st and 2nd choice only)
Cotton	_____	_____
Cotton & Dacron	_____	_____
Lace	_____	_____
Nylon	_____	_____
Cotton & Lace	_____	_____
Nylon & Lace	_____	_____
Cotton & Dacron blend & Lace	_____	_____

5. A brassiere manufacturer wants to make a garment that you are able to wear. (one which will be made in your size).....He has two types in mind which are described below:

   Type A: - A brassiere that could be worn by everyone (Mother, Aunt, older sister as well as yourself.
   Type B: - A brassiere which is designed specifically for the teen-ager and young adult only. (Check the type you would most likely purchase.)
   Type A: - Brassiere for everyone ☐
   Type B: - Brassiere for teen-ager or young adult only ☐

6. Have you worn a strapless brassiere in the past 12 months?   Yes ☐   No ☐

   The first six questions have dealt with the brassiere you are currently wearing.
   Now, lets go back to the first time you wore a brassiere.

   Was the first brassiere you wore?   Padded ☐   Unpadded ☐

Note: The number "7" was not used in original survey numbering.

8. Did the first brassiere you wear come   Packaged ☐   Unpackaged ☐

9. What was the brand of the first brassiere you wore? _____
                                                         (write in)

10. Where did you buy your first brassiere?

      Department store   ☐
      Specialty store in the major
      shopping area of your town   ☐
      A local specialty store   ☐
      Variety store 5 & 10¢   ☐
      Other _____
                  (specify)

10a. What was the name of the store and city and state where the store was located.

      Name of store _____ City _____ State _____

  b. If you checked "dept. store" in question 10, in which department of the store was your first brassiere
     purchased?

      Foundation/corset dept.   ☐
      Junior or teen dept.   ☐
      Notion department   ☐
      Main floor   ☐
      Basement   ☐
      Other _____
                  specify

11. In question 1 you checked the type of brassiere you most regularly wear now....in question 7 you checked
    the type of brassiere you first wore. If you have switched types that is: you now regularly wear a padded
    brassiere, yet your first was unpadded or vice-versa, please try to tell us why you switched.

    _____

12. Do you ever wear a girdle?   Yes ☐   No ☐

    If "No" _____ Why don't you wear a girdle? _____

    If "Yes"   a. What brand of girdle did you last purchase? _____
               b. About how much did this girdle cost? _____
               c. Was it a pantie or regular girdle?   Pantie ☐   Regular ☐

    General Information

    a. What size brassiere do you wear? (Please write in both numerical and letter description i.e., 36 AA,
       34 A, 36 B, etc. _____
                          (write in size you wear)

    b. Check the size of girdle you wear?
                          Extra small ☐   Large   ☐
                          Small   ☐   Extra Large ☐
                          Medium   ☐

    c. How tall are you? feet _____ inches _____

    d. How old are you? years _____ months _____

Appendix C:
Maidenform "I dreamed" Ads

1949 I dreamed I went shopping (walking with shopping bag)
1949 I dreamed I went shopping (seated with mirror)
1949 I dreamed I went strolling
1949 I dreamed I went skating
1949 I dreamed I went cycling
1950 I dreamed I danced a ballet
1950 I dreamed I danced the Charleston
1950 I dreamed I had a screen test
1950 I dreamed I lived on the moon
1950 I dreamed I was bewitching (witch's hat & broom)
1950 I dreamed I went cruising
1950 I dreamed I went sightseeing
1950 I dreamed I went to the theater
1950 I dreamed I went to the zoo
1951 I dreamed I broke the bank in Monte Carlo
1951 I dreamed I got caught in the rain
1951 I dreamed I had a lovelier figure
1951 I dreamed I sang Carmen
1951 I dreamed I starred on television
1951 I dreamed I was Cinderella
1951 I dreamed I was a Lady Ambassador
1951 I dreamed I was a lady editor (strange hat)
1951 I dreamed I was a mermaid
1951 I dreamed I was a toreador
1951 I dreamed I was an artist
1951 I dreamed I was bewitching

1951 I dreamed I was on television
1952 I dreamed I joined the circus
1952 I dreamed I led the Easter Parade
1952 I dreamed I opened the World Series
1952 I dreamed I played Cleopatra
1952 I dreamed I rode a street car
1952 I dreamed I stopped at a Sidewalk Café
1952 I dreamed I stopped traffic
1952 I dreamed I was bewitching—Genie
1952 I dreamed I was given the keys to the city
1952 I dreamed I went skiing
1952 I dreamed I went to the races
1952 I dreamed I won the election
1953 I dreamed I arrived in Paris
1953 I dreamed I rode a gondola
1953 I dreamed I went on a tiger hunt
1953 I dreamed I lived like a Queen
1953 I dreamed I rode a roller coaster
1953 I dreamed I was a fireman
1953 I dreamed I was sawed in half
1953 I dreamed I was the queen of hearts
1953 I dreamed I was voted best dressed
1953 I dreamed I went square dancing
1953 I dreamed I went to the circus
1953 I dreamed I went to the flower show
1953 I dreamed I won an academy award
1954 I dreamed I danced the hours away
1954 I dreamed I flew a kite
1954 I dreamed I played lawn tennis
1954 I dreamed I sailed for Europe
1954 I dreamed I was a cigar store Indian
1954 I dreamed I was a jack-in-the-box
1954 I dreamed I was a living doll
1954 I dreamed I was a private eye
1954 I dreamed I was an Eskimo
1954 I dreamed I went on a safari
1954 I dreamed I went to a masquerade
1954 I dreamed I went to the opera
1955 I dreamed I lived in a house of mirrors
1955 I dreamed contest entry
1955 I dreamed I climbed the highest mountain

1955 I dreamed I rode a magic carpet
1955 I dreamed I went to see "Silk Stockings"
1955 I dreamed I went to see "The French Comedy"
1955 I dreamed I went to see Maurice Chevalier's "Songs and Impressions"
1955 I dreamed I was a designing woman
1955 I dreamed I was a mad hatter
1955 I dreamed I was a social butterfly
1955 I dreamed I was a valentine
1955 I dreamed I was queen of the westerns
1955 I dreamed I went back to school
1955 I dreamed I went to see "Plain and Fancy"
1955 I dreamed I went to see "The Boyfriend"
1955 I dreamed I went to see "Fanny"
1955 I dreamed I went to see "Can-Can"
1955 I dreamed I went to see "The Vamp"
1955 I dreamed I went up in a balloon
1955 I dreamed I was Venus De Milo
1956 I dreamed I had spring fever
1956 I dreamed I went to see "The Lark"
1956 I dreamed I went to see "No Time for Sergeants"
1956 I dreamed I was a work of art
1956 I dreamed I went to see the "Damn Yankees"
1956 I dreamed I was an international figure
1956 I dreamed I was being followed
1956 I dreamed I was twins
1956 I dreamed I went whistle stopping
1957 I dreamed I crashed the headlines
1957 I dreamed I had tea for two
1957 I dreamed I played chess
1957 I dreamed I posed for a fashion ad
1957 I dreamed I raced with the wind
1957 I dreamed I was a Jigsaw Puzzle
1957 I dreamed I was lost in a London Fog
1957 I dreamed I was an outdoor girl
1958 I dreamed I made an impression
1958 I dreamed I made sweet music
1958 I dreamed I was a midsummer night's dream
1958 I dreamed I was made over
1959 I dreamed I accentuated the positive
1959 I dreamed I got a lift
1959 I dreamed I looked in a mirror (relates to "and saw myself")

1959 and saw myself (relates to "looked in a mirror")
1959 I dreamed I was a heavenly body
1959 I dreamed I was tied to the telephone 25 hours a day
1959 I dreamed I sang a duet at the met
1959 and a solo (refers to sang a duet at the met)
1959 I dreamed I set a record
1959 I dreamed I was bookends
1960 I dreamed I conducted myself beautifully
1960 I dreamed I covered the Paris Collections
1960 I dreamed I played in an all-girl orchestra
1960 I dreamed I was a beauty shop quartet
1960 I dreamed I was a lady editor
1960 I dreamed I was a medieval maiden
1960 I dreamed I was a real dish
1960 I dreamed I was a vamp
1960 I dreamed I was cut out for fun
1960 I dreamed I was enchanted
1960 I dreamed I was sugar and spice and everything nice
1960 I dreamed I was wanted
1960 I dreamed the leaves fell for me
1961 I dreamed I was arrested for indecent exposure
1961 I dreamed I bowled them over
1961 I dreamed I drove them wild
1961 I dreamed I flipped
1961 I dreamed I had a stylish carriage
1961 I dreamed I walked a tight rope
1961 I dreamed I was a knockout
1961 I dreamed I was a siren
1961 I dreamed I was an autograph hound
1962 I dreamed I barged down the Nile
1962 I dreamed I barged down the Nile (British Version)
1962 I dreamed I caught the brass ring
1962 I dreamed I charmed the spots off a leopard
1962 I dreamed I stole the show
1962 I dreamed I stopped them in their tracks
1962 I dreamed I took the bull by the horns
1962 I dreamed I was a trademark
1962 I dreamed I was all decked out
1962 I dreamed I was tickled pink
1963 I dreamed I cheered the team on
1963 I dreamed I had a swinging time

1963 I dreamed I painted the town red
1963 I dreamed I swayed the jury
1963 I dreamed I took the cue
1963 I dreamed I was the center of attention
1963 I dreamed I was wild in the West
1963 I dreamed I went to blazes
1964 I dreamed I was way out
1964 I dreamed I went to work
1964 I dreamed I won a college scholarship
1965 Who is that dream in the Maidenform Swim Suit?
1965 I dreamed I lived in a castle in Spain
1965 I dreamed I switched on the stars
1965 I dreamed I was a classic beauty
1964 I dreamed Paris was at my feet
1965 This is the dream you can be (Let yourself show)
1966 I dreamed I turned on the magic of Venice
1966 This is the dream you can be (You'll never yank at a girdle again)
1967 I dreamed I had the world on a string (lime green bell bottoms)
1967 I dreamed I had a mod mod world on a string
1967 I dreamed I had the world on a string (half slip and bra)
1968 I dreamed I was a new dimension color
1968 I dreamed I was a new dimension in action
1968 I dreamed I was a new dimension in POW
1968 I dreamed I was a new dimension in shape
1968 I dreamed I was a real cool treat
1968 I dreamed I was a sketch
1968 I dreamed I was here and there
1968 I dreamed I swung to a new beat
1969 I dreamed I felt free
1969 I dreamed I felt free, really free
1969 I dreamed I looked shapely at any angle
1969 I dreamed I made more of myself
1969 I dreamed I shaped up in an instant
1969 I dreamed I stretched from here to there
1969 I dreamed I was somewhere over the rainbow
1969 I dreamed it's me
1969 I dreamed there was no end to me

Bibliography

Adorno, Theodor and Max Horkheimer. "The Culture Industry: Enlightenment as Mass Deception." *Dialectic of Enlightenment*. New York: Continuum, 1987. [1944]

Althusser, Louis. "Ideology and Ideological State Apparatus." *For Marx*. New York: Vintage, 1970.

Armstrong, Pat and M. Patricia Connelly, eds. *Feminism, Political Economy and the State: Contested Terrain*. Toronto: Canadian Scholars Press, 1999.

Arnold, Rebecca. *Fashion, Desire and Anxiety: Image and Morality in the 20th Century*. New Brunswick, NJ: Rutgers University Press, 2001.

Ash, Juliet and Elizabeth Wilson, eds. *Chic Thrills: A Fashion Reader*. Berkeley: University of California Press, 1992.

Aubry, Erin J. "The Butt." *Body Outlaws: Young Women Write about Body Image and Identity*, edited by Ophira Edut. Seattle: Seal, 2000.

Banner, Lois. *American Beauty*. New York: Alfred A. Knopf, 1983.

Barthes, Roland. *Elements of Semiology*. 21st Printing. New York: Hill and Wang, 1999.

———. *The Fashion System*. Berkeley: University of California Press, 1983.

———. *Mythologies*. Trans. Annette Lavers. New York: Hill and Wang, 1972.

Bartky, Sandra. *Femininity and Domination: Studies in the Phenomenology of Oppression*. New York: Routledge, 1990.

———. "Foucault, Femininity, and the Modernization of Patriarchal Power." *Feminism and Foucault: Reflections on Resistance*, edited by Irene Diamond and Lee Quinby. Boston: Northeastern University Press, 1988.

Baudrillard, Jean. *For a Critique of the Political Economy of the Sign*. Trans. and Intro. by Charles Levin. St. Louis: Telos Press, Ltd., 1981.

Beauvoir, Simone de. *The Second Sex*. New York: Vantage, 1989.

Benstock, Shari and Suzanne Ferris, eds. *Footnotes: On Shoes*. New Brunswick, NJ: Rutgers University Press, 2001.

———, eds. *On Fashion*. New Brunswick, NJ: Rutgers University Press, 1994.

Bordo, Susan. *Unbearable Weight: Feminism, Western Culture, and the Body*. Berkeley: University of California Press, 1993.

Bourdieu, Pierre. *The Logic of Practice*. Stanford, CA: Stanford UP, 1990.

———. *Masculine Domination*. Stanford, CA: Stanford UP, 2001.

———. *Outline of a Theory of Practice*. Cambridge: Cambridge UP, 1977.

Brennan, Teresa. "A Structural Connection among Race, Gender, Class." *Gender and Political Economy*, edited by Ellen Mutari, Heather Boushey, and William Fraher IV. London: ME Sharpe, 1997.

Bressler, Karen W., Karoline Newman, and Gillian Proctor. *A Century of Lingerie*. Edison, NJ: Chartwell Books, 1997.

Brumberg, Joan Jacobs. *The Body Project: An Intimate History of American Girls*. New York: Random House, 1997.

Bruzzi, Stella and Pamela Church Gibson, eds. *Fashion Cultures: Theories, Explorations and Analysis*. London: Routledge, 2000.

Burton-Nelson, Mariah. *Are We Winning Yet? How Women are Changing Sports and Sports are Changing Women*. New York: Random House, 1991.

Butler, Judith. *Bodies that Matter: On the Discursive Limits of "Sex."* New York: Routledge, 1993.

———. "The Body Politics of Julia Kristeva." *Hypatia* 3, no. 3(Winter 1989): 104–117.

———. *Excitable Speech*. New York: Routledge, 1997.

———. "Foucault and the Paradox of Bodily Inscriptions." *The Journal of Philosophy* 86, no. 11 (November 1989): 601–614.

———. "Gender as Performance: An Interview with Judith Butler." *Radical Philosophy* 67, no. 3(Summer 1994): 32–39.

———. *Gender Trouble*. Revised edition. New York: Routledge, 1999.

———. "Gendering the Body: Beauvoir's Philosophical Contribution." *Women, Knowledge and Reality: Explorations in Feminist Philosophy*, edited by Ann Garry and Marilyn Pearsall. New York: Routledge, 1989.

———. "Imitation and Gender Insubordination." *Inside/Out: Lesbian Theories, Gay Theories*, edited by Diana Fuss. New York: Routledge, 1991.

———. "On Speech, Race and Melancholia: An Interview with Judith Butler." *Theory, Culture & Society* 16, no 2 (1999): 163–174.

———. "Variations on Sex and Gender: Beauvoir, Wittig and Foucault." *Feminism As Critique: On The Politics Of Gender*, edited by Seyla Behabib and Drucilla Cornell. Minneapolis: University of Minnesota Press, 1987.

Cahn, Susan. *Coming on Strong*. New York: The Free Press, 1994.

———. "From the 'Muscle Moll' to the 'Butch' Ballplayer: Mannishness, Lesbianism, and Homophobia in U.S. Women's Sports." *The Politics of Women's Bodies: Sexuality, Appearance, and Behavior*, edited by Rose Weitz. Oxford: University Press, 1998.

Coleman, Barbara J. "Maidenform(ed): Images of American Women in the 1950s," *Genders 21: Forming and Reforming Identity*, edited by Carol Siegel and Ann Kibbey. New York: New York UP, 1995.

Costa, D. M. and Guthrie S. R. *Women and Sport: Interdisciplinary Perspectives*. Champaign, IL: Human Kinetics, 1994.

Craik, Jennifer. *The Face of Fashion: Cultural Studies in Fashion*. London: Routledge, 1994.

Crane, Diana. *Fashion and Its Social Agendas*. Chicago: University of Chicago Press, 2000.

———. "Gender and Hegemony in Fashion Magazines: Women's Interpretations of Fashion Photographs." *The Sociological Quarterly* 40, no. 4 (1999): 541–563.

Creedon, Pamela J. *Women Media and Sport*. London: Sage, 1994.

Damon-Moore, Helen. *Magazines for the Millions*. Albany: SUNY Press, 1994.

Davis, Angela Y. "Afro Images: Politics, Fashion, and Nostalgia." *Critical Inquiry* 21, no. 2 (Autumn 1994): 37–45.

Davis, Fred. *Fashion, Culture, and Identity*. Chicago: University of Chicago Press, 1992.

Davis, Kathy. *Embodied Practices*. London: Sage, 1997.

———. *Reshaping the Female Body: The Dilemma of Cosmetic Surgery*. New York: Routledge, 1995.

De Lauretis, Teresa. "The Female Body and Heterosexual Presumption." *Semiotica*. 67, no. 3 (1987a): 259–279.

———. "The Lure of the Mannish Lesbian." *The Practice of Love: Lesbian Sexuality and Perverse Desire*. Bloomington: Indiana UP, 1994.

———. *Technologies of Gender: Essays on Theory, Film and Fiction*. Bloomington: Indiana UP, 1987b.

Duggan, Lisa and Kathleen McHugh." A Fem(me)inist Manifesto." *Women and Performance* 8, no. 2 (1996): 150–160. Special issue "Queer Acts," edited by José Munoz and Amanda Barrett.

Edut, Ophira, eds. *Body Outlaws*. Seattle: Seal Press, 2000.

Ehrenreich, Barbara and Deidre English, eds. *For Her Own Good: One Hundred Fifty Years of Experts' Advice to Women*. Garden City: Anchor Press, 1978.

Emberly, Julia. "The Fashion Apparatus and the Deconstruction of Postmodern Subjectivity." *Canadian Journal of Political and Social Theory* 11, no. 1–2 (1987): 38–50.

Engels, Frederick. *Origin of the Family, Private Property and the State*. New York: International, 1942. [1884]

Enstad, Nan. "Fashioning Political Identities: Cultural Studies and the Historical Construction of Political Subjects." *American Quarterly* 50, no. 4 (1998): 745–782.

Entwistle, Joanne. "'Power Dressing' and the Construction of the Career Woman." *Buy This Book: Studies in Advertising and Consumption*, edited by Mica Nava et al. London: Routledge, 1997.

———. *The Fashioned Body*. Cambridge: Polity Press, 2000.

Entwistle, Joanne and Elizabeth Wilson, eds. *Body Dressing*. Oxford: Berg, 2001.

Epstein, Julia and Kristina Straub. *Body Guards: The Cultural Politics of Gender Ambiguity*. New York: Routledge, 1991.

Ewen, Stuart. *Captains of Consciousness: Advertising and the Social Roots of Consumer Culture*. New York: McGraw-Hill, 1976.

Ewen, Stuart and Elizabeth Ewen. *Channels of Desire: Mass Images and the Shaping of American Consciousness*. New York: McGraw-Hill, 1982.

Ewing, Elizabeth. *Dress and Undress: A History of Women's Underwear*. New York: Drama Book Specialists, 1978.

——. *Everyday Dress: 1650–1900*. New York: Chelsea House Publishers, 1984.

——. *History of 20th Century Fashion*. 3rd Edition. Lanham, MD: Barnes & Noble, 1992.

Faludi, Susan. *Backlash: The Undeclared War against American Women*. New York: Crown, 1991.

Farrell-Beck, Jane and Colleen Gau. *Uplift: The Bra in America*. Philadelphia: University of Pennsylvania Press, 2002.

Faurschou, Gail. "Fashion and the Cultural Logic of Postmodernity." *Canadian Journal of Political and Social Theory* 11, no. 1–2 (1987): 68–82.

Fausto-Sterling, Ann. "The Five Sexes: Why Male and Female Are Not Enough." *The Sciences* 33, no. 1 (1993 March/April): 20–25.

——. *Myths of Gender: Biological Theories about Women and Men*. Revised edition. New York: Basic Books, 1992.

Featherstone, Mike, ed. *Body Modification*. London: Sage, 2000.

Featherstone, Mike, Mike Hepworth, and Brian S. Turner, eds. *The Body: Social Process and Cultural Theory*. London: Sage, 1991.

——. *Stone Butch Blues: A Novel*. New York: Firebrand, 1993.

Feinberg, Leslie. *Transgender Liberation: A Movement Whose Time Has Come*. New York: World View Forum, 1992.

——. *Transgender Warriors*. Boston: Beacon Press, 1996.

Ferguson, Marjorie and Peter Golding, eds. *Cultural Studies in Question*. Thousand Oaks, CA: Sage, 1997.

Festle, Mary Jo. *Playing Nice*. NY: Columbia UP, 1996.

——. *An Intimate Affair: Women, Lingerie and Sexuality*. Berkeley: University of California Press, 2007.

——. "Fighting the Corsetless Evil': Shaping Corsets and Culture," 1900–1930." *Journal of Social History* 33, no. 2 (1999): 355–384.

Fields, Jill. "The Production of Glamour: A Social History of Intimate Apparel, 1909–1952." Diss. USC, 1997.

Finch, Casey. "Hooked and Buttoned Together: Victorian Underwear and Representations of the Female Body." *Victorian Studies* 34, no. 1(Spring 1991): 337–363.

Fiske, John. "Down under Cultural Studies." *Cultural Studies* 10, no. 2 (1996): 369–374.

Fogarty, Anne. *Wife Dressing*. New York: Julian Messner, 1959.

Foucault, Michel. *Herculine Barbin: Being the Recently Discovered Memoirs of a Nineteenth-Century French Hermaphrodite*. Trans. by Richard McDougall. New York: Pantheon Books, 1980.

——. *Discipline and Punish*. New York: Vintage, 1995.

——. *History of Sexuality. Vol I*. New York: Vintage, 1990.

——. *History of Sexuality. Vol II*. New York: Vintage, 1990.

——. *History of Sexuality. Vol III*. New York: Vintage, 1990.

Fraad, Harriet, Stephen Resnick and Richard Wolff, eds. *Bringing It All Back Home: Class, Gender, and Power in the Modern Household*. London: Pluto Press, 1994.

Frader, Laura L. "Bringing Political Economy Back In: Gender, Culture, Race and Class in Labor History." *Social Science History* 22, no. 1 (1988): 21–55.

Frith, Katherine Toland, ed. *Undressing the Ad: Reading Culture in Advertising*. New York: Peter Lang, 1997.

Fuss, Diana. "Fashion and the Homo-spectatorial look." *Critical Inquiry* 18, no. 2(Summer 1992): 713–737.

Gaines, Jane and Charlotte Herzog, eds. *Fabrications: Costume and the Female Body*. New York: Routledge, 1990.

Gallop, Jane. *Thinking through the Body*. New York: Columbia UP, 1988.

Gamber, Wendy. *The Female Economy: The Millinery and Dressmaking Trades, 1860–1930*. Urbana, IL: University of Illinois Press, 1997.

Garnham, Nicholas. "Cultural Studies vs. Political Economy—Is Anyone Else Bored with This Debate? Reply to Grossberg and Carey." *Critical Studies in Mass Communication* 12, no. 1 (1995): 95–100.

———. "Political Economy and Cultural Studies: Reconciliation or Divorce?" *Critical Studies in Mass Communication* 12, no. 1 (1995): 62–71.

Gilroy, Susan. "The Embody-ment of Power: Gender and Physical Activity." *Leisure Studies* 8, no. 2 (1989): 163–172.

Gimlin, Debra L. *Body Work: Beauty and Self-Image in American Culture*. Berkeley: University of California Press, 2001.

Ginsberg, Elaine K, ed. *Passing and the Fictions of Identity*. Durham, NC: Duke UP, 1996.

Gluckman, Amy and Betsy Reed, eds. by *Homo economics: Capitalism, Community and Lesbian and Gay Life*. New York: Routledge, 1997.

Goffman, Erving. *Gender Advertisements*. New York: Harper & Row, 1979.

Gordon, Linda, ed. *Women, the State and Welfare*. Madison: University of Wisconsin Press, 1990.

Gramsci, Antonio. *Selections from the Prison Notebooks*. London: Lawrence and Wishart, 1971.

Green, Michael, "The Centre for Contemporary Cultural Studies." *Re-Reading English*, edited by Peter Widdowson. London: Methuen, 1982.

Griffin, Pat. *Strong Women, Deep Closets: Lesbians and Homophobia in Sport*. Champaign, IL: Human Kinetics, 1998.

Grossberg, Lawrence. "Cultural Studies vs. Political Economy: Is Anybody Else Bored with This Debate?" *Critical Studies in Mass Communication* 12, no. 1 (1995): 72–81.

Grosz, Elizabeth A. *Volatile Bodies: Toward a Corporeal Feminism*. Bloomington: Indiana UP, 1994.

Grosz, Elizabeth and Elspeth Probyn, eds. *Sexy Bodies: The Strange Carnalities of Feminism*. London: Routledge, 1995.

Guy, Ali, Eileen Green and Maura Banim. *Through the Wardrobe: Women's Relationships with Their Clothes*. Oxford: Berg, 2001.

Guy, Alison and Maura Banim. "Personal Collections: Women's Clothing Use and Identity." *Journal of Gender Studies* 9, no. 3 (November 2000): 313–327.

Haber, Honi Fern. "Body Politics and the Muscled Woman." *Feminist Interpretations of Michel Foucault*, edited by Susan Hekman. University Park: Penn State University Press, 1996.

———. "Muscles and Politics: Shaping the Feminist Revolt." *Exercising Power: The Making and Remaking of the Body*, edited by C. Cole and M. Mezner. Albany: SUNY, forthcoming.

Hale, Jacob. "Are Lesbians Women?" *Hypatia* 2, no. 2 (Spring 1996): 94–121.

Hall, Margaret Ann. *Feminism and Sporting Bodies*. Champaign, IL: Human Kinetics, 1996.

Hall, Stuart. "Cultural Studies and the Centre: Some Problematics and Problems." *Culture, Media, Language*, edited by S. Hall, D. Hobson, A. Lowe and P. Willis. London: Hutchinson, 1980, 15–47.

———. "Encoding/Decoding." *Culture, Media, Language*, edited by S. Hall, D. Hobson, A. Lowe and P. Willis. London: Hutchinson, 1980, 128–138.

———. "The Problem of Ideology: Marxism without Guarantees." *Marx: A Hundred Years On*, edited by B. Matthews. London: Lawrence and Wishart, 1983.

———. "Race, Articulation, and Societies Structured in Dominance." *Black British Cultural Studies: A Reader*, edited by Houston Baker, Manthia Diawara, and Roth H. Lindenborg. Chicago: University of Chicago Press, 1996.

Hall, Stuart and Tony Jefferson, eds. *Resistance through Rituals: Youth Subcultures in Post-War Britain*. London: Routledge, 1993 [1976].

Halprin, Sara. *Look at My Ugly Face: Myths and Musings on Beauty and Other Perilous Obsessions with Women's Appearance*. NY: Penguin, 1996.

Hanson, Karen. "Dressing Down Dressing Up—The Philosophic Fear of Fashion." *Hypatia* 5, no. 2(Summer 1990): 107–121.

Hargreaves, Jennifer. *Heroines of Sport*. London: Routledge, 2000.

———. *Sporting Females: Critical Issues in the History and Sociology of Women's Sports*. London: Routledge, 1994.

Hawthorne, Rosemary. *Stockings and Suspenders*. London: Souvenir Press, 1993.

Hebdige, Dick. *Cut 'n' Mix: Culture, Identity and Caribbean Music*. London: Comedia, 1987.

———. "From Culture to Hegemony." *The Cultural Studies Reader*, edited by Simon During. London: Routledge, 1993.

———. *Subculture: The Meaning of Style*. London: Routledge, 1978.

Hekman, Susan, ed. *Feminist Interpretations of Michel Foucault*. University Park: Pennsylvania State University Press, 1996.

Hennessy, Rosemary. *Profit and Pleasure*. New York: Routledge, 2000.

Hennessy, Rosemary and Chrys Ingram, eds. *Materialism Feminism: A Reader in Class, Difference, and Women's Lives*. New York: Routledge, 1997.

Heywood, Leslie. *Bodymakers: A Cultural Anatomy of Women's Body Building*. New Brunswick: Rutgers UP, 1998a.

———. *Pretty Good for a Girl*. New York: Free Press, 1998b.

Heywood, Leslie and Jennifer Drake. *Third Wave Agenda: Being Feminist Doing Feminism*. Minneapolis: University of Minnesota Press, 1997.

Heywood, Leslie and Shari Dworkin, eds. *Built to Win: The Female Athlete as Cultural Icon*. Minneapolis: University of Minnesota Press, 2003.

Hollander, Anne. *Seeing through Clothes*. New York: Viking, 1978.

Hong, Fan. *Footbinding, Feminism and Freedom*. Portland, OR: Frank Cass, 1997.

hooks, bell, ed. *Black Looks: Race and Representation*. Boston: South End, 1992.

——. "Is Paris Burning?" *Black Looks: Race and Representation*, edited by bell hooks. Boston: South End, 1992a.

——. "Selling Hot Pussy: Representations of Black Female Sexuality in the Cultural Marketplace." *Black Looks: Race and Representation*, edited by bell hooks. Boston: South End, 1992b.

"How We Dress." *American Scholar* 68, no. 1(Winter 1999): 10.

Howard, Vicki. "'At the Curve Exchange': Postwar Beauty Culture and Working Women at Maidenform." *Beauty and Business: Commerce, Gender, and Culture in Modern America*, edited by Philip Scranton. New York: Routledge, 2001.

Hoy, David Couzens. "Critical Resistance: Foucault and Bourdieu." *Perspectives on Embodiment*, edited by Gail Weiss and Honi Fern Haber. New York: Routledge, 1999.

Irigaray, Luce. *An Ethics of Sexual Difference*. Trans. by Carolyn Burke and Gillian C. Gill. Ithaca, NY: Cornell UP, 1993.

——. *This Sex Which Is Not One*. Trans. by Gillian C. Gill. Ithaca, NY: Cornell UP, 1985a.

——. *Speculum of the Other Woman*. Trans. by Gillian C. Gill. Ithaca, NY: Cornell UP, 1985b.

Jaggar, Alison M. and Iris Marion Young, eds. *A Companion to Feminist Philosophy*. Malden, MA: Blackwell, 1998.

Juffer, Jane. *At Home with Pornography: Women, Sex, and Everyday Life*. New York: New York UP, 1998.

——. "A Pornographic Femininity? Telling and Selling Victoria's (Dirty) Secrets." *Social Text* 14, no. 3 (1996): 27–48.

Kaiser, Susan. "Minding Appearances: Style, Truth and Subjectivity." *Body Dressing*, edited by Joanne Entwistle and Elizabeth Wilson. Oxford: Berg, 2001.

Keenan, William J. F., eds. *Dressed to Impress: Looking the Part*. Oxford: Berg, 2001.

Kennedy, Elizabeth Lapovsky, and Madelaine Davis. *Boots of Leather and Slippers of Gold: The History of a Lesbian Community*. New York: Routledge, 1993.

Kessler, Suzanne J., and Wendy McKenna. *Gender: An Ethnomethodological Approach*. Chicago: University of Chicago Press, 1990.

Kidwell, Claudia Brush and Valerie Steele, eds. *Men and Women: Dressing the Part*. Washington, D.C.: Smithsonian Institution Press, 1989.

Kilbourne, Jean. *Killing Us Softly 3: Advertising's Image of Women*. Media Education Foundation, 2000.

Kipnis, Laura. "(Male) Desire and (Female) Disgust: Reading Hustler." *Cultural Studies*, edited by Cary Nelson, Paula Treichler and Lawrence Grossberg. New York: Routledge, 1992, 373–389.

Kitch, Carolyn. *The Girl on the Magazine Cover: The Origins of Visual Stereotypes in American Mass Media*. Chapel Hill: The University of North Carolina Press, 2001.

Ko, Dorothy. *Every Step a Lotus: Shoes for Bound Feet*. Berkeley: University of California Press, 2001.

Kollontai, Alexandra. *Selected Writings of Alexandra Kollontai*, edited by Alix Holt. New York: Norton, 1977.

Kristeva, Julia. *Powers of Horror*. Trans. L. S. Roudiez. New York: Columbia University Press, 1982.

Kunzle, David. "Dress Reform as Antifeminism: A Response to Helene E. Roberts 'The Exquisite Slave: The role of Clothes in the Making of the Victorian Woman'." *Signs: Journal of Women in Culture and Society* 2, no. 3 (Spring 1977): 570–579.

———. *Fashion and Fetishism: A Social History of the Corset, Tight-Lacing and Other Forms of Body Sculpture in the West*. New Jersey: Rowman and Littlefield, 1982.

Lacan, Jacques. *Feminine Sexuality*, edited by Juliet Mitchell and Jacqueline Rose. New York: Norton, 1982.

Laclau, Ernesto and Chantal Mouffe. *Hegemony and Socialist Strategy: Towards a Radical Democratic Politics*. London: Verso, 1985.

Lancaster, Roger. *Life Is Hard: Machismo, Danger, and the Intimacy of Power in Nicaragua*. Berkeley: University of California Press, 1992.

———. *Thanks Be to God and the Revolution*. New York: Columbia University Press, 1988.

Lancaster, Roger N. and Micaela Di Leonardo, eds. *The Gender/Sexuality Reader: Culture, History Political Economy*. NY: Routledge, 1997.

Laqueur, Thomas. *Making Sex: Body and Gender from the Greeks to Freud*. Cambridge, MA: Harvard University Press, 1990.

Lauer, Jeanette C. and Robert Lauer. *Fashion Power: The Meaning of Fashion in American Society*. New Jersey: Prentice-Hall, 1981.

Lears, T. J. Jackson. *Fables of Abundance: A Cultural History of Advertising in America*. New York: Basic Books, 1994.

Leder, Drew. *The Absent Body*. Chicago: University of Chicago Press, 1990.

———. "Girl-friendly Sport and Female Values." *Women in Sport and Physical Activity Journal* 3, no.1 (Spring 1994): 35–45.

Lenskyj, Helen. *Out of Bounds: Women, Sport and Sexuality*. Toronto: Women's Press, 1986.

———. "Sport and the Threat to Gender Boundaries." *Sporting Traditions* 12, no. 1(November 1995): 47–60.

Leonardo, Micaela Di and Roger Lancaster. "Gender Sexuality, Political Economy." *New Politics* 5, no. 1 (Summer 1996): 29–43.

Lloyd, Moya. "Feminism, Aerobics and the Politics of the Body." *Body & Society* 2, no. 2 (1996): 79–98.

Lock, Margaret. "Cultivating the Body: Anthropology and Epistemologies of Bodily Practice and Knowledge." *Annual Review of Anthropology* 22 (1993): 133–155.

Lorber, Judith. "Believing Is Seeing." *The Politics of Women's Bodies: Sexuality, Appearance, and Behavior*, edited by Rose Weitz. New York: Oxford University Press, 1998.

———. Paradoxes of Gender. New Haven, CT: Yale UP, 1994.

Lorde, Audre. "The Master's Tools Will Never Dismantle the Master's House." *This Bridge Called My Back: Writings by Radical Women of Color*, edited by Gloria Anzaldua and Cherrie Moraga. NY: Kitchen Table, Women of Color Press, 1983.

Lynch, Annette. *Dress, Gender and Cultural Change: Asian American and African American Rites of Passage*. Oxford: Berg, 1999.

MacKinnon, Catharine A. "Desire and Power: A Feminist Perspective." *Marxism and the Interpretation of Culture*, edited by Cary Nelson and Lawrence Grossberg. Urbana: University of Illinois Press, 1988.

———. *Toward a Feminist Theory of the State*. Cambridge, MA: Harvard UP, 1989.

Marchand, Roland. *Advertising the American Dream: Making Way for Modernity, 1920–1940*. Berkeley: University of California Press, 1986.

Marx, Karl. *Capital*. Vol. 1. Intro. by Ernest Mandel. Trans. by Ben Fowkes. New York: Vintage Books, 1977. [1867]

———. *Capital: A Critique of Political Economy*. Vol. 2. Intro. by Ernest Mandel. Trans. by David Fernbach. London: Penguin Books, 1978. [1868]

———. *Economic and Philosophic Manuscripts of 1844*. Trans. by Martin Milligan. New York: Prometheus Books, 1988. [1930]

———. *The Eighteenth Brumaire of Louis Bonaparte. The Marx and Engel's Reader*, edited by Robert Tucker. 2nd Ed. New York: W. W. Norton and Company, 1978. [1852]

———. *The Grundrisse. The Marx and Engel's Reader*, edited by Robert Tucker. 2nd Ed. New York: W. W. Norton and Company, 1978. [1939]

———. *Preface to A Contribution to the Critique of Political Economy. Marxist Literary Theory, edited by* Terry Eagleton and Drew Milne. Cambridge, UK: Blackwell, 1996. [1859]

———. *Theses on Feuerbach. The Marx and Engel's Reader*, edited by Robert Tucker 2nd Ed. New York: W. W. Norton and Company, 1978. [1888]

Marx, Karl and Frederick Engels. "Manifesto of the Communist Party." *The Marx and Engel's Reader* edited by Robert Tucker. 2nd Ed. New York: W. W. Norton and Company, 1978. http://www.anu.edu.au/polsci/marx/classics/manifesto.html[1848].

Matthaei, Julie. *An Economic History of Women in America: Women's Work, the Sexual Division of Labor, and the Development of Capitalism*. New York: The Harvester Press, 1982.

———. "Surplus Labor, the Household, and Gender Oppression." *Rethinking Marxism* 2, no. 4 (1989): 70–78.

McRobbie, Angela. *Feminism and Youth Culture*. Boston: Unwin Hyman Inc., 1991.

———. *In the Culture Society: Art, Fashion and Popular Music*. London: Routledge, 1999.

———. "Post-Marxism and Cultural Studies: A Post-script." *Cultural Studies*, edited by Lawrence Grossberg, Cary Nelson and Paula A. Treichler. New York and London: Routledge, 1992: 719–730.

————. "Shut Up and Dance: Youth Culture and Changing Modes of Femininity." *Nordic Journal of Youth Research* 1, no. 2 (1993).

Melinkoff, Ellen. *What We Wore*. New York: Quill Publishing, 1984.

Merleau-Ponty, Maurice. *Phenomenology of perception*. London: Routledge & Kegan Paul Ltd., 1962.

Morgan, Kathryn Pauly. "Woman and the Knife." *The Politics of Women's Bodies: Sexuality, Appearance, and Behavior*, ed. Rose Weitz. New York: Oxford University Press, 1998.

Mulvagh, Jane. *Vogue: History of 20th Century Fashion*. New York: 1988.

Mutari, Ellen, Heather Boushey and William Fraher IV, eds. *Gender and Political Economy*. London: M.E. Sharpe, 1997.

Nelson, Carey and Lawrence Grossberg, eds. *Marxism and the Interpretation of Culture*. Urbana: University of Illinois Press, 1988.

Nicholson, Linda J. *Feminism/Postmodernism*. New York: Routledge, 1990.

Ong, Aihwa. *Spirits of Resistance and Capitalist Discipline*. Albany: SUNY Press, 1987.

Peiss, Kathy. *Hope in a Jar: The Making of America's Beauty Culture*. New York: Metropolitan Books, 1998.

Poulton, Terry. *No Fat Chicks: How Big Business Profits by Making Women Hate Their Bodies—and How to Fight Back*. Seacaucus, N.J.: Carol Publishing Group, 1997.

Presley, Ann Beth. "Fifty Years of Change; Societal Attitudes and Women's Fashions, 1900–1950." *The Historian* (Winter 1998): 307–324.

Rabine, Leslie W. "A Woman's Two Bodies: Fashion Magazines, Consumerism and Feminism." *On Fashion*, edited by Shari Benstock and Suzanne Ferriss. New Brunswick, NJ: Rutgers, 1994.

Roberts, Helene. "The Exquisite Slave: The Role of Clothes in the Making of the Victorian Woman." *Signs: Journal of Women in Culture and Society* 2, no. 3 (Spring 1977): 554–569.

Rosenberg, Justin. *The Follies of Globalisation Theory*. London: Verso, 2000.

Rubin, Gayle. "The Traffic in Women: Notes on the 'Political Economy' of Sex." *Toward an Anthropology of Women*, edited by Rayna R. Reiter. New York and London: Monthly Review Press, 1975.

————. "Sexual Traffic. Interview." *Feminism Meets Queer Theory*, edited by Elizabeth Weed and Naomi Schor. Bloomington: Indiana UP, 1997.

Salus, E. W. "Madonna, the Lingerie Look, and Postmodernism." *Semiotics* (October 1992): 143–148.

Scanlon, Jennifer. *The Ladies' Home Journal, Gender, and the Promises of Consumer Culture*. New York: Routledge, 1995.

Scranton, Philip, ed. *Beauty and Business: Commerce, Gender, and Culture in Modern America*. New York: Routledge, 2001.

Shiebinger, Londa. Nature's Body: *Gender in the Making of Modern Science*. Boston: Beacon Press, 1993.

Shoemaker, Leigh. "Part Animal, Part Machine. *Third Wave Agenda: Being Feminist, Doing Feminism*, edited by Leslie Heywood. Minneapolis: University of Minnesota Press, 1997.

Simmel, Georg. "Fashion." *On Individuality and Social Forms*, edited by Donald N. Levine. Chicago: University of Chicago Press, 1971 [1904].

Smith, Paul. *Discerning the Subject*. Minneapolis: U of Minn. Press, 1988.

——. Introduction to Cultural Studies course lecture, "Althusser's Repressive State Apparatus and Ideological State Apparatus," English 676. George Mason University, Fairfax, VA, 24 Sept 1996.

——. *Madonnarama: Essays on Sex and Popular Culture*. Pittsburgh, PA: Cleis Press, 1993.

——. *Millenial Dreams: Contemporary Capital in the North*. London:Verso, 1997.

Spalter-Roth, Roberta. *What Works! The Working Women Count Honor Roll Report*. Washington: U.S. Dept. of Labor, Women's Bureau, 1997.

Squiers, Carol. "Lingerie: A Brief History." *American Photo* 6, no. 5 (September–October 1995): 46–57.

Stabile, Carol. "Feminism without Guarantees: The Misalliances and Missed Alliances of Postmodernist Social Theory." *Marxism in the Postmodern Age: Confronting the New World Order*, edited by Antonio Callari, Stephen Cullenberg and Carole Biewener. New York: Guilford Press, 1995.

——. *Materialist Feminism and the Politics of Difference*. New York: Routledge, 1993.

——. ""Postmodernism, Feminism, and Marxism: Notes from the Abyss." *Monthly Review* 47, no. 3 (July/August 1995): 45–67.

Steele, Valerie. *The Corset: A Cultural History*. New Haven: Yale University Press, 2001.

——. *Fashion and Eroticism: Ideals of Feminine Beauty from the Victorian Era to the Jazz Age*. New York: Oxford University Press, 1985.

——. *Fetish: Fashion, Sex, and Power*. New York: Oxford University Press, 1996.

——. *Fifty Years of Fashion*. New Haven: Yale UP, 1997.

Steinem, Gloria. "The Politics of Muscle." *Moving beyond Words*, edited by Gloria Steinem. New York: Simon & Schuster, 1994.

Stull, James. "The Maidenform Campaigns: Reaffirming the Feminine Ideal." *Connecticut Review* 16, no. 2 (Spring 1992): 1–7.

Theberge, Nancy. *Higher Goals: Women's Ice Hockey and the Politics of Gender*. Albany: State University of New York Press, 2000.

Valdivia, Angharad N. "The Secret of My Desire: Gender, Class and Sexuality in Lingerie Catalogs." *Undressing the Ad: Reading Culture in Advertising*, edited by Katherine Frith. New York: Peter Lang, 1997.

Warwick, Alexandra and Dani Cavallaro. *Fashioning the Frame: Boundaries, Dress and the Body*. New York: Berg, 1998.

Wax, Murray. "Themes in Cosmetics and Grooming." *American Journal of Sociology* 62 (May 1957): 588–593.

Weiss, Gail. *Body Images: Embodiment as Intercorporeality*. New York: Routledge, 1999.

Weiss, Gail and Honi Fern Haber, eds. *Perspectives on Embodiment: Intersections of Nature and Culture*. New York: Routledge, 1999.

Weitz, Rose, ed. *The Politics of Women's Bodies: Sexuality, Appearance and Behavior*. Oxford: Oxford University Press, 1998.

182   *Bibliography*

Wilchins, Riki Anne. *Read My Lips: Sexual Subversion and the End of Gender.* Ithaca, NY: Firebrand Books, 1997.
Williamson, Catherine. "Swimming Pools, Movie Stars: The Celebrity Body in the Post-War Marketplace." *Camera Obscura* 38, no.4 (1996): 4–30.
Willis, Deborah and Carla Williams. *The Black Female Body: A Photographic History.* Philadelphia: Temple University Press, 2002.
Wilson, Elizabeth. *Adorned in Dreams: Fashion and Modernity.* New York: Virago, 1985.
———. "All the Rage." *Fabrications: Costume and the Female Body,* edited by Jane Gaines and Charlotte Herzog. New York: Routledge, 1990.
Wittig, Monique. "One Is Not Born a Woman." *The Straight Mind and Other Essays.* Boston: Beacon Press, 1992.
Workman, Nancy V. "From Victorian to Victoria's Secret: The Foundations of Modern Erotic Wear." *Journal of Popular Culture* 30, no. 2 (1996): 61–73.
Yoder, Janice D. "Women at West Point: Lessons for Token Women in Male-Dominated Occupations." *Women: A Feminist Perspective,* edited by Jo Freeman. 4th ed. Palo Alto, CA: Mayfield, 1989.
Young, Iris Marion. "The Exclusion of Women from Sport: Conceptual and Existential Dimensions. *Philosophy in Context* 9 (1979): 44–53.
———. *Intersecting Voices: Dilemmas of Gender, Political Philosophy, and Policy.* Princeton: Princeton UP, 1997.
———. "Throwing Like a Girl." Pp. 51–70 in *The thinking muse: Feminism and modern French philosophy,* edited by Jeffner Allen and Iris Marion Young. Bloomington: Indiana University Press, 1989.

Market Research

Carter, Jeff. *Seventeen Magazine.* Intimate Apparel Buying among Subscribers. August 1995.
Kalish, Allan. *Woman's Day.* Shoptalk Bra Survey. Jan. 1995.
Specialists in Business Information, Inc. *SBI Market Profile: Women's Undergarments.* New York: Specialists in Business Information, 1995.
Victoria's Secret. *Strategic View of the Line 2001: Foundations.* Dec. 1999.
Victoria's Secret. *1999 Market Patterning: Total Bras.* Apr. 20, 2000.
Victoria's Secret. *1999 Market Patterning: Total Bras.* Apr. 20, 2000.

Trade Journal Articles

Braus, Patricia. "Boomers against Gravity." *American Demographics* Feb. 1995: 50–57.
Chandler, Susan and Theresa Ann Palmer. "Remember When Bras Were for Burning?" *Business Week* 16 Jan. 1995: 37.
Corwin, Pat. "More Space, Variety Build Intimate Apparel Sales." *Discount Merchandiser* Oct. 1995: 48–51.

"Go Figure: Shapewear Sheds Inhibitions." *Discount Store News* 6 May 1996: 20.

Monget, Karyn. "Bodyslimmers Stretching Out." *WWD* 18 Nov. 1996: 12.

——. "Foundations: Strategy Time." *WWD* 8 Jan. 1996: 18.

——. "Fresh Ideas Spark Shapewear Market." *WWD* 18 Nov. 1996:16.

——. "Intimate Apparel/Sleepwear: The Fairchild 100." *WWD* Nov 1995: 44.

——. "Little Nothings Are Big Business." *WWD* 15 Nov. 1997:48.

——. "Microfiber for the Millennium." *WWD* 22 June 1998: 8.

——. "Nancy Ganz Body Bar Brings Self-Service to Shapewear." *WWD* 12 May 1997: 19.

——. "A New Direction for Shapewear." *WWD* 15 Nov. 1999: 12.

——. "Shapewear Defines Its Targets." *WWD* 10 June 1996: 8.

——. "Shapewear Strategy: Aiming at Young and Old." *WWD* 18 Sept.1995: 24.

——. "Sizing Up Sales." *WWD* 19 June 1995: 8–9.

——. "Soft Dressing Wins Day for Mom." *WWD* 12 May 1997:19.

——. "Warnaco and BodySlimmers : Execs Like the Fit." *WWD* 22 July 1996: 14.

"70% of Women Do Not Enjoy Bra Shopping." *About Women & Marketing* Nov. 1996: 15.

"The Shape of Things to Come: Victoria's Secret Launches Sexy Controlwear Targeted at a Younger Audience." *Body Fashions Intimate Apparel* Nov. 1996: 16.

"Smooth Move: Bodyslimmers Engineers Shaper Excitement with Tactel Plus Lycra." *Body Fashions Intimate Apparel* Aug. 2000: 6.

"What Names Do Consumer's Know Best?" *WWD* Nov. 1997: 11+.

Newspaper Articles

Blumner, Robyn E. "One who Remembers Girdles Says: Don't Cinch Me In." *St. Petersburg Times* 16 Nov. 1997, 6D.

Elliot, Stuart. "Maidenform's Ad Direction Changes." *New York Times* 12 Mar. 1997. members.aol.com/aster314/nytimes.html.

"A Good Figure Costs American Women $65,000,000 a Year." *Life* 8 Feb. 1937: 64–67.

Rittenhouse, Susan. "Girdles: Little Torture Chambers Made of Lycra." *The Pantagraph* Bloomington, IL 23 July 1997, sec. A5: 1.

Seipel, Tracy. "Although in Decline Girdles Still Have Their Place." *The Denver Post* 4 May 1989, sec. D1: 3.

Strom, Stephanie. "When Victoria's Secret Faltered, She Was Quick to Fix It." *The New York Times* 21 Nov. 1993: 10.

Wright, Vevlyn. "The Shape of Fashion Today Is Sometimes a Matter of Selecting the Right Girdle." Quincy, MA: *The Patriot Ledger* 23 Feb. 1998:15.

Popular Women's Magazine Articles

"Are You a Corset Contortionist?" *Ladies' Home Journal* Apr. 1938: 68.

"Asset Management: Tips on Making the Most of Your Figure—Learning Curve." *In Style* June 2003: 106.

Baum, Joan. "How to Choose the Right Foundation for You." *Woman's Home Companion* Feb. 1956: 94–95.

"Build Your Own Silhouette." *Woman's Home Companion* Feb. 1956: 92–93.

"Bras and Girdles for Teen-Agers." *Good Housekeeping* Nov. 1956: 289.

Chance, Julia. "Form and Function." *Essence* April 1996: 36.

Darnton, Nina. "The Ultimate Squeeze Play." *Newsweek* 13 May 1991: 63.

Dixon, Jane. "Fitting the Feminine Form." *Hygeia* Aug. 1942: 621–622.

Eaton, Jeanette. "Corset Comfort." *The Parents' Magazine* Apr. 1935: 74–75.

Fenstermacher, Jack. "The Do's, Don'ts and Dressing Room Decorum of Buying Bras and Girdles." *Seventeen* Oct. 1964: 67.

"Fashion 101: All-Reason Thongs." *In Style* Feb. 2002: 103

"Fashion 101: New Problem-Solvers." *In Style* Oct. 2004: 252.

"Fashion 101: Problem Solvers." *In Style* Feb. 2000: 116.

"Fashion 101: Selecting the Right Body Shaper." *In Style* Oct. 2004: 256.

"Fashion 101: Sexy Looks." *In Style* Feb. 2000: 122.

"Fashion Prop Kit." *In Style* Nov. 2006: 186.

"Foundations for Figure Types." *Practical Home Economics* Dec. 1955: 14–16.

Goldberg, Hyman. "The Big Squeeze." *Cosmopolitan* Sept. 1954: 22–25.

Hogeland, Ruth. "A Girdle Is a Girl's Best Friend." *Country Gentleman* June 1954: 99.

"How to Fit a Foundation." *Woman's Home Companion* Oct. 1948: 164–166.

Howard, Miriam. "The Fitting Room." *Mademoiselle* June 1953: 26.

"Is Your Figure a Problem to Fit?" *Woman's Home Companion* Mar. 1954: 88.

"It's a Perfect Fit that Counts in Foundation Garments." *Good Housekeeping* Nov. 1954: 79–83.

Livingstone, Janet. "How to Tell Whether You're Wearing the Wrong Girdle & Bra." *Good Housekeeping* Feb. 1958: 68–71.

Mapes, Shirley W. "Choosing Foundation Garments." *Good Housekeeping* Mar. 1949: 300–303.

McMichael, Carrie S. "Signs of the Times: Fitting Foundation Garments." *The Journal of Home Economics* Jan. 1941: 29–30.

Mower, Sarah. "The Bottom Line: Is There Any Way a Modern Woman Can Be Persuaded into a Girdle?" *Harper's Bazaar* Feb 1995: 68.

Obolensky, Helen. "The Best Silhouette." *Redbook* Jan. 1964: 50–51.

Quinn, Erin. "Style 101: Under Studies." *Allure* June 2006: 84–86.

"Right Girdle and Bra." *Good Housekeeping* Mar. 1968: 172–174.

Shields, Jody. "Inside Out." *Vogue* Nov. 1990: 342–347.

Sommerfeld, Edna. "Buying and Wearing a Foundation Garment." *Consumers' Digest* Feb. 1941: 26–28.

"Stretch the Life of Your Girdle 3 Ways." *Woman's Home Companion* Dec. 1952: 98.

Swartz, Mimi. "A Day in the Life of a Victoria's Secret." *Mademoiselle* Apr. 1990: 238–239.

"Testing Body Shapers." *Good Housekeeping* Jan 1999:54.

"The Most Valuable Players in Your Sports Wardrobe Are Foundations that Make You Look Like a Winner." *Seventeen* May 1964: 206.

"We Thank Our Supporting Cast." *Good Housekeeping* Nov. 1950: 72–73.
Woodman, Sue. "Victoria Reigns . . . Again." *Working Woman* Sept. 1991: 77.

Personal Articles Posted on the Web

"You're Asking Me about Girdles?" *Zona: The Girdle Zone.* 1999. www.girdlezone
.org/women.htm (7 May 1999).
"My First Girdle" *Zona: The Girdle Zone.* 1999. www.girdlezone.org/thefirst.htm (12
Sep 1999).

Interviews

Barowski, Vita. Personal interview. 13 Oct. 2002.
Benevides, Judy. Personal interview. 12 Nov. 1999.
Brebner, Kristin. Personal interview. 15 Nov. 2002.
Brent, Ashly. Personal interview. 17 Nov. 2002.
Bryson, Janet. Personal interview. 13 Oct. 2002.
Burns, Kathy. Personal interview. 13 Oct. 2002.
Cain, Terry. Personal interview. 14 Oct. 2002.
Casabianca, Lynn. Personal interview. 9 Nov. 1999.
Chadwick, Anne. Personal interview. 12 Oct. 2002.
Chase, Heidi. Personal interview. 13 Nov. 2002.
Clements, Ashley. Personal interview. 10 Nov. 1999.
Davis, Laurie. Personal interview. 14 Oct. 2002.
Dragiewicz, Molly. Personal interview. 1 Nov. 2002.
Duke, Sheryl. Personal interview. 15 Oct. 2002.
Gunnerson, Carrie Anne. Personal interview. 13 Nov. 2002.
Harper, Donna. Personal interview. 14 Oct. 2002.
Harris, Ashley. Personal interview. 17 Nov. 2002.
House, Erika. Personal interview. 13 Nov. 2002.
Hutson, Joy. Personal interview. 14 Oct. 2002.
Kallini, Kristina. Personal interview. 23 Nov. 2002.
Kelly, Bonnie. Personal interview. 4 Nov. 1999.
Kenrick, Meaghan. Personal interview. 12 Nov 2002.
Lawhorn, Jennifer. Personal interview. 16 Nov. 2002
Leggat, Pam. Personal interview. 8 Nov. 1999.
Mallory, Marva. Personal interview. 14 Nov 2002.
Marchessault, Lori. Personal interview. 9 Dec. 2002.
May, Frances. Personal interview. 28 Nov. 1999.
May, Katy. Personal interview. 28 Nov. 1999.
McLoone, Tracy. Personal interview. 10 Nov. 2002
Millis, Sara. Personal interview. 12 Nov. 2002
Nguy, C.J. Personal interview. 20 Nov. 2002.

Powell, Morgan. Personal interview. 12 Nov. 2002.
Randall, Adrienne. Personal interview. 11 Nov. 2002
Rishforth, Sara. Personal interview. 28 Dec. 2000.
Rousch, Nancy. Personal interview. 30 Oct. 1999.
Sas, Brinna. Personal interview. 11 Nov. 2002.
Shaver, Sarah. Personal interview. 12 Nov. 2002
Somlar, Shelly. Personal interview. 17 Nov. 2002.
Trur, Teryn. Personal interview. 12 Oct. 2002.
Wood, Carol. Personal interview. 3 Nov. 1999.

Catalogs

Victoria's Secret. Christmas Specials 1999.
Victoria's Secret. Fall 2000.
Victoria's Secret. Holiday 2000.
Victoria's Secret. Spring Fashion Issue 2000.
Victoria's Secret. Spring 2000.
Victoria's Secret. Christmas Specials 2000.

Index